ADVANCE PRAISE FOR
MATTERS OF LIFE AND DEATH:
The remarkable journey of Dr. Philip Merkle

"A compelling intermingling of fiction and non-fiction which relates a treasure trove of insightful information about the fascinating life of Philip Merkle in an eventful historical setting."

Marianne Lamonaca is Chief Curator and Associate Gallery Director, Bard Graduate Center, Bard College, NY and Author/ Editor of Liberty, Equality, and Fraternity.

"Matters of Life and Death: the remarkable journey of Dr. Philip Merkle aptly draws the reader into 19th century life in America. Throughout the work, the author's knowledge of leadership is portrayed by the main character whose undertakings display and educate through his exemplary actions."

Marshall Goldsmith is the New York Times #1 bestselling author of Triggers, Mojo, and What Got You Here Won't Get You There.

"From Freinsheim, a little township in Germany, to the New World: the narratives of Henrich Antes, emigrated in 1720 to Pennsylvania and Michael Harm, emigrated in 1857 to Cleveland, are already told (by Arthur J. Lawton and Claire Gebben). And now we learn about the story of Philip Merkle, who emigrated to New York City in 1833, by the fascinating novel of Bruce H. Seger - fantastic !"

Dr. Hans-Helmut Görtz is an author and historian of Freinsheim, Germany.

"Superb depiction of 19th century New York City and vivid descriptions of the relentless leadership of Philip Merkle. His actions seeking equality and inclusion, wonderfully portrayed by the author, pull the reader into the scenes and actions as the main character pursues his visions."

"A creative presentation of events that shaped 19th century Germany, New York and Missouri bringing forth every emotion from sad and depressing to joyful and humorous interspersed with delightful anecdotes. Portraying events through the eyes of an immigrant whose life was a mission to bring about acceptance, inclusion, equality, and tolerance makes it wonderfully engrossing. Thoroughly enjoyable."

Matters *of* Life *and* Death

The Remarkable Journey of Dr. Philip Merkle

BRUCE SEGER

World Renoun Publishing
Islandia, New York

World Renoun Publishing

Islandia, New York

For more information or to order go to: www.worldrenounpublishing.
com or www.bruceseger.com

Matters of Life and Death The Remarkable Journey of Dr. Philip Merkle
Copyright © 2019 by Bruce Seger

ISBN: 978-1-54398-501-6 (print)
ISBN: 978-1-54398-502-3 (ebook)

LCCN - 2019916069

Printed in the United States of America

CONTENTS

ACKNOWLEDGMENTS

My heartfelt thanks to my parents, grandparents, aunts, uncles, and cousins, who regaled me with stories of our ancestors and their struggles and accomplishments. An ancestor of interest is Philip Merkle. The information and memorabilia that was relayed regarding him was intriguing. It set me on the road to this adventure and project which commenced over four years ago.

My appreciation and thanks to co-chairpersons Paul Beaudin, Cynthia Eaton and the other members of the college-wide Sabbatical Review Committee for selecting my proposal.

I am pleased that in my position as a library science and paralegal professor at Suffolk County Community College, New York, I have access to so many knowledgeable librarians, other colleagues, and friends in the academic community with specific mention of Christopher Adams, Johanna Boutcher, Paulette Brinka, Danielle DiMauro-Brooks, Kerry Carlson, Rocco Cassano, Donna Ciampa, Christine Clifton, Christine Crowe, Peter DiGregorio, Jeanmarie DeLanty, Susan DeMasi, Ronald Feinberg, Donald Ferruzzi, Christopher Gherardi, Anita Greifenstein, Lisa Hamilton, Dawn Tracy-Hanley, Alphonses Heraghty, Virginia Horan, Yvon Joseph, Alexander Kasiukov, James Keane, Mary Kim, Jeralynn McCarthy, Kevin McCoy, Erikka Mendez, Rajni Misra, Fabio Montella, Dante Morelli, William O'Connell, Victoria Pendzick, Priscilla Pratt, Deborah Provenzano, Jason Ramirez, Hector Sepulveda, Gayle Sheridan, Sean Tvelia, Rebecca Turner-Wallace, and Deborah Wolfson.

A special thank you to Kevin Peterman for his ongoing support.

My gratitude and appreciation to David Conrad 2nd great grandson of Friederike Merkle Conrad (sister of Philip Merkle) for his kind sharing of family information and photos.

My gratitude to the librarians and archivists at the National Archives and Records Administration, New York City Municipal Archives, the New York Public Library, New York Historical Society, New York Genealogical and Biographical Society, Half Hollow Hills Community Library, (Melville Branch) Patchogue-Medford Public Library, The State Historical Society of Missouri, Missouri Historical Society, St. Louis (MO) Public Library, The Free Library of Philadelphia, Landesarchiv (state archives) Speyer, Germany, Landesbibliothek (state library) Speyer, Germany, and Institut fur Pfalzische Volkskunde in Kaiserslautem, Germany.

A special thank you to the following librarians or archivists, Paul Friedman (The New York Public Library), Jaime Ellyn Bourassa (Missouri Historical Society), Rachel Forester (The State Historical Society of Missouri), Amanda Bahr-Evola (St. Louis Public Library Special Collections), and Dr. Christian Decker (Institut fur Pfalzische Volkskunde) for his wonderful find of the publications of Edgar Soss (inaugural dissertation for a doctoral degree at Johannes Gutenberg University).

Thank you to journalist Joe Holleman of the *St. Louis Post-Dispatch* for leading me on the trail to locate Michael Keevil, 3rd great grandson of William Henry Keevil, the proprietor of three 19th century hat stores in St. Louis, MO.

Thank you to 3rd great grandson Mike Keevil for his kind response and assistance.

My gratitude to genealogist Mary Ann D'Napoli for her help in the difficult task of locating the will and land deed of Marie Merkle.

Thank you to Martin Greulich for providing translations.

Appreciation to Dr. Richard Haberstroh for his kind assistance.

Thank you to Gabriele Indinemao for procuring records regarding Philip Merkle's university education.

Appreciation to Dr. Stanley Nadel for his kind assistance.

Thank you to Dr. Thomas Anastasio for his suggestions and sharing his knowledge regarding manuscript conversion.

My heartfelt gratitude to historian Dr. Hans-Helmut Görtz for giving me a better understanding of the history of Philip Merkle's life in Germany, for walking me through documents from the archives and library in Speyer, for translating materials, for finding the deeds and location of Philip Merkle's home in Freinsheim, for sending photos of the area, and for kindly and patiently answering my questions.

My thanks and gratitude to my first manuscript reader Joyce Gabriele for her suggestions, encouragement, and support.

My heartfelt thanks and appreciation to my former colleague and dear friend Kathleen Martin for her innovative illustration suggestions, and outstanding sketches.

My thanks to my friend and colleague William Eppig, Esq. for discussing his ancestors' breweries.

My sincerest gratitude and appreciation to Mary Daniello for her advice, sharing her expertise, offering valuable support, counsel, and guidance through the production process.

My thanks and appreciation to Cara Daniello for sharing her knowledge of composition and offering suggestions regarding writing fiction.

My thanks to family members and friends for their encouragement with this project.

Finally my love and heartfelt gratitude to my dear parents Teresa and Henry for their support, inspiration, and encouragement with this project and for always providing unconditional love in a thought-provoking environment.

PREFACE

Through genealogical research, I learned that Dr. Philip Merkle was part of my family history. As I perused information about him, references abounded: numerous 19th century newspaper articles, bibliographies which included his name and led to information about him from various sources, and even a doctoral thesis written in 1956 Germany which included his actions against oppression in Germany. During his education at Gymnasium and the University of Heidelberg, his life's mission and philosophy to eradicate injustice, bias, and intolerance, took form.

His actions in Germany forced his emigration, and he adopted America as his country. During his lifetime in the United States, he attained positions as pharmacist, physician, examiner of drugs, interpreter, excise commissioner, coroner, civic leader, and theologian in New York City (where he lived for the majority of his life). This allowed for his ongoing pursuit of equality for humanity.

By authoring the book in an autobiographic, historical novel format, it allows the main character to narrate, comment, and offer opinions. The book is a blend of fiction and nonfiction. The 19th century characters, events, and articles presented are nonfiction, including information about Philip's personal life (incarceration, conflict, tragedy, and infidelity). However, many of the viewpoints of the narrator are gleaned from the anecdotes and memorabilia passed down to me by prior generations. The assumptions drawn from those reminiscences and other findings about his life's actions are relayed in an interpretive style.

The volume depicts life and events during 19th century Germany, New York City, and St Louis, Missouri where some of his relatives settled. The stage is set throughout to immerse the reader in the time frame and offer a backdrop of imagery to experience 19th century life: aromas of vineyards and flowers, smells of animal and human waste, overcrowded tenements, infidelity, poverty, rampant disease, epidemics, outhouses, attire, artistic events, inventions, horse drawn carriages, the founding of the Metropolitan Museum of Art, Carnegie Hall, Mercantile Library, Lenox Library, New York Public Library, Central Park, Fraunces Tavern, Delmonico's Restaurant, the introduction of popcorn, bananas, lager beer, Fleischmann breads, economic depressions, the inception of bread lines and more.

I am sure Philip would be amazed to witness New York City and the rest of the nation 120 years after his death: over 5,000,000 increase in New York City population, computers and other technological inventions, men, women, and children's attire, modes of transportation, the 1919 ratification of the Eighteenth Amendment prohibiting intoxicating liquors, the 1933 passage of the Twenty-first Amendment repealing the Eighteenth Amendment, the Nineteenth Amendment granting women the right to vote, and many other changes. He would also be pleased to observe the continued mission for inclusion of all differences (but saddened regarding the slow pace at which it is occurring), disheartened to witness the ongoing poverty, the relentless anti-immigrant sentiment, and political views that resemble the Know Nothing movement.

CHAPTER 1

Upheaval in Germany

IT WAS A BEAUTIFUL SPRING DAY IN MAY 1895. I HAD BEEN READ-ing my diaries, which I began writing after arriving in America. It occurred to me that the observations I recorded recount intriguing and engaging experiences. Therefore, I decided to author an autobiog-raphy. In it, I would incorporate many events from my life in the hope that it will be a meaningful and compelling volume about my personal history and the state of affairs in 19th century Germany and America.

I was born in Freinsheim, a small town in southwest Germany, west of the beautiful green Rhine River, with a picturesque view of orchards. In my mind, I can still see the village, with its lovely gardens and vineyards blooming with beautiful flowers in spring, vibrant colors in autumn, and bountiful fruit during harvest time.

Over the years, the townspeople of Freinsheim have overcome many calamities. At the end of the 17th century, they suffered tremen-dous destruction from the Nine Years' War waged with France. Not much more than a decade later, in 1709, they faced a horrible freeze that killed many of the village's inhabitants, caused livestock and poultry, as well as other wildlife, to freeze to death, and destroyed the region's productive grapevines.

Freinsheim's location near the border of France is a major disad-vantage. For centuries, Germany was part of the Holy Roman Empire, which was often at war with France. When the French were aggressors, the routes to their destinations were through Freinsheim. This was the case when France invaded Germany during the French Revolution from 1789 to 1793 and during the reign of Napoleon Bonaparte from 1804-1815.

During his reign, the people of Freinsheim were subject to the Napoleonic Code, a series of liberal policies that influenced Germany and other nations. The laws within the code affirmed equality of men before the law, freedom of religion, and the abolition of feudalism. My parents were in favor of those ideas and spoke specifically about equality of the law, whereby judges were forbidden from applying case law to civil cases, rather than evaluating each case on its own merit. This discouraged judges from favoring the upper class.

Despite their approval of certain Napoleonic policies, my parents were disturbed by his establishment of the supremacy of men over women (the generally accepted legal position in most of Europe at the time). In essence, women were considered chattels of their fathers and, once married, of their husbands. In fact, Napoleon, when comparing men to women, reportedly stated that nature had made women men's slaves!

My parents settled in Freinsheim during Napoleon's reign. Perhaps the simple reason that Father chose the location was that he was able to find employment there. Another reason might have been that my paternal grandmother, Kristina Friederike Kulhhoefir (whose father was a minister in Freinsheim) had married my grandfather, Johann Gottlieb Merkle (an itinerant Evangelical minister) who was preaching in Freinsheim at the time of their meeting. My grandparents spoke favorably about the town, stating that the Freinsheim townspeople were known to be a mix of classes, religions, and educational levels. Such differences were important to my parents, who instilled in their children tolerance for dissimilarity and intolerance for social injustice.

Father was always in favor of the education of the human race and, therefore, ignored the decree forbidding literacy for women. He taught Mother to read, write, and do arithmetic and, my mother, in turn, taught my sisters, Catherina and Friederike. Father believed that, in spite of some positive aspects of the Napoleonic Code, Napoleon had become a tyrannical leader who wished to rule all of Europe and needed to be stopped.

Since I was born during Napoleon's reign, my civil birth record is in French. The English translation is:

In the year one-thousand eight-hundred eleven, on March twenty-first at ten o'clock in the morning, in front of me, Jakob Werner, mayor and officer of civil affairs of the community of Freinsheim, canton of Dürkheim, département (district) of Donnersberg, appeared Mr. Karl Merckle, surgeon, thirty-two years old, residing in Freinsheim, who has presented to us a child of male sex, born on March twenty-first, (son) of him and of Elisabeth Fischer, his wife, and he declared to give him the name Philipp Daniel.

Although my birth name is Philipp Daniel Merckle, later I adopted a slight change in spelling and omitted my middle name wishing to be known as Philip Merkle.

My father, Johann Karl Auguste Merckle (listed in French records as Charles Merckle) was born 1779 in Hochhauser, Germany about 100 kilometers from Freinsheim. Father was of medium height and slender build with light brown hair, blue eyes, and had a commanding presence. His occupations were surgeon and barber. At the time, barbers (a respected profession) often performed minor surgeries. In addition to practicing medicine, Father was well-versed in the sciences, literature, and the arts.

Before I was a decade old, I recall, Father occasionally inviting my brother Johann Gottlieb and me to take walks around our delightful town of Freinsheim.

He taught us about items that we observed: plant-life, animals, architecture, and enlightened us about the history of our town and surrounding areas. I was particularly proud as we passed people along the route who greeted Father with great respect and often thanked him for a medical diagnosis or cure he had offered. Later, during Gymnasium holidays, Father allowed Johann Gottlieb and me to accompany him to his medical office or the barber shop to quietly observe his procedures. I was fascinated observing the surgeries and discussing them afterward. As a result of these events, I knew that my chosen profession would be medical doctor and perhaps even surgeon.

Mother, Klara Elisabette Fischer, the daughter of a vintner, was born in 1789. She was beautiful: small in stature with long brown hair and large brown eyes, a caring, hardworking, intelligent woman, who was reserved, but occasionally outspoken about certain issues, such as, the Napoleonic Code regarding women. What I most recall is her cheerful demeanor: constantly smiling and laughing easily. I will always remember when I was a young lad, returning from play or school, and detecting the wonderful aroma of her home-baked goods. She always allowed me to sample a small portion while we engaged in lighthearted conversation. As much as I enjoyed Father's serious conversations, I looked forward to time with Mother.

After early schooling at the Latin School in Durkheim, I attended Gymnasium (an advanced secondary school) in Speyer and then transferred to Gymnasium in Zweibrucken. I credit the political discussions with Father and my time in Gymnasium and the surrounding area of Zweibrucken (a growing area of supporters of the democratic movement in Germany) for opening my mind to those ideals.

On several occasions, Johann Gottlieb and I indicated to Father our passion and intrigue with science and medicine and hoped to be doctors. Then during one of our visits home from Gymnasium, Father spoke to us about our future education. He told my brother that he must prepare for a medical career and I must be a minister. I was shocked and angry. Father saw my reaction and when we were alone explained that although my brother and I had a great deal of self-taught medical knowledge in addition to information learned from him which could ultimately result in our becoming excellent doctors, he saw something more in me. He continued that I reminded him of his father, a minister, who was intelligent, compassionate, and had a desire to improve the plight of humankind. Grandfather had helped many people through difficult events and was always outspoken in his quest and advocacy for equality. I told Father that I could certainly combine Grandfather's advocacy with a medical vocation, but he said that I must focus on one profession, otherwise I will perform both inadequately. It always disturbed me that, in spite of Father's liberal views, he dictated our professions. At the time, it was not unusual for heads of families to determine the professions of their children, but I found this practice inconceivable and was disappointed that Father would follow this unfair custom.

Sadly, in 1826, upon one of my infrequent visits home from Gymnasium, I learned that Mother was an invalid (bedridden and uncommunicative). I spoke with Father about the diagnosis and he responded that he was unable to find any physical malady. Despite this, until her death, my mother was an invalid and my sisters, Catherina, age 18 and Friederike, age 16, assumed the household duties and the care of Mother. I always felt badly about my sisters' added responsibilities, but they accepted them without complaint.

Johann Gottlieb and I traveled home as frequently as possible to visit Mother and give support to Father, Catherina, and Friederike. When I entered her sickroom, she seemed to enjoy seeing me, always giving a faint smile, but she would quickly become disinterested in my comments. It was difficult to accept that her demeanor, which had been inquisitive, personable, and joyful, had become so detached.

When it was time for me to enroll in university, unbeknown to my father and against his wishes, I registered at the University of Wurzburg, a secular research-teaching university with an outstanding faculty. I enrolled in the pre-medical program and excelled in the courses. My father learned what I had done and insisted I leave and enroll at the University of Heidelberg (another research-teaching university) to study theology, and I obeyed.

In 1831, I received a correspondence informing me that Mother had died at home on November 24th. She was 42 years of age and for several years had no quality of life. Nevertheless, I was deeply saddened, especially while remembering the wonderful years prior to her affliction. I immediately traveled home, where I remained for a short time to attend funeral services and her interment.

When I returned to Heidelberg University, the student association in which I was active was discussing potential actions to express our displeasure with the government. At the time, Germans were again living under oppressive conditions enforced by the King of Bavaria.

We learned of an event that was being organized and would meet our criteria. Beginning May 27, 1832, a three-day gathering, the Hambach Festival, was planned to be a political rally disguised as a festival. Professors and students at the University of Heidelberg arranged to take part. The idea spread and people were enthusiastic about possible changes that would result in a united democratic country with freedoms for all classes. I was eager to participate in the event.

Through correspondence with my father, I learned that he, his brother (my Uncle Philip Daniel), my brother Johann Gottlieb, and my sister Friederike were also going to take part in the demonstration. My sister Catherina, who had married two months prior to the planned festival, was not going to be in attendance. The last Johann Gottlieb, Friederike, and I had seen her was at Mother's funeral service. (We had not been invited to her wedding.) Father had attended the marriage ceremony and informed us that the only others in attendance were her fiance's parents. Johann Gottlieb, Friederike, and I believed that to be puzzling since we had a wonderful relationship with our sister.

My family and I, along with other attendees of the Hambach Festival, met in the town of Neustadt where the festival committee had arranged for a procession to Hambach Castle. We were quite early and had time to converse. Besides some insignificant conversation, we discussed some medical and political topics as we had when I lived at home. I will always recall those enjoyable sessions and Father welcoming our opinions. However, Mother had alerted us to never broach personal matters with Father so we avoided those subjects.

We were interrupted a few times when local vendors greeted and spoke briefly with Father. I wondered how they were acquainted. Although I did not question, Father must have seen my quizzical demeanor, was silent for a short time, and then explained that he had been an assistant to the town doctor of Neustadt before moving to Freinsheim. I wondered why he had never mentioned that. Then he added that he had met Mother in that town, was so smitten, that whenever he wasn't working, he was with her. We were surprised he divulged such personal information, but happy that he would share those remembrances. Then he continued that after knowing Mother for a while, he learned that she had a daughter, Catherina. We were shocked that our sister Catherina was actually our half sister! I asked if Mother was a widow when they met, and again, Father paused, probably pondering if he should say more. Then he added that Mother was not a widow and he did not know the identity of Catherina's father. I was astounded, but tried not to show any emotion.

Mother bore Catherina out of wedlock! Johann Gottlieb, Friederike, and I had to become accustomed to this news although it did not change our love for Mother or our sister. It might also explain the reason Catherina did not invite us to the marriage ceremony since her surname would be stated as Fischer, Mother's maiden name rather than Merkle as she had been known by us. Perhaps Father told us this personal information so that we would not be offended by not having been invited to the marriage ceremony. Telling us these facts was probably easier since Mother was deceased.

Contemplating this information, I felt badly that perhaps Catherina, a wonderful person, might have been ashamed that she was conceived out of wedlock. Johann Gottlieb, Friederike, and I agreed to visit her after the festival, of course speak nothing of what we had learned, but offer her and her husband our congratulations.

In pondering further about this newly learned information, I recalled reading that during the 1800s in southern Germany, there were strict legal rules governing marriage, e.g., the father had to show an income indicating his ability to support his prospective family. As a result between 15 and 20% of women had children out of wedlock. The father is occasionally listed on documents (although he was not the husband) but in many cases, simply listed as unknown. I never read the particulars of those marriage regulations since they were not of much interest at the time. I now wondered, "Is it possible that Mother became an invalid because of her secret being revealed to Catherina prior to her marriage, which perhaps caused great distress?" That is a conjecture since there was yet to be a cogent medical explanation for a person becoming an invalid.

I was so engrossed reflecting on this newly learned information that I didn't notice the tremendous number of people gathering for the procession. It was later reported that the estimated attendance was an impressive 30,000. There were thousands on horseback, thousands in carriages, and many others on foot (as were we) interspersed with marching bands. The various delegations carried banners in the national colors, (black, red, and gold) and many ladies wore scarves with those colors. What a magnificent procession it was!

As we approached the top of the hill where Hambach Castle is located, there was a spectacular panoramic view: the green waters of the Rhine, the picturesque villages along the river, and the expanse of mountain ranges as a backdrop.

Citizens came from all areas of Germany, along with many from other countries. Among the speakers were prominent Germans and notable individuals from Poland, Austria, Switzerland, and France.

They spoke about the sad state of affairs in Germany, which suffered from economic depression and the importance of preserving freedom of the press. What impressive and convincing speakers! I was amazed to see Lucien Ray, the distinguished French journalist, who gave an eloquent speech congratulating the Germans on their endeavor to obtain constitutional freedom. Unfortunately, some of the speakers were later arrested.

An exciting moment that helped solidify the purpose of the festival occurred when the attendees were asked to hold their hands up and repeat an oath, only part of which I can recall:

"We swear we will be free as were our sires, and sooner die than live in slavery." This was followed by tremendous cheers. I have observed many rallies and protests since I have been in America, but never have I seen a greater organized demonstration of unbounded enthusiasm.

The Hambach Festival was an informal protest against Bavarian rule (a call for freedom and a unified, democratic Germany) but it did not accomplish as much as had been hoped. However, it planted a seed and laid the groundwork for the 1848-1849 uprising in which many again fought (albeit unsuccessfully) for freedom from religious and political censorship. After both the 1832 festival and the 1848-1849 uprising against the government, there were mass emigrations to America.

The day after the festival, freedom trees were dedicated in some German towns to further protest injustices by the Bavarian Regime. They followed the example of the Liberty Tree in Boston, Massachusetts, which was a symbol of unity with the Sons of Liberty. Many townspeople throughout southern Germany were consecrating the trees as symbols of their displeasure with the government.

Despite the risk of severe punishment for such behavior, I led the placing of one in Freinsheim. A few of us brought a tree from the nearby forest and stood it in the town. When guards appeared, Freinsheim's Mayor, Peter Reis, warned us there would be consequences, so we temporarily laid it down. The townspeople were encouraging us to reposition it, so we did. Once again, the mayor insisted we take it down, but this time many townspeople became boisterous and demanded his resignation. He refused.

Suddenly all the riotous behavior became subdued. I turned and saw guards approaching. My heart started pounding rapidly because, as leader of the tree raising, I knew I would be the one arrested. My father, my uncle Philip Daniel and my sister Friederike were observing the event and when the guards began walking toward me, Father stepped in front of one, pleading for leniency. The guard shoved him aside and continued toward me accompanied by another guard. In that instant, for the first time, I saw a side of Father that I had never witnessed: his display of love and empathy for me by bravely confronting the guard and risking arrest. That public act of affection I have never forgotten. As expected the guards roughly grabbed me and briskly escorted me to prison.

Imprisonment was a horrible experience and one I can never totally put out of my mind. I was harshly tossed into an overcrowded jail cell in which the unsanitary conditions were abhorrent. A small bowl of food was given once a day which was barely edible. Others who had been in the cell longer than I were becoming weak and ill. The stench of dead bodies not yet removed was dreadful. It was a paramount example of man's inhumanity to man. On June 2, 1832, there were witness hearings in which the Freinsheim mayor gave details of the freedom tree event and I was sentenced to a year in prison.

After a few months, some prisoners had the opportunity to plead their cases before the Appellationsgericht in Zweibricken, which is somewhat like the Supreme Court in America. It was difficult to come to terms with my decision, but I thought, "Am I better in here where I can never do anything worthwhile, or shall I go before the court and perhaps be freed?" I always have believed if your chances to oppose injustice are impossible in a current venue, try to discover another opportunity elsewhere.

I saw several who tried pleading and returned having been beaten by prison guards. Nevertheless, I requested a hearing, spoke before the judges, and my sentence was overturned. I think, perhaps, I was released because I did not mention anything political in the hearing, but simply indicated that I was sorry for any disturbance I had caused and wished to finish my degree in theology. I heard later that the judges were releasing insignificant prisoners to make room for more notable ones.

Today when I reflect about the Hambach Festival and my leadership in erecting the freedom tree, I realize how daring and foolishly fearless my actions were and how over-idealistic my thinking was.

After being released, I returned to university, completed the final semester and received a degree in theology, graduating second in my class. During that time, I became acquainted with a family who provided a dormitory for students. The father was deceased, and the mother and her grown children were managing the house. In speaking with the family, I learned they had plans to emigrate to America. I became fond of the oldest daughter, Anna, who was born the same year as I. She was lovely in appearance, with long flowing blonde hair, blue eyes, and a delightful smile. Her mother wisely bartered with some of the university students and professors who boarded at the dormitory to teach her daughters to read, write, and do arithmetic. Anna became a voracious reader and I enjoyed discussing many classic books with her. I found myself managing to find more and more time to spend with her and realized I had fallen in love. Did she have the same feelings? I finally mustered the courage and told her how deeply my feelings were for her and asked if she had affection for me? She threw her arms around me and said, "Yes, yes." We embraced and kissed. I was ecstatic. We had such high hopes and began to plan for the future.

In spite of having a doctor of divinity degree, I could not gain a position as a clergyman in Germany. My tenth interview was with an elderly minister who kindly told me that I was on a government black-list because of my arrest record and would not gain employment in any church. I had wasted 6 months attempting to gain employment always believing I was not providing the expected responses in the interviews.

After speaking with the minister, I worried even more acutely about the horrific state of affairs in Germany: governmental threats, intimidating behavior of regime guards and soldiers throughout the country, journalists being censured, and advocates for change being jailed or executed. What had happened to my country? At that point, I decided to prepare for emigration to America, where there would be opportunities to contribute to positive causes without the risk of incarceration or execution.

CHAPTER 2

Germany to America

I INFORMED MY FAMILY OF MY PLANS TO EMIGRATE AND A FEW days later my father, Friederike, and Uncle Philip Daniel announced that they too wished to emigrate to America. My brother, Johann Gottlieb, had already departed in late 1832, and had settled in St. Louis, Missouri. Father commented that he had felt such frustration and discontent with the government leaders and anticipated sadness regarding the emigration of his children and brother.

He needed to sell properties and other possessions. Besides our expansive home, which included two iron stoves for cooking, one kettle, and two heating stoves as well as a cellar and stables underneath, he had to dispose of several other properties: parcels with trees, and three vineyards. He either sold his belongings or gave them to those in need. Father was well-compensated for his property holdings and I was pleased that it would allow him financial stability while he acclimated to his new country.

I left Germany prior to Father, Uncle Philip Daniel, and Friederike. Anna, her family, and I sailed to America and arrived at the port of New York during the summer of 1833.

It was a grueling and wearisome journey across the Atlantic, especially when high winds and storms occurred. During the voyage many became ill and some perished. When we arrived in America, all passengers were left at a dock on Manhattan's East Side and there were no customs agents to greet us. As I perused the dock, many had no one meeting them and looked frightened and bewildered. I also noticed some unscrupulous people standing about who I am sure were there to take advantage of the newly arrived immigrants. Fortunately, Anna, her family, and I were greeted by her relatives from New Jersey.

Arrangements had been made for me to stay with Anna's cousin while she and her family resided with her aunt and uncle.

Meanwhile, Father and Friederike were staying with friends in Freinsheim until Uncle Philip Daniel was ready to emigrate. They finally arrived in New York City December 1833. Anna's cousin (with whom I was staying) and I met them at the New York City dock and I convinced them to remain in New Jersey until the weather would be conducive for pleasant travel to St. Louis, Missouri. They were tired from the long journey so it was not difficult to persuade them to stay. Anna's cousin had ample room and my father and uncle compensated him fairly. It was wonderful having family with me, although they were intent on ultimately moving to St. Louis.

Finally, after eight months in America, I was successful in procuring a position as minister of St. John's Evangelical Lutheran Church in Newark, New Jersey. My appointment commenced in April 1834, and Anna and I married a month later. The same month, Father and Uncle Philip (both educated medical doctors) gained temporary employment in a local clinic and remained with us until the fall of 1834, when they and Friederike departed for St. Louis.

I will explain the reason my family was so anxious to settle in St. Louis. Many Germans who wished to immigrate were intrigued by what they read and heard from Gottfried Duden, a lawyer and author, who in 1824 had traveled from Germany to the St. Louis, Missouri area, purchased farmland in the Missouri River Valley, and remained there for three years. After returning to Germany, he published, *Report on a Journey to the Western States of North America* in which he encouraged immigration to Missouri. His description was appealing, especially because the conditions in Germany were so horrific. In the book, he compared the Missouri River to the lauded Rhine River in Germany and likened the climate and land to that of the most beloved areas of Germany.

Thousands of copies of Duden's publication were purchased resulting in tremendous numbers immigrating mostly to the area, he suggested, between St. Louis and Hermann, Missouri, where they established farms and vineyards. Others who were not successful in those endeavors made their way to urban areas such as St. Louis.

The imagery in Duden's writings resulted in a continuous flow of immigrants to the Missouri region beginning in the 1830s when my brother Johann (which he now preferred as his given name) settled there. Like many others, known as Duden's followers, Father, Uncle Philip Daniel, and Friederike determined to settle there and could not be dissuaded.

Those who chose Missouri (like those of us who immigrated to the east coast of America) had diverse religions with mostly Catholic, Protestant, and Jewish backgrounds. In addition, they represented a range of professions, including those who were highly educated, and others with developed skills.

In September 1834 Anna, her family, and I bade farewell to my father, uncle, and sister and wished them well in their journey to St. Louis. Their itinerary was designed to take them from New Jersey to Pittsburgh, Pennsylvania, where they would board a steamship and travel the Ohio River to Cairo, Illinois, (the point at which the Ohio River meets the Mississippi River) and from there, journey on the Mississippi to St. Louis. We were unable to contact Johann about their approximate arrival date, but I was not concerned because they were traveling together and could locate him when they arrived in St. Louis. Friederike promised to write as soon as they were settled. About a month later, I received a missive from Friederike.

Beloved Brother,

I take pen in hand to give you the news about our journey. We arrived safely in Pittsburgh, boarded a steamboat and began a relaxing ride on the Ohio River. The weather was beautifully sunny and the cool river breezes felt delightful against our skin. As the boat moved along the river, we viewed some lovely sights of our new country. We also enjoyed some wonderful conversation about our time in New Jersey with you, Anna, and her family. Father and Uncle Philip spoke of their time working together in the New Jersey clinic and how they were looking forward to opening a medical clinic in St. Louis. Father added that he would like to settle near a hospital so that eventually he might be able to resume a position as a surgeon.

The conversations among us seemed to cause the voyage to go quickly until shortly before reaching Cairo, Illinois, the unthinkable occurred. The boiler of the steamboat exploded, scalding Father and Uncle Philip Daniel. We were rescued by a kind person in an open barge, but unlike the warm rays of the sun and light breezes of the river against their skin, now the sun's rays beat against their horribly burned bodies causing Father and Uncle Philip's already unbearable pain to become exacerbated. Both became unconscious and approximately three hours later when we reached the dock in St. Louis, Uncle Philip Daniel had died. Father had regained consciousness, but was in a great deal of pain.

Upon arrival, I ran up the levee to the first store in view, a bake shop. There I relayed to the owner our ordeal and need for lodging. He introduced himself as Enoch Conrad and kindly offered rooms in the rear of his store. He summoned a doctor to treat Father, but there was little that could be done except for medication to lessen the pain.

I have been caring for Father, as best I can, but he has lost most of the vision in his eyes, his hands are so badly burned that he has little use of them, and he is barely ambulatory. His hope for a new beginning in America has been shattered. Father seldom speaks and not only suffers physically, but seems to have lost his desire for life.

I hope you, Anna, and her family are well.

Affectionately yours,
Your sister, Friederike

In the year following the accident, Friederike and I learned that steamboats had no safety regulations and it was not unusual for their boilers to explode. In fact, it was reported that annually, riverboat accidents killed about 400 people, not including those severely injured, like Father!

Father and Friederike remained with Enoch Conrad where my sister cooked, helped with the bakery, and cared for Father. Enoch and Friederike fell in love and married in October, a few weeks after her arrival in St. Louis.

In a later correspondence, Friederike wrote that the descriptions of the Missouri area were exaggerated and the opportunities for employment were lacking. Many immigrants remained and succeeded, while others lost all or most of their savings and suffered serious hardships. She added that she believed some of the problems were resultant from the rapid increase in population. When my brother Johann settled in Missouri in 1832, there were about 200 Germans in the state. By 1834, just two years later, when Father and Friederike arrived, there were about 3,000.

According to Friederike, Father was grateful to Enoch for his kindness and offered to give Friederike her inheritance early in order for Enoch to purchase land on which to build. In 1835, Enoch purchased over four acres of land on which they had an eight room dwelling built. There, they established The Rising Sun Tavern and an adjacent beer garden named The Serene Garden. The location was very close to a stage coach stop catering to 49ers headed to the Gold Rush. It was also near the western terminus of an omnibus line and a Pony Express station, so their business flourished. When I received this news, I was so pleased to learn of their prosperity.

CHAPTER 3

Acclimating to America

MY EMPLOYMENT AT THE EVANGELICAL LUTHERAN CHURCH didn't offer much opportunity to preach my philosophy of religion, so in October 1835 (about a year and a half after accepting the position as a Lutheran minister), I resigned. I decided I'd like to live on Manhattan's Lower East Side, where my brother Johann had recently moved and where I believed I could make positive contributions to the community. Anna reluctantly agreed to move but wanted to stay in New Jersey for a while longer to care for her ill mother.

Mid-December 1835, her mother regained health, but we had to postpone our journey to Manhattan because the city had experienced a devastating fire. It occurred December 16th, on a frigid, windy night with a reported temperature of 17 degrees below zero.

The newspapers provided many accounts of the fire. The inception occurred in a commercial area of factories and warehouses but, because of the high winds, the flames spread quickly. The East River appeared to be on fire resulting from large containers of turpentine from some factories blowing and rolling into the river. People displaced from their homes suffered from the extreme cold and from severe irritation to their eyes and nostrils as a result of the embers which blew from the flames. The smell of smoke and burning chemicals permeated their clothing and the atmosphere.

The local fire departments that responded found that the water in the pumps was frozen, so the attempts to quell the fire were fruitless. The fire raged out of control for two days. Finally, Marines were called to blow up buildings on Wall Street creating a rubble wall to stop the flames. It was successful!

During the fire at least 600 or more factories and warehouses were leveled along with many buildings in the financial district. Because New York was a center of import/export, many of the destroyed warehouses contained expensive goods readied for export. Essentially all of lower Manhattan had been destroyed. This was a tremendous loss for businesses, but fortunately only a few lives were lost.

The cost to rebuild that part of the city was approximately $20,000,000 which was funded by a minimal amount of aide provided by the federal government and substantial loans from the Erie Canal Authority. The canal, (built ten years earlier) was the main connection for raw materials and commercial interests between the Midwest and lower Manhattan. As such, the authority had a vested interest in an expedited reconstruction. We remained with Anna's family until some of the restoration of Manhattan had been completed

In January 1836, we received the news that Father had died. I was planning to visit him as soon as we were settled in New York City and my employment was established, but sadly he died before I was able to journey there. I am pleased that he did stay with us in New Jersey when he first came to America where I enjoyed about nine months of his company.

After his death, Friederike sent Father's bequest to me. I was amazed by the sizable inheritance. Friederike explained that Father had monies bequeathed to him from his father and grandfather, and as a result of those bequests, his personal savings, proceeds from properties, and frugality, Friederike, Johann Gottlieb, Catherina, and I received sizable inheritances.

In March 1836, Anna and I ventured into Manhattan to see the status of the Lower East Side and to visit Johann. We had been unable to contact him and had only learned the status of the city through newspaper reports. It was wonderful to learn that he had not suffered personal, physical, or property damage.

The progress of rebuilding was amazing. We found two edifices to our liking, one for a home on Broome Street and the other for a business on Grand Street. They were not our first choices because of several factories and warehouses nearby, but they had other advantages. They were located near the Grand Street ferry service at the bend in the East River. This would allow Anna to easily travel to Williamsburg, Brooklyn to visit relatives. It would also be a good location for a drugstore which I had decided to open since I had a great deal of knowledge, mostly self-taught, in the fields of medicine and pharmaceuticals.

We moved to Manhattan in April 1836. The area in which we settled had a preponderance of Germans-approximately 25,000. The adjacent area was known as Five Points because of the way five streets merged. It was inhabited mainly by Irish who lived in extreme poverty. When Five Points was seen by author Charles Dickens, he was incredulous. A description was recorded in his travelogue, *American Notes*, in which he characterized the area as, "All that is loathsome, drooping, and decayed."

About two years prior to our move to the Lower East Side, a section was set aside for a park which was named Tompkins Square Park. It was the only open space in the area where families could gather for relaxation and enjoyment. It also became the meeting place for organizing protests and riots. We witnessed one such protest that had been organized in the park in 1837 which became known as the Flour Riot.

At the time, unemployment was rampant, there was a food shortage, and prices had risen tremendously. A barrel of flour had more than doubled in cost. As a result, an angry crowd of about 5,000 people in our area marched on two flour companies that they accused of hoarding flour. The crowd destroyed hundreds of barrels of flour and wheat. Fortunately, they were quickly subdued. The civil disobedience of the Flour Riot occurred within a month of the admission by the federal government that not only New York City, but the entire country was in a financial and economic crisis. This became known as the Panic of 1837 and lasted about eight years.

In addition to the economic crisis, with the increase in population, the city water supply was no longer sufficient and was becoming more and more polluted. Adding to the problem was the dumping of waste from the factories and warehouses which contaminated the waters and caused the spread of disease. New York City residents suffered cholera, typhoid, and yellow fever in the 1830s. During that time, it was estimated that one person in 39 died of disease.

The tremendous loss of life emphasized the need for a clean water supply. Several of us volunteered to meet, study, and suggest a plan for improved water. Our recommendation, which was accepted by city and state governments, was to establish a method of water transport from upstate New York. Engineers designed what became known as the Croton Aqueduct System. The construction took five years and was a network designed to use gravity to move uncontaminated water from the Croton River in upstate New York into reservoirs in Manhattan. Our goal was reached in the early 1840s when clean water reached the city. However, my concern was that, in the future, constantly increasing population might require even more reservoirs for which there had been no plan. For now the problem was solved and the water supply seemed to be greatly improved.

Although I volunteered to assist with that endeavor, there always seemed to be other projects that needed attention. I constantly pondered what ways I could best help.

Meanwhile, it seemed Anna was incessantly complaining about my increased frequency being away from home. Admittedly I was, but Anna was aware before we married that I intended to pursue avenues to serve humanity; yet she was angry and often did not speak to me when I returned home. There was increasing marital strife, but we ignored the differences as much as possible and carried on with our lives.

CHAPTER 4

Anti-immigrant Sentiment

ONE HOT SUMMER DAY, AT EVENFALL, I WAS AS USUAL LOCKING my drugstore for the day; but this evening was different. Suddenly I noticed commotion at the end of the street where there were several women sitting outside their dwellings, I assume to get some relief from the sweltering temperatures of the interiors of their tenements. There was a group of men speaking to them and the women hurriedly took refuge in their homes. I continued watching and within a minute or two, the men who also lived in those tenements came around the corner returning from work. That is when the uproar started and the voices of those awaiting them became boisterous. They shouted at the men, "Go back to the countries you came from" and "You are not part of our country." After some profane comments, they added, "This country does not accept immigrants; it is a country of native-born Americans!" A few even shoved some of the men who quickly entered their dwellings without responding to the hecklers. I was pleased by the immigrants' behavior and appalled by what I had seen and heard. The next few days I walked the neighborhood and learned that these abusers were part of the American Party and the Know Nothing movement. (What an appropriate title they had bestowed on themselves!) Their mission was vengefulness and abusiveness toward immigrants.

After our move to Manhattan, we had observed occasional shunning of some of us but now the anti-immigrant sentiment seemed to be increasing exponentially. Those organizations which professed anti-immigrant tenets made it clear, in word and action, that they believed current immigrants were inferior and should return to their countries of origin.

I learned that this sentiment was not unique to the Lower East Side but existed throughout the United States in all levels of government.

The cause was primarily the result of prejudicial views endorsed by some political movements which espoused the belief that immigrants should not be granted citizenship for a long period of time, should not have the right to vote, should not be permitted to hold public office, and preferably should return to their countries of origin.

I could never abide complacency when there was injustice and discrimination. To this end, I concluded that the establishment of fraternities might help solve the problem in offering the appearance of strength in numbers which, I hoped, would lessen the incidence of bias and bigotry. In essence, the fraternities would be support systems against prejudice and redirect fear and negative feelings.

Besides the horrific anti-immigrant sentiment, I also observed that certain customs were disappearing. Several of my friends and I spoke four or five languages, yet many of the immigrants who only spoke German were so intent on learning to speak English, that their German language fluency and customs were not being preserved or passed to the next generation. Assimilating is of utmost importance, but having the ability to speak more than one language is an asset, and preserving customs is a tribute to one's heritage.

Another of my concerns was the unhappiness and even despair among many of the hard-working Germans who endured terrible living and workplace conditions. In my opinion, they needed an outlet which would offer an enjoyable and community oriented venue. I was known and respected in the Lower East Side community and hoped I would be successful in convincing the men to join a social organization which would address needed reforms.

Therefore, in 1840, with the assistance of a few friends, I formed the Order of the Sons of Hermann. The organization was named for a German liberator who successfully fought the Roman Empire. Our purposes were to preserve traditions, (including the German language), pursue freedom from prejudice, and perform charitable acts. We discussed and developed the objectives for the group and established its main goal as the quest for justice and freedom through knowledge and labor for the betterment of humanity. One could join whether or not he had religious or political affiliations, as long as he was of good character, spoke German, and, was loyal to the American government.

Admittedly, by nature, fraternal organizations often limit the involvement of all. However, there are times that purpose must supersede certain admittances. I also believed that by selecting some members to be greeters at the door, if any anti-immigrant persons attempted to enter, the greeters could ascertain if they spoke German and if not, refuse their entrance.

We established as one of the member benefits, a non-profit, low-cost insurance policy. This was aptly overseen by several members especially Rabbi Emanuel Gerechter who was invaluable as an insurance advisor to the Sons of Hermann. This policy was of great assistance to many members and I was pleased we had initiated it.

The fraternity grew quickly and spread nationwide. Within the first year, membership had reached about 1,000 in New York City.

The following year (1841) I was naturalized in New York City Marine Court and have since been a proud American citizen.

I would be remiss in not mentioning another important fraternity which began in 1843 also in New York City known originally as the Children of the Covenant, but shortly after, as B'Nai B'rith. It was founded by Heinrich Jonas (later anglicized to Henry Jones) and 11 other German Jewish immigrants. I was impressed by its founders' insights and became acquainted with the group of 12. They met regularly in Sinsheimer's Cafe on Essex Street, a cozy place, just a short distance from where I lived, and where I occasionally enjoyed a meal.

I learned they and I had emigrated from Germany about the same time and we all had small, but successful businesses on the Lower East Side. They appreciated the fraternity of which I was a founder (two of the 12 were already members of The Sons of Hermann) but in addition realized the necessity of establishing a Jewish fraternity to preserve Jewish tradition while embracing American ways. Their main goals were similar to the goals of The Sons of Hermann. They wished to address anti-German sentiment and embrace charitable endeavors. In addition, the 12 had astutely observed that Jewish immigrants were becoming Americanized and discarding their Jewish culture. That was of concern to them, and I agreed.

The group of 12 opened its membership of B'nai B'rith to all Jews regardless of Jewish religious affiliation (or lack thereof). Jones said that the focus was intended to be on communal activities for all in need. He asked me if I could arrange for them to use the nearby Masonic Hall at Oliver and Henry Streets for their meetings. I will tell you about my affiliation with the Freemasons shortly, but on behalf of the Freemasons, I had been renting the Masonic Hall to other organizations and welcomed Jones' request. The Masonic Hall was where they met and named the lodge, the B'nai B'rith New York Lodge Number I.

In less than a decade, there were 12 B'nai B'rith lodges and in two decades there were 70 with 6,000 members nationwide. About a decade later, they had an impressive building erected in New York City named Covenant Hall which served as a community center.

The organization also offered non-profit insurance policies in order to help widows and orphans. Among their other charitable deeds benefitting the inhabitants of New York City were the establishment of Maimonides Library (open to the public) and the founding of the Jewish Hospital which offered free care for the poor. Another success-ful fraternal endeavor.

In 1844, Anna and I no longer rented on Broome Street but instead made our home behind my drugstore on Grand. It was a rela-tively large dwelling with a parlor, kitchen, and three bedrooms with windows throughout.

Since the Sons of Hermann was successful, I, with the assistance of friends founded another fraternity in 1847 known as the Order of Harugari. The focus again was intended as a venue for the working class and its name references the meeting place of the ancient defend-ers of German freedom from injustice. The purpose of the organization is in part the same as that of the Sons of Hermann: to resist anti-Ger-man sentiment, preserve German culture, but be foremost a charitable organization not only for the German community, but for others suffering national and international tragedies. Differences in religion, social standing, and political affiliation were never mentioned, nor considered. The Order of Harugari professes brotherhood of all mankind and the importance of working for the good of society, not self.

Based on the model established by Rabbi Emanuel Gerechter, the other founders and I arranged mutual benefits for the members of the Order of Harugari which provided from $500 to $1,000 upon the death of a member to support his widow and children and $5 per week in case of sickness.

For both the Sons of Hermann and the Order of Harugari, there were membership dues of $6 annually, but if this fee presented a hardship, it was waived. Those of us who could offer more financial support did so. This allowed for a sufficient budget to affect the desired objectives.

I could not possibly attend and preside over all fraternal meetings so I suggested the members vote for leaders. I am pleased that those selected possessed insight and prudence. I sporadically attended the meetings and the goals were being met.

My wife Anna was active in our community and received positive reactions from the neighborhood ladies who reportedly commented that the fraternities were alleviating the anger and depression that had been growing among the men who were being verbally and physically assaulted by anti-immigration groups. As time passed, the immigrant abuse lessened and the main goal of the fraternities became charitable works.

As a result of the lack of success of the 1848-1849 uprising in Germany, many more Germans immigrated to America and settled on the Lower East Side. As part of the migration, my nephew, Frederick Bechtel arrived in America and asked if he could live with us while he pursued a career in music. Of course, we obliged. He is an outstanding musician and I was confident that he would have success in this endeavor. He and the many others who emigrated after the 1848-1849 conflict joined the fraternities, and the membership continued to grow.

I believe that the other founders and I met our objectives in establishing fraternities as seen by the continuous growth and reported good works.

CHAPTER 5

Freemasons and Landmark Dedications

DURING THE 1840S I ALSO BECAME A MEMBER OF THE FRATERNAL organization of Free and Accepted Masons. Joining this organization was important to me because the Freemasons have a long history in Europe and have always performed impressive charitable works. My father belonged to the Freemasons and I recall that he and other members of his lodge were involved in altruistic undertakings and seeking ways to enact positive change. I also thought joining the Freemasons would be a tribute to my father.

The interest in the organization in New York City grew to the extent that, by the early 1850s, there was a need for more lodges. I organized two additional ones in which I served in a leadership capacity, and some years later, I assisted in establishing four others.

The Freemasons are respected, not only in New York State, but nationally and internationally. As a result, they were invited to be part of many events and celebrations. Shortly after I became a member, George Washington, a Freemason, was selected to be memorialized with a monument in Washington D.C. Freemasons were invited to preside over the dedication of the cornerstone and a group of us from New York attended. The cornerstone weighed over 240,000 pounds and was laid on July 4, 1848. In attendance was a gathering of approximately 20,000 people, including President James Polk, Mrs. James Madison, Mrs. Alexander Hamilton, and George Washington Parke Custis (the step- grandson of George Washington).

By 1854, the construction of the monument was about one- third completed, but an anti-immigrant action caused future progress to be temporarily curtailed. A storage facility contained stones contributed by various countries intended to be used in the construction of the structure as a symbolic gesture of peaceful co-existence.

Unfortunately, anti-immigration groups removed a large block of black marble that was labeled as a gift from Rome. It had been sent by Pope Pius IX, but a protestant minister, John Weishampel, through his writings and addresses, attempted quite successfully, to incite Protestants throughout the country to rally against the use of the Pope's gift. They were indoctrinated with the belief that the large number of Irish and German Catholic immigrants threatened "native Americans" and that the Pope was attempting, through the Catholic German and Irish immigrants, to take over the United States by affecting a Catholic uprising. The Know-Nothing movement proudly claimed responsibility for the theft and it was also suspected that they stole funds intended for the project. They caused such turmoil that Congress ceased the construction of the monument for about 30 years. It was finally completed in 1888. I attended the dedication and it was a wonderful ceremony.

Besides being invited to be part of national historic dedications outside New York City, the Freemasons within the city presided over the installation of many New York City landmarks. One such example is the obelisk nicknamed Cleopatra's Needle which now resides in Central Park. The obelisk was originally erected in the 1400s B.C. in the city of Heliopolis, Egypt and later moved to Alexandria from which the transport took place. It was a gift from the leader of Egypt to the people of the United States.

The United States was responsible for arranging and financing the transport of the obelisk from Egypt to New York City and, ultimately, Central Park. Through newspaper accounts, especially *The New York World*, I followed the progress of the transport and the obelisk's final placement in Central Park.

The journey began in June 1880 and the red granite obelisk arrived in America a little over a month later. It was docked at the banks of the Hudson River in Staten Island, then transported slowly (estimated at a rate of one block per day) through the city on specially constructed rail tracks and finally advanced with a steam engine across a specially built trestle bridge from Fifth Avenue to Central Park. From the time of its arrival in America, until it reached its destination at the east side of Central Park, it took 112 days. Railroad Magnate William Henry Vanderbilt, paid the transport expenses which exceeded $100,000.

Before the obelisk could be placed, its cornerstone had to be set. The cornerstone and steps weighed 50 tons and had been hauled to the park using 32 horses. The laying of the cornerstone took place October 2, 1880. For the occasion, I joined about 9,000 Freemasons who marched up Fifth Avenue from 14th Street to 82nd Street. It was estimated that about 50,000 people stood along the parade route and gave ovations as we passed. When we reached our destination, besides the laying of the cornerstone, a time capsule with a copy of the Declaration of Independence, Webster's Dictionary, and the 1870 Census were buried under the base.

The populace of New York City was enamored with the accounts of the obelisk, and "Egyptomania" ensued. Local restaurants offered Obbylish cocktails, vendors sold souvenirs, and even a replica of the obelisk was manufactured by Tiffany and Company for those who were most notable in bringing the project to fruition.

It was realized that the desire for souvenirs had become out of control so it was necessary to place an iron railing around the obelisk and have it guarded. Some people of unscrupulous nature were surreptitiously chipping pieces of the obelisk to retain or sell as mementos. There were even some who came from locations outside the city with chisels and hammers, hoping to chip substantial pieces to sell in other areas. The most incredible account I read was that, while the obelisk was still in Egypt, an Arab stonecutter was regularly chipping pieces to sell as souvenirs. He threatened to sue the United States government for damages after the monolith was removed from his country, eliminating his livelihood!

The installation onto the base was delayed slightly due to a blizzard but, finally, in January 1881, the beautiful hieroglyph-covered obelisk was positioned. Tens of thousands, including many of us Freemasons were in attendance.

The obeslisk stands vertically at a height of about 70 feet, weighs approximately 200 tons, and is the oldest manmade structure in

Central Park. In the distance, from its location, can be seen the newly opened Metropolitan Museum of Art.

It was a moving occasion and best described in a delightfully written account in *The New York Times* that was published January 23, 1881, the day after the event. Here are some excerpts:

THE OBELISK IN POSITION
YESTERDAY'S CEREMONY IN THE CENTRAL PARK.

The original Egyptian and only American
obelisk is at this moment standing erect in Central
Park, stately and lonely, and very cold.
It was lowered from its uncomfortable position
in the air upon the stone foundation, and
here it is to stand until something happens to upset it.
If it stands in the Central Park
as long as it stood in the brick-yard behind the railroad station in Alexandria, it will no doubt see the
Brooklyn bridge finished and the electric light almost perfected.
Ample preparations for the great
event had been making for some time in the
Brooklyn Navy-yard; the marine bands had been
practicing "Hail Columbia," the tune that was to
make the air of the Park vibrate at the supreme
moment.
The obelisk was accustomed to a warm climate and
the day, as everybody knows, proved warm and
damp, and the needle was believed to be in the best
of humors. Everything, in fact, looked so favorable for a successful launch that the Egyptian birds
carefully carved near the peak are said to have
been seen to smile.
At high noon, the stone was to be dropped into place
and everybody was cautioned to be on hand
exactly on time, for the business was to be done
promptly and the eager New Yorker might never

have an opportunity to see an
obelisk lowered again. The work was done
promptly, and those unfortunate people who were
15 minutes late lost the golden opportunity.

Another impressive event over which we Freemasons were asked
to preside was the laying of the cornerstone for the Statue of Liberty.
Freemasons were very much involved with that endeavor.

The statue was a wonderful gesture by the French people to the
populace of the United States, but most do not realize that the statue
was conceived by a French professor, Freemason Edouard de Laboulaye
who perhaps had an ulterior motive, albeit a virtuous one. He was
impressed with America, especially after the Civil War, because of the
emancipation of slaves and the nation's republican ideals. The statue,
he hoped, would plant a seed for those ideals in the minds of the citizens of France to seek a similar republic.

Meanwhile, he would avoid antagonizing the monarchy if he
presented the concept in America, rather than in France. Freemason
Frederic Auguste Bartoldi was the artist who designed the statue and
Freemason Gustave Eiffel provided the structural framework. The
Masonic organization in France successfully raised over 3,000,000
francs to support the endeavor.

In August 1884, a celebration was planned for the laying of the six-
ton cornerstone. The Grand Lodge of Free and Accepted Masons of
the State of New York was asked to perform the ceremony. Although
it went well, we were deluged by torrential downpours. The inclement
weather resulted in many invitees not attending.

Nevertheless, there were an estimated 1,500 people on Bedloe's
Island, about one- third of them French. The steamship, *Bay Ridge*
was decorated with French and American flags and transported the
guests from Manhattan to the island. Among the guests, there were
about 100 Freemasons. On the island, a band played "Hail Columbia"
and "The Marseillaise" while the stone was lowered.

As is often tradition, a copper time capsule was housed in an opening behind the cornerstone. Some items chosen to be placed in the box were cards with the names of the people present at the cornerstone ceremony, a copy of the Declaration of Independence, a copy of George Washington's Farewell Address, bronze medals of 20 United States presidents who were Freemasons, a parchment that listed the Grand Lodge officers, copies of New York City newspapers, and a portrait of Bartholdi. It was an inspiring ceremony.

I remember the problems that occurred regarding the completion of the statue's pedestal. Americans had to pay for the pedestal and the American Committee for the Statue of Liberty was given the responsibility of raising the needed funds. They announced that they needed yet another $100,000 and, until the pedestal was installed, the statue would not be transported. A funding campaign was undertaken in 1885 by Joseph Pulitzer, the publisher of the *New York World*. He asked citizens to contribute to the cause. Any amount was gratefully accepted and people who donated $1 or more received a model of the anticipated Statue of Liberty. Those who gave $5 or more received a larger model of the statue.

An editorial that appeared in Pulitzer's newspaper read:

"We must raise the money! The *World* is the people's paper, and now it appeals to the people to come forward and raise the money. The $250,000 that the making of the Statue cost was paid in by the masses of the French people- by the working men, the tradesmen, the shop girls, the artisans- by all, irrespective of class or condition. Let us respond in like manner. Let us not wait for the millionaires to give us this money. It is not a gift from the millionaires of France to the millionaires of America, but a gift of the whole people of France to the whole people of America."

The plea resulted in an outpouring of donations not only from Americans, but also from others throughout the world. The appeal was so successful that, in six months, Pulitzer, with the assistance of the members of the American Committee of the Statue of Liberty, had raised the necessary money. It is estimated that over 200,000 people donated and Pulitzer, being a clever businessman, published donors' names in his newspaper, which resulted in greatly increased circulation of his publication. I was, of course, happy that the goal was realized.

The construction of the pedestal resumed. Freemason Richard Morris Hunt, a talented and innovative artisan, was chosen as the architect of the pedestal. He had designed many New York City mansions and landmarks including the New York Tribune Building, the facade of the Metropolitan Museum of Art, and the Lenox Library. When it was completed, the Statue of Liberty pedestal was transported to Bedloe's Island. The pedestal and foundation stand 154 feet high, just a few feet taller than the statue, which is 151 feet tall!

The pedestal and statue were ready for dedication October 28, 1886. The day before the event, people arrived from cities throughout the United States and throughout the world to witness this momentous event.

The New York Times reported,

"All day yesterday people came to the city in droves to participate in to-day's celebration. Extra heavily loaded trains, much behind schedule time, were the rule on every railroad entering the city. Every hotel was crowded to its utmost capacity last night, and there was hardly one of the better known hotels which did not have to turn away hundreds of would be guests."

The day of the dedication was declared a holiday in New York City and a parade of 20,000 people including many masons boarded the steamer to Bedloe's Island. Once on the island, Freemason Henry Potter, Episcopal Bishop of New York, gave the invocation, Freemason Chauncey DePew, a United States Senator, gave the main address; and President Grover Cleveland accepted the statue on behalf of the United States. Then, Freemason Bartholdi, the artist of the statue, removed the tricolor French flag from the statue's face.

After the unveiling, I was overwhelmed by the power of this huge, meaningful work of art, which held a torch of freedom and a book of law with the inscription, "July 4, 1776." It so aptly represents what the United States exemplifies to so many of us immigrants.

The principle aims of fraternities created during the 1800s and earlier have been preserving traditions and addressing the needs of the less fortunate. As the century progressed, more fraternities were formed, but always with specific ethnic or religious affiliations. I believe and hope these organizations were influenced and inspired by the success of the ones that I and a few others founded. One of the most recent of which I have become aware is the Knights of Columbus formed in the 1880s, and has a Roman Catholic affiliation. As with those I founded, the focus of their members is assistance to the needy.

CHAPTER 6

Medical Schools and Resurrectionists

19TH CENTURY UNITED STATES MEDICAL SCHOOLS

IN 1841, THE NEW YORK UNIVERSITY MEDICAL COLLEGE WAS founded. I was fortunate and excited that it opened in a convenient location and my schedule allowed for me to enroll and attain a medical degree. It was a two-year program. The curriculum was definitely less strenuous than any renowned medical schools in Europe, and clinical experience was lacking. However, the professors were, for the most part, well-chosen and aware of the shortcomings of the curriculum.

When I attended the Medical College, there were only six professors in the medical department. The one who most inspired me was Dr. Valentine Mott. He had gained his medical education at King's College, New York, and at several European locations. His reputation as an incredible surgeon who had performed thousands of successful operations, even several dozen on carotid arteries, was impeccable.

I will tell you a little about the other five professors whose courses were required for the degree:

Dr. John Revere was the youngest son of Revolutionary War hero Paul Revere. He gained his medical knowledge from Boston physicians and attained a medical degree from the University of Edinburgh, Scotland in 1811. He taught theory and practice of medicine at New York University.

Dr. Martyn Paine was a graduate of Harvard and gained practical medical experience in Montreal, Canada. He taught courses in materia medica, (medical cures), but was not open-minded in discussing the options available.

Dr. Granville Sharp Pattison was educated in Europe and taught in medical schools in both Europe and the United States. He was volatile and intolerant if anyone disagreed with him, and had been forced to leave several employments due to his actions. Many accounts of his exploits were reported in newspapers here and in Europe and I was disturbed about the activities that were disclosed. During his lectures, he kept a pair of pistols on his desk. He challenged other physicians and surgeons to duels (but was refused) and was accused of several instances of incompetence. I was not convinced it was a wise hiring, but I admit his anatomical lectures offered some insights.

Dr. Gunning S. Bedford, Jr. attained his medical degree from Rutgers College, New Jersey and then studied for several years in Europe. He specialized in diseases of women and children, was innovative in improving standards in childbirth, and introduced the option of caesarean birth. In New York City, he established a successful practice and was devoted not only to his field, but to the plight of the poor. The clinic which he established (acknowledged to be the first of its kind in the country) served a dual purpose: to avail women unable to pay, a venue for safe treatment, and to provide practical experience for his students. I read that his clinic served about 10,000 women each year.

Dr. John William Draper graduated from University College, London, attained a medical degree from the University of Pennsylvania, and a doctorate in law from The College of New Jersey. He was an outstanding chemist and his knowledgeable and motivating lectures inspired me.

In 1843, I was granted a medical degree and, although I would have preferred a more extensive curriculum, most of the professors imparted a great deal of information. I also gained much additional knowledge through constant interaction with my brother Johann and some of his colleagues who were well- read and stayed current in the medical field. I maintained a formal practice for a few years but due to other commitments, I later limited treatment to family and friends.

Disturbingly, during most of the 1800s, United States' medical schools were prejudicial especially against women and colored people.

Not only were women not accepted in most medical schools, but even nursing was almost exclusively an occupation for men, except when wars occurred; then, women were permitted to serve as nurses.

I do remember reading that Elizabeth Blackwell graduated with a medical degree from Geneva Medical College in New York State in the late 1840s. She was acknowledged to be the first woman graduate of a medical college in the United States. In spite of her degree, graduating first in her class, and attaining further medical experience in Europe, she struggled to be accepted in the medical profession in the United States. She finally opened what became the very successful New York Infirmary for Indigent Women and Children.

Since women were not admitted into the male dominated medical schools, there were a few philanthropic and concerned individuals who acted to attempt to solve the problem by opening medical colleges exclusively for women. The earliest, the Boston Female Medical College (later renamed the New England Female Medical College) was established in the late 1840s by Drs. Samuel Gregory and Israel Tisdale Talbot.

Of the graduates, many are now successful women doctors. One whose career was of particular interest was Rebecca Crumpler, a colored woman who had graduated from the college in the 1860s and is believed to be the first woman of her race to become a medical doctor in the United States. She worked for the Freedmen's Bureau to care for freed slaves and then contributed to the care of indigent women and children in the Boston area (accepting little or no remuneration). Her publication, *A Book of Medical Discourses* which focused on medical care for women and children is outstanding and enlightening. In spite of her selfless contributions, it was reported that she withstood much criticism and harassment from many men in the medical profession, not only because of being a woman, but also because of race.

The second institution was the Female Medical College of Pennsylvania, which was established about 1850 by Quaker women and businessmen to also address the prejudice against women. It graduated many dedicated and proficient women doctors over the years, one of whom was Rebecca Cole, a colored woman who tolerated the same abuse and discrimination as Crumpler.

Throughout the 1800s, women medical doctors continued to have difficulty in gaining employment. It was reported in a medical journal that in 1860, the United States had approximately 54,000 physicians, of which only 300 were women.

It was also difficult for colored men to be accepted in medical schools. In 1865, philanthropist Henry Martin Tupper established Raleigh Institute in North Carolina (later named Shaw University to honor its donor, Elijah Shaw). November 1, 1881, the university expanded to include a medical and pharmaceutical school giving the opportunity for colored men to become medical doctors. It is recognized as the first four-year medical school in the United States.

Although Tupper's dedication to the education of freedmen is tremendous, there were those who vehemently opposed his contributions and achievements which resulted in his home being totally burned by members of the Ku Klux Klan. Fortunately, he survived the fire. Over the years, during talks or discussions, I would often highlight Crumpler and Cole as examples of overcoming adversity and persecution to advance the greater good of the human race.

Johns Hopkins University School of Medicine opened in Baltimore, Maryland in 1893, and I believe it to be the first medical school in America to equal the standards of the best in Europe. The administrators only accept exceptional students who are required to complete a difficult curriculum. Professors do not simply teach, but are also research scientists; and students are required to intern in the affiliated hospital before being granted degrees. The university administration advocates egalitarian principles so long as the entrance requirements are met. Johns Hopkins University's teaching-research program is modeled after the University of Heidelberg, my alma mater.

What a sad commentary on some people in my adopted country who allowed such prejudice against women and colored people. They prevented those with potential in the medical field from pursuing their careers and assisting those in need.

Resurrectionists

During my tenure in medical school, the professors constantly advocated for reform in clinical experience especially anatomical practice, but procuring bodies was an issue. I was aware that many surgeons, professors, and their students were taking part in body snatching for anatomical dissections and they believed the end justified the means. Those in the medical profession insisted that to find new treatments and cures for illnesses, the dissection of bodies was important. They added that if legislators would pass acts to allow for more bodies to be accessible, snatching would not be necessary.

In New York, medical faculty attempted to convince the state legislature to enact a law to allow for the legal procurement and dissection of bodies. Finally, in 1854, the legislature passed "An Act to Promote Medical Science and Protect Burial Grounds" better known as "The Bone Bill." Until that point, New York State law allowed for only the bodies of executed criminals to be used for dissection, but the legislature now also permitted vagrants whose bodies were not claimed within 24 hours, be donated for dissection. The rationale was that by their deaths, they would finally be contributing to society, something they failed to do during their lives. The law was still too limiting.

In addition, authorities were lackadaisical in their enforcement of laws forbidding the stealing of corpses and if a snatcher were caught and found guilty, the penalty was a misdemeanor, a small fine, and perhaps a short time in jail. I understood the need, but for me, there were ethical and moral implications that prevented me from such illegal undertakings.

With minimal penalties imposed, some resurrectionists (professional body snatchers) were especially inventive and brazen. One in particular was a man named Cunningham, (known by many as Old Cunny or The Ghoul). After exhuming a body, he transported the corpse in his carriage to the purchaser, but not before he dressed the cadaver and seated it next to him in the wagon. As he traveled through the streets en route to his destination, he would engage in a one-sided conversation with the corpse.

At first, most of the resurrectionists pilfered from potter's fields because the graves were shallow and the deceased's bodies had not been claimed. As more medical colleges were founded, the exhumations increased and resurrectionists emerged in great numbers. It was a lucrative endeavor and so successful that New York grave snatchers became the illegal source of cadavers for not only New York medical schools, but also medical colleges in other states. Many medical schools had funds to purchase corpses and, when their orders were delivered, they did not want details about their origins.

Another source of corpse snatching was from experienced southern resurectionists. There were even arrangements with some of them to transport corpses to northern medical schools. One such arrangement was made by an anatomy professor in New England who, during the 1880s and 1890s, admitted to having a dozen bodies shipped each semester. The corpses were placed in barrels labeled *turpentine* and shipped to a hardware store from which they were transported to the college.

As more cadavers were requested, the resurrectionists not only exhumed bodies from potter's fields, but all cemeteries where they found access. When the public became aware, they were outraged. Cemeteries hired more watchmen, but it was learned that they and undertakers could be easily bribed.

No matter how secure a burial site was, bodies were still snatched. I read that during the late 1870s, the body of one of the prominent Harrison family was exhumed, namely Congressman John Scott Harrison (son of United States President William Henry Harrison and father of United States President Benjamin Harrison). One of John Scott Harrison's sons offered to help a friend locate the corpse of his family member, whose body had been taken. They went uninvited to the cellar of the Ohio Medical College, but did not find the friend's family member's corpse. To Harrison's astonishment, he and his friend found the body of Harrison's father hanging naked on a hook!

Harrison's son was shocked and angry because the family had taken precautions to prevent exhumations: a brick vault placed around the coffin, the gravesite filled with heavy rocks, and a watchman employed to check the grave every hour.

The populace looked for other means of protecting the graves of family members. Those who had the financial ability sought security measures to protect the graves of the deceased. They became willing customers of newly formed businesses that offered a range of products: expensive lead and cast-iron coffins, specialty locks, screws, and nails, and wired alarms that would sound if the casket were moved. A few years ago, about 1896 or 1897, a coffin torpedo was invented. It can be placed inside the casket and, if the lid is lifted, the torpedo is triggered and the snatchers are either injured or killed.

My brother Johann, our friends in the medical profession, and I have discussed the need for more legislation to regulate and protect the public. However, to this point little has taken place. Hopefully in the 20th century more monitoring of the profession will occur.

CHAPTER 7

19th Century Medical Progress

I WILL IMPART A SYNOPSIS OF THE PHILOSOPHIES, PRACTICES, and some outstanding contributors to the field of medicine during the 1800s. In that way, you will better understand the evolution and advances in medicine during my lifetime.

The long-accepted philosophy that body and spirit must be in balance to achieve optimum wellness had been the assumption for thousands of years by Chinese, Indian, Islamic, and European practitioners. Most immigrants, medical practitioners, and doctors who arrived in America during the 1700s and the first half of the 1800s embraced that theory and treated those who were ill by administering heroic depletion methods, most notably bloodletting, purging (using calomel), and sweating to rid the body of impurities. Through the remainder of the 1800s, there was an ongoing quest to discover other methods, treatments, and cures for the ailing so the body could return to wellness.

An early proponent of the heroic depletion theory was Dr. Benjamin Rush, (born 1746) in Pennsylvania and died there in 1813 (two years after I was born). He was a favorite of Thomas Jefferson and, on Jefferson's behalf, readied Meriwether Lewis for the Lewis and Clark Expedition. Rush instructed Lewis about the illnesses he and his corps should expect to encounter and the methods to counteract them. Medical supplies were provided by Rush including opium, wine, medications to induce vomiting, and his specially prepared laxatives nicknamed *thunderclappers*.

There were those who were critical of Rush's methods and he was even accused of accelerating the death of Benjamin Franklin through bloodletting. At one point, a critic denounced Rush's treatments, but Rush responded by suing for libel. He was victorious, and awarded $8,000. His methods were lauded during the first half of the 19th century.

Another was surgeon J. Marion Sims, born about the same time as I, but in the state of South Carolina. He is credited with developing surgical procedures to repair complications of obstructed childbirth. Southern masters agreed to donate women slaves to serve as test subjects so that Sims could perfect his techniques. He performed his unproven methods in an unsanitary backyard building and repeatedly performed painful procedures (with no anesthesia) on the same women. One in particular endured the procedure 30 times during a four- year period. The women suffered constant infections after surgery until Sims experimented with the use of metal sutures, which proved successful.

Even after perfecting his techniques, his practice did not flourish in South Carolina. He moved to New York City, expecting to easily find employment because of the publishing of his innovative methods, but doctors here did not need his personal expertise since they could follow the procedures from reading his publications. Although he couldn't gain employment in the city, and was financially lacking, he did convince some New York City societal women to finance a hospital, which was subsequently named New York Women's Hospital. Sims was the first administrator.

Johann and I have discussed the work of Sims. Although Sims developed procedures to help correct gynecological problems, we believe his lack of humanity was appalling. We have heard others defend Sims by stating that sacrifices of some must be made for the sake of progress in medical knowledge, but Johann and I cannot abide such a rationale.

In the 1840s, Reservoir Square Park was established in Manhattan. In the 1880s, the park was renamed Bryant Park to honor the abolitionist William Cullen Bryant. I was pleased to learn that this man who tirelessly and diligently worked to assist slaves attain freedom, was being recognized. Then I read in the early 1890s, that a statue of J. Marion Sims was being erected in Bryant Park. Many of us voiced our objections, but others believed the success of his gynecological experiments, no matter how achieved, afforded him a place of honor in a park. What an insult to humanity!

Many of the contributions to medical advances have been accomplished by European scientists, doctors, and surgeons because they had attended long- established medical schools, some of which dated back to the 1200s or earlier. Those schools offered challenging curricula, excellent professors, research facilities, and centers for internships.

Since the United States is such a young country, medical progress here is still in its early developmental stage. During my lifetime, I have seen progress, but I must add that it is often due to the outstanding doctors, surgeons, and scientists who have gained much of their medical knowledge in European medical schools. In addition, many European physicians and scientists contributed scholarly written findings, which have been published here and have also assisted in our medical progress. I will mention some of them who particularly have impressed me.

At the turn of the 19th century and until his death in 1829 at age 51, the work of English scientist Humphry Davy is notable. He isolated and studied the actions and ramifications of elements such as potassium, sodium, calcium, and magnesium. As a result of his experimentation with nitrous oxide, he realized its potential as an anesthetic. (During those experiments he was caused to laugh, resulting in its nickname "laughing gas.") In addition to students and colleagues attending his intriguing lectures and fascinating demonstrations, elite English men and women enjoyed the presentations, and his lectures became a popular venue for their entertainment.

Doctor and Mrs. Syntax, with a party of friends, experimenting with laughing gas.
Credit: Wellcome Collection.

In spite of his authoring a scholarly book about nitrous oxide and its use as an anesthetic for minor surgical procedures, the idea was not accepted until the 1840s. However, during his lifetime, not only were his demonstrations and lectures popular but the inhalation of the gas also became a recreational event at social gatherings.

Other outstanding European scientists, surgeons, and doctors are: Rene Laennec, inventor of the stethoscope (a definite improvement over simply placing one's ear against the patient's chest), surgeon James Blundell, an obstetrician, who introduced the concept of blood transfusions and performed the first successful human to human one, and physician Samuel Hahnemann, who introduced the theory of homeopathy. Hahnemann experimented on himself (a healthy person) by ingesting a substance which was known to cause malaria symptoms. When the symptoms manifested themselves, he was convinced that if ill persons ingested a diluted amount of a substance that was known to cause their disease, they would be cured. (His law is referred to as "Like Cures Like.")

My brother worked at the German Dispensary and befriended many respected doctors who practiced there. He met with them periodically to discuss medical concerns. I enjoyed meeting Johann's medical friends. One in particular was Dr. Abraham Jacobi, who had immigrated to America after the 1848 uprising. On the Lower East Side, Jacobi had a small practice in which he focused his care on the treatment of children. He called this practice *pediatrics*, a term that eventually came to be used universally. At the German Dispensary where he and Johann, met, Jacobi was impressed that those who could not pay were treated free of charge, regardless of race, ethnicity, or any other difference. He became a physician and teacher there and began a Department for Children's Diseases, the first such in the nation.

Jacobi was in demand. He accepted positions, as his schedule permitted, to work or teach at Jews' Hospital, Bellevue Hospital, New York University Medical College, and City University of New York. Before he left Jews' Hospital, he oversaw several changes. They include the hospital becoming non-sectarian, adopting a new charter, being renamed the Mount Sinai Hospital, adding a department of pediatrics, and a school of nursing.

During the 1880s, German scientist Robert Koch, a proponent of germ theory, discovered the bacteria responsible for tuberculosis (consumption). At the time, one in seven people were dying of the disease. He also isolated the bacteria responsible for cholera by performing autopsies on the victims. This was another lauded discovery since each cholera epidemic in the United States was claiming thousands of lives.

During the same decade, the Spanish physician Jaime Ferran, a student of Louis Pasteur created a cholera vaccine. He successfully administered mass vaccinations to about 50,000 people in Spain during an epidemic.

British surgeon Joseph Lister was convinced of the importance of sterile surgery and introduced carbolic acid as an antiseptic to sterilize surgical instruments, sanitize operating rooms, and disinfect hands before surgical procedures. His supposition was correct and the transmission of diseases within hospitals and the incidence of postoperative infections declined significantly after the introduction of sterilization.

Rudolf Ludwig Virchow, a German physician, scientist, and pathologist was the chair of pathological anatomy for a period of time at the University of Wurzburg, Johann's alma mater. Johann's medical friends in Germany always kept him informed of Virchow's amazing accomplishments.

My brother and I also read any publications authored by Virchow that were available to us in this country and those sent by Johann's friends. Virchow wrote, "Medicine is a social science and the physician is the natural attorney of the poor." He believed that epidemics had their inception in social arenas, not medical, resulting in some progress and success in his pleas for public health.

In 1896, Johann received a letter from a friend at the University of Wurzburg about a discovery by the chair of the current physics department, Wilhelm Conrad Röntgen. Professor Röntgen had detected electromagnetic radiation, which became known as Röntgen rays or X-rays. They enabled views of the interior of the body. What an incredible diagnostic tool!

Many wonderful advances have taken place during the 1800s, and Johann, our medical friends, and I have discussed the possibilities of many more diagnostic and surgical tools to enable more detailed surgeries and to treat specific diseases. In my musings about the medical progress during my lifetime, I can't help but envision the possibilities of a future in which many diseases will be eradicated.

CHAPTER 8

Indigent and Orphaned Children

ANNA AND I WERE UNABLE TO HAVE CHILDREN. THEN, IN 1842, one of Anna's sisters and her husband were killed in a carriage accident and we agreed to adopt their two children, Julia, age seven, and Augustus, age two. Amazingly, there was nothing we needed to do to make the adoptions official. Since colonial times, children of deceased parents were informally transferred to willing relatives or friends, and if those options were not available, they were placed in orphanages or meandered the streets.

Within a few months of adopting Julia and Augustus, Anna and I realized the tremendous responsibility we had undertaken. As a result, we became more cognizant of the treatment of other children, not only in orphanages, but also those living with families, friends, or wandering the streets.

We witnessed instances in which birth parents or adoptive parents sent children, younger than age eight to work, not allowing for their education or childhood activities. Child labor was an ever-increasing problem. By the late 1860s, more than 100,000 children were working in New York City and neighboring areas. Many were working 10 to 12 hours per day.

I understood that some families needed additional income, but there were other methods, including charitable organizations, from which assistance could be sought. Anna and I remained vigilant of any situations in which we observed behavior that was inappropriate. Often, tactful conversations with parents or guardians resulted in improvement, but, at times, there was resentment for intruding.

Another concern Anna and I shared was the tremendous number of indigent children. Some members of fraternal organizations and I were serving on orphanage committees that discussed possible solutions. Some wives of members (including Anna) were either employed or volunteered in orphanages.

Unfortunately, in spite of advocacy, most governmental agencies were not responsive to the problem. There were several private orphanages that had been founded in the early 1800s and others were evolving, but they often had insufficient supervisory personnel. Those directly involved with overseeing the care of indigent children were reportedly not always the most compassionate.

Eventually there was more monitoring of the employees who dealt directly with the children. At some of our fraternity meetings, members who were involved with this mission would share their experiences and seek others to lend support. This was part of our charitable work.

The members directly involved in the orphanage work told us how difficult the job was. It took tremendous patience and caring to gain trust from many of the children, who had been wandering the streets and begging or stealing in order to survive. Some were from households in which the parents were abusive while others were sent into the streets because of the lack of food and clothing in the home. There were also many parents, who resulting from either unemployment or the death of a spouse, found institutionalizing their children the best alternative.

By the mid-1800s, there were about 30 orphanages in New York City, albeit not all well administered. Fortunately, more and more devoted people were becoming involved in overseeing the care and treatment of children in such institutions. In spite of the number of orphanages, it was reported that there were yet over 30,000 homeless children meandering the streets of New York City.

The fraternities, in which I was a member, identified charitable support of the needy as a main goal. Here are stories about three of the outstanding orphanages, in which our fraternity members or their families volunteered.

The Orphan Asylum Society in the City of New York began in the early 1800s before we settled in New York City. It was the first private orphanage in the city and was founded by philanthropists Isabella Graham and Elizabeth Hamilton, (the wife of founding father Alexander Hamilton). The two women's insightfulness resulted in an orphanage in which destitute children were accepted, regardless of race. The children were placed in a caring atmosphere that resembled a loving family environment and would also attend to their educational needs. Couples wishing to be employed in this environment were interviewed in order to select ones that would be nurturing to the children. The first of these orphanages was located on the Lower East Side. It was a small dwelling where a caring married couple and six orphans were domiciled.

This endeavor was so successful that within a year, with public and private assistance (but maintaining the same prototype), they established a larger home to house 200 children. The Orphan Asylum continues to this day doing outstanding work.

Another orphanage in which some of our fraternity members volunteered was the Colored Orphan Asylum. It was founded in the 1830s by three white Quaker women. This was reportedly the first institution of its kind in America and even had a colored medical director, Dr. James McCune Smith, who was a licensed medical doctor. He not only attended the medical needs of the children, but counseled and encouraged the graduates to obtain further education.

Smith published erudite articles in response to the political climate (especially in the south) opposing freedom for colored people. Other articles were in refutation to those who professed the inferiority of colored individuals. For example, Dr Samuel Cartwright of New Orleans wrote in the *Southern Medical Reports* that colored people wishing to flee servitude were suffering from "Drapetomania," a mental illness similar to madness. Another disease Cartwright invented was "Dysaesthesia Aethiopica," also known as "Rascality," that he asserted caused the lack of work ethic among slaves and was even more prevalent among freed ones. Another example are the claims of John C. Calhoun, a member of the United States Congress, who declared that freedom of colored people caused vice, pauperism, deafness, blindness, insanity, and idiocy. Dr. McCune Smith was not only an astute, intuitive thinker, but also virtuous, and altruistic. I am grateful that he and I became friends and worked towards similar goals.

In the mid-1850s, The Children's Aid Society was established under the direction of the philanthropist Charles Loring Brace. He introduced the innovative concept that orphanages should go beyond feeding, clothing, and giving shelter and should prepare children for life outside the institutions. To this end, he established educational programs that not only taught literacy, but also trained children for what he called "emigration from the institution."

Brace arranged for children to be transported on what was known as the Orphan Trains to farms in many parts of the country. There, host families could give them basic needs in a more personal setting. They would live surrounded by fresh air and be employed on the farms. As much as possible, he tried to have the host families screened to assess the success of the placements.

His plan also emphasized that these children were not indentured and had the right to leave an uncomfortable situation at any point. I believe the premise was a good one, but monitoring each situation was difficult. Fortunately, evaluation from many adults who had experienced the farm opportunity was positive and had prepared them for other endeavors. During Brace's approximately 40-year tenure as director of The Children's Aid Society, other orphanages requested taking part in Brace's "emigration plan."

Two other persons, Isaac Hopper and his daughter, Abigail Hopper Gibbons, deserve mention. The goal of both Hopper and Hopper-Gibbons was the avoidance of recidivism, and their advocacy resulted in much progress in this needed area of reform.

By the time I met Hopper in the 1840s, he was a leader of the Prison Association of New York State and was successful in working through the New York State Legislature to effect several positive changes in the prison system. In 1851, he and several other New Yorkers founded the New York Juvenile Asylum, a home for children who had been in trouble with the law. The asylum offered housing, education, and eventual placement in apprentice positions. Some of these young people were also given the opportunity to emigrate on the Orphan Trains.

Abigail Hopper-Gibbons advocated for improvements in women's prisons. She established the Women's Prison Association and founded the Isaac T. Hopper Home to assist in preparing released women prisoners to re-enter society as contributory citizens.

I was pleased that I had the opportunity to contribute to some of the orphanage programs and, of course, to offer a loving and nurturing home to Julia and Augustus, the children we adopted. Julia grew into a lovely young woman. She and my nephew Frederick Bechtel (who as I mentioned, was living with us) were spending a great deal of time together and announced they were going to wed. I performed the marriage ceremony, which took place, October 1, 1853.

By 1854, Julia was with child and gave birth in September of that year. My newborn grandchild and my daughter Julia were having difficulties during the birth. The newborn was having respiratory problems so I quickly summoned my prior professor Dr. Bedford and our friend Dr. Jacobi. In spite of their incredible knowledge, the child only survived a few hours and Julia died the following day. It was a tremendous shock. Anna, Frederick, and I were grief-stricken.

I often think that if some of the scientific findings of the later 1800s had been discovered sooner perhaps Julia and her child could have been saved. My brother, Johann consoled me saying that he and I were aware of the latest medical advances, but there are times that we cannot reverse a condition or situation with the present knowledge.

There were many people who arrived at our home to offer their condolences. Fortunately, Anna has a large extended family and they were at our home every day for several weeks bringing food and making sure Augustus was not forgotten in all the sadness.

Anna insisted we buy a large lot in Greenwood Cemetery. I didn't see the need for such an expansive one, but Anna could be relentless when she wanted something. We purchased an area on a hill, nicely landscaped, with a lovely view of the city.

Greenwood Cemetery, a rural cemetery in Brooklyn, New York, had opened in 1838. By the 1840s, an expansion of several hundred additional acres was added through the efforts of Almerin Hotchkiss, the innovative landscape gardener and first superintendent of the cemetery. The cemetery then covered an area of almost 500 acres located on a picturesque site with lovely uneven terrain, accented throughout with ponds, many trees (to beautify and offer shade), and roadways and pathways attractively integrated into the landscape. It is such a beautiful setting that, in addition to a cemetery, it is considered a park and picnic site. *The New York Times* reported some years after we purchased the lot that New Yorkers wished to live with the upper class on Fifth Avenue and sleep with their fathers in the elite Greenwood Cemetery.

Julia and her child were interred there. Anna and her family have Jewish, Protestant, and Catholic religious affiliations so she was able to offer our lot to them for burials because it is a non-sectarian cemetery.

The death of my grandchild made me even more cognizant of the various causes of infant death. In the United States during the 1850s, the infant death rate (children under age one) was over 20%. Therefore, I will mention one other orphanage, The New York Foundling, established in the late 1860s by the Sisters of Charity, a division of the Roman Catholic Church. The organization focused on caring for ill and abandoned infants. In addition, it also offered an alternative to the widespread incidence of infanticide. The sisters reported that after two years of accepting children, there had been 2,500 babies left with them. They also arranged to send infants and other young children on the Orphan Trains, but only permitted them to be adopted by Catholic families. Their dedication was admirable, but although a private charity, it was still saddening that religion was an impediment that prevented many children from receiving needed parenting.

The population of New York City almost quadrupled from the time we had moved to the Lower East Side until the time of Julia's death (approximately 20 years). The area had become extremely noisy and lacked fresh air, but we remained because of my service to the community. Our lot at Greenwood did offer an open space with fresh air and a lovely setting, where Anna regularly invited family and friends for weekend picnics. I attended only two of the many outings because I was otherwise engaged. Anna always indicated her displeasure when I didn't attend and ceased communication with me for a few days on each of those occasions.

CHAPTER 9

Tales of Two Cities

FRIEDERIKE AND I CORRESPONDED FREQUENTLY, KEEPING EACH other apprised of family news and events in our cities. I will mention some information contained in those letters from the 1840s to the 1860s.

The immigrants in St. Louis were experiencing similar treatment by the Know- Nothing movement to those in New York City. She sent an article from the anti-immigrant newspaper, the *Native American Naturist*, in which it was recommended that citizenship for immigrants be raised from 5 to 20 years (which the group actually brought before Congress). Friederike explained that this was extremely upsetting to the immigrants in the St. Louis area (as it was for me upon reading about it).

According to Friederike, the lodges of Hermann, Harugari, and B'nai Brith that had been established in Missouri had burgeoned. Enoch and many of his friends were members of the Hermann and Harugari lodges and pleased about the success of both.

There were serious environmental and economic problems in both cities which resulted from similar causes. The lodgings were mostly tenements containing four, five, and six floors with many families living on each floor in small quarters. There were few windows so the lighting and ventilation were poor, and the lack of heating in the winter, and fresh air in the summer presented further problems. At times, during the summer, desperate measures were taken to alleviate the stifling conditions and many would sleep on rooftops. Because of the crowded conditions, some would fall from the roofs to their deaths.

In 1845, I received the exciting news that Friederike had given birth to a child she named for me. Then more exciting news arrived in

1850 that another son was born who was named John Ferdinand and nicknamed JF. I had two nephews! Hopefully someday I would meet them in person.

The year before JF was born and Philip was only 4 years of age, Friederike wrote that in May 1849, there was a dreadful fire in St. Louis. Its inception was a steamboat fire on the Mississippi River which spread to over 20 other steamboats and vessels. The fire spread to dwellings along the levee and into the city destroying about 15 city blocks. The description reminded me of the destruction of the 1835 fire in New York City. In spite of horrific fires in both cities, it was not until the 1850s in St. Louis and the mid-1860s in New York City that professional fire departments with better equipment and trained personnel were established.

Friederike and Catherina wrote to each other frequently. Catherina indicated that she was happy in her marriage, and enjoyed helping with her husband's employment as baker and innkeeper. However, she added that there was no improvement in the leadership of Germany, there was always military presence, and a feeling of uneasiness felt by her and her husband. On several occasions, Friederike suggested they immigrate, but never received a response to that particular idea. In May 1847, a short message arrived from Catherina that she had become a widow. Then another correspondence was received the same year from a friend of Catherina informing us that our sister had died in September (four months after her husband). Our sister was only 39 years of age, but we never learned the cause of her death.

Two years after the regretful news of our sister's death, both New York and St. Louis suffered cholera epidemics. It was a frightening and horrible period of time. Sadly, more than 5,000 people died in each city, but we were fortunate that none in our immediate families succumbed.

I corresponded about the poverty stricken Five Points section (our neighboring area). By the mid-1800s it had become even more populous when additional Irish settled there after escaping the oppressive English landlords and the accompanying famine.

Hoping for a better life, they came to America, but unfortunately few possessed university educations or trades. Living among them were impoverished colored people and small groups of other ethnicities. The area was not only known for its horrific living conditions and poverty, but also for its ruthless gangs and widespread crime. Many political leaders were from that area and could always enlist the gangs to serve their unscrupulous needs.

Friederike responded that similar to the Five Points area, there was an area of St. Louis populated by Irish, known as the Kerry Patch. Like those in New York, most living in the Kerry Patch were uneducated and either unemployed, worked on the riverfront, or in factories. There were also vicious gangs in the Patch who were always ready to act at the behest of St. Louis' unscrupulous leaders.

We discussed in correspondences the ongoing problem of waste removal in both cities. From the time we arrived in America, solutions for waste removal were woefully lacking in both cities until late in the century. Waste was left in the streets by animals, especially horses. Transportation was mostly by horse drawn carriages which increased every decade in New York City until they numbered over 100,000. I remember being shocked when I learned that each horse left about 25 pounds of manure in the streets every day which of course left a horrible stench and an accompanying health hazard. Other animals such as pigs, dogs, cattle, and sheep freely wandered the streets and also left their waste. When animals died, their carcasses were often not discarded for a year or more especially those of horses which were left to decompose so their weight would be manageable. At times in New York City, the waste in the streets reached two feet high.

Besides the animal waste, human waste was also a concern. During the night, chamber pots were used rather than going to the overflowing outhouses. The contents from the pots were supposed to be deposited in the outhouses in the early morning hours. Instead, many tenants (especially those living on the upper floors of the tenements) would toss the waste from a window to the street. I recall hurriedly walking the streets trying not to inhale the disgusting stench and always wearing a hat with a brim in case I had chosen an inopportune time when the contents of a chamber pot were being thrown out a window. The hat did protect me to an extent, but over the years I must have disposed of about a dozen soiled hats. Friederike added that the horrific, unsanitary conditions on ships bringing passengers to St. Louis via the Mississippi River exacerbated the overall problem there.

Solutions were proposed such as using St. Louis' limestone sinkholes and caves as repositories for waste. Unfortunately, large rainstorms caused the sinkholes to overflow allowing human waste to float in the open. Another solution, in both cities, was for waste to be dumped in waterways, such as the Mississippi River and the East River. The installation of sewers and indoor plumbing was begun in the mid-1800s in both cities. However, outhouses were not sealed and were essentially open cess-pits that permitted wastewater to seep out from under the foundation walls of homes and other buildings. This allowed raw sewage to continue to flow without constraint. Repositories for most waste continued to be outhouses, on streets, and in waterways.

In other correspondences, my sister wrote about the *Dred Scott v. Sandford* lawsuit which had commenced during the 1840s in St. Louis and lasted into the 1850s. She believed that since Missouri was a border state (and was divided between pro-slavery proponents and abolitionists) the case received a great deal of attention from the citizenry.

In the event that the reader is not aware of the case, I will explain. Scott, a slave was seeking freedom on the basis that he and his family had lived with their master in free territories. Prior to the *Dred Scott* case, there had been several precedent cases heard in Missouri courts, such as *Rachel v. Walker* in the 1830s (Missouri Supreme Court) which had a positive outcome for the plaintiff.

The *Dred Scott* case was initially unsuccessful because of a technicality of a witness statement, but was reheard a few years later when a jury found in Scott's favor. In her letter, Friederike expressed jubilation and believed that the case represented the freedom that all should enjoy as part of the human race.

Then the case was appealed several times in the Missouri Supreme Court and the verdict was reversed and remained so. The Court held that Scott should have sued while residing in a Free State. In the 1850s, he appealed the decision to the United States Supreme Court. The court found against Scott on the basis that he was a slave, therefore not a citizen. They further ruled that the Missouri Compromise of 1820 (which prohibited slavery in Northern Territories) was unconstitutional!

I wrote to Friederike that newspapers in New York City were reporting the details of the case and I expected the same was occurring throughout the country. She and I were incredulous about the outcome. We couldn't help but wonder how the U.S. Supreme Court would defend their finding against the provisions set forth in the United States Constitution. There was outrage by many in New York City. Friederike and I agreed that it had exacerbated an already tense issue and that it might provoke violence. Of course, we never anticipated a civil war some years later.

The population explosion in both cities was amazing as shown by the numbers we exchanged. I informed Friederike that in 1850, New York City had about 350,000 Germans and about 174,000 Irish together representing about three-quarters of the city's population. In fact, in 1850, Germans in New York City occupied the third largest German population of any city in the world. Friederike responded that in 1850, the population of Germans in St. Louis had reached approximately 25,000 and the Irish about 10,000 together representing about 45% of the population of the city. In both cities their presence was definitely evident.

My sister and I enjoyed attending concerts and corresponded about them. There were many renowned European artists whose concerts included performances in New York City and St. Louis during the mid-1850s, but I will mention only one.

Probably the most extraordinary concertizing was that of Jenny Lind, the soprano known as the Swedish Nightingale. She was reticent to tour the United States until convinced by the promoter and businessman, P.T. Barnum. He offered to pay her $200,000 to come to the United States and a percentage of the ticket sales.

Lind arrived in America in 1850 and the anticipation and excitement was termed "Lind Mania." The ship bringing her arrived at the pier in New York City and was met by 30,000 to 40,000 people, several of whom were severely injured by the crushing crowds.

Her concerts in New York City (and for that matter in any hall in which she sang) were always sold out and in some instances tickets were auctioned for as much as $600. We were fortunate to get tickets through my nephew Frederick. He, Anna, and I attended Lind's first New York concert at Castle Garden, September 11, 1850. After her New York performance, she traveled by private train car and concertized in many other eastern cities. Then she journeyed by ship to southern and mid-western cities including St. Louis, Missouri.

At some point, Lind terminated her contract with Barnum, apparently because she was unhappy with some of his promotional tactics as well as his practice of charging too high ticket prices.

Friederike wrote giving details of Lind's time in St. Louis. She had traveled via the Mississippi River on the steamboat *Lexington* from her concert in Memphis to St. Louis and arrived at 4 a.m. to a large crowd that had assembled at the levee to get a glimpse of her. (Several years after, the *Lexington's* boiler exploded while making the same trip on the Mississippi. This brought back memories of Uncle Philip and father's horrific ordeal.)

Friederike wrote that the total ticket sales for Lind's five concerts in St. Louis, were $40,000. She added that thousands assembled within auditory range in various places outside the theater and even were seen on housetops.

Her tour ended in 1852 in New York City. Anna surprised me saying that she was going with some of her relatives and had not purchased a ticket for me because, she said, sarcastically, that I was so often otherwise occupied. Fortunately, my nephew Frederick was able to purchase tickets and he and I attended Lind's final concert, another sold out one at Castle Garden.

It was reported in *The New York Times* that it was the largest concert audience ever assembled in New York City. Those without tickets congregated on all walkways, passageways, and the bridge leading to the Battery, to hear what they could of her final concert. Soon after the concert, Jenny Lind with her accompanist and husband Otto Goldschmidt returned to Europe permanently. I was so pleased we had the opportunity to hear her and I enjoyed both concerts immensely.

After Lind's visit, I read that her donations included a substantial amount to New York City and St. Louis charitable organizations. Besides her musical talent, she was certainly a philanthropic person.

Sadly, I received a cable in 1859 that Friederike's husband, Enoch had died suddenly. I immediately traveled to St. Louis for the funeral. Although I was aware that the United States is 28 times larger than Germany, I did not comprehend this fact until I traveled to Missouri. What a beautiful and expansive country my adopted land is, with so much diverse terrain!

I had never met Enoch (who died before his 50th birthday), but I learned at the funeral, upon meeting many of his friends, that he was an intelligent, affable, kind person, and obviously a successful businessman. After the funeral, we had a lovely lunch at the tavern he had owned. The restaurant was appointed tastefully with wood-paneled walls, and a large fireplace. Those at the luncheon commented that Enoch had been accommodating in making his guests comfortable and served the best food (often prepared by Friederike) and liquor. Friederike told me that Enoch always believed he should give the customers the best and that, combined with his congenial personality, led to his success.

Correspondences continued after I returned to New York. My sister not only had to adjust to the loss of Enoch and raise the children alone, but she also learned when the property deed was transferred from Enoch to her, there was a legal error that resulted in the property belonging to the heirs of the seller. The owners made an arrangement that Friederike and her children could remain in their home, but must make monthly payments to purchase the property. To accomplish this, Friederike worked diligently, her son JF worked in a grocery store after school to contribute, and I sent some financial help each month. Eventually the land was recovered.

On several occasions, I suggested that she and the children move to New York City, but she declined. She was fortunate after Enoch's death because she had so many excellent friends to assist her. Her frequent letters to me always indicated that she and the children had acclimated well.

She wrote that it was important for the children to enjoy family outings and told about three. One was to the Missouri Botanical Garden which she reported was magnificent. The garden opened in 1859, has a herbarium and library, and is praised as one of the best in the world. I responded that it was my hope that someday New York City would also have a botanical garden.

Friederike and the children also attended the 1860 St. Louis Fair, which had become an event of note throughout the world. She wrote that before the fair officially opened, the Prince of Wales visited St. Louis. It was estimated that at least 150,000 people gathered to get a glimpse of him. The fair offered wonderful educational, innovative, and entertaining displays.

The other pleasurable outing to which she took the children was to Bellefontaine Cemetery. It had opened in 1850, but by the 1860s, more acreage and horticultural splendor had been added. It was interesting to learn that Almerin Hotchkiss who had designed Greenwood Cemetery in Brooklyn, New York designed Bellefontaine Cemetery. She penned that Bellefontaine is regarded as a cemetery-arboretum because of the tremendous number of trees, shrubs, and flowers of various species, probably several thousand. According to Friederike, it was a perfect setting for a picnic.

She also mentioned that she frequently accompanied friends in attending productions and exhibits on the Mississippi showboats.

Friederike said they were outstanding productions and the exhibits were wonderful.

We discussed the improvements in transportation. Prior to the railroads, steamboats were the main means of transportation of passengers and goods to convenient ports. New York City received goods via the Erie Canal and the Hudson River to New York Harbor where ships were unloaded and then reloaded with other goods to transport to eastern seaports. Similarly, St. Louis had access via the Mississippi River for transport of goods to and from southern ports.

During the 1800s, the progress in transportation provided options by boat or railroad. Certainly railroads opened the door for considerably faster passenger and freight travel. They were in use in the eastern United States and from there to the Mississippi, opposite St. Louis. Ferries brought products across the Mississippi to St. Louis. As a result of the two modes of transportation, economic growth in both cities began to flourish. It was an exciting time and Friederike and I hoped with improved, easier, and less costly travel, we would eventually have the opportunity to visit each other frequently.

Receiving correspondences from her kept me apprised of the welfare and happenings of my family and the state of affairs in St. Louis. I looked forward to each letter.

CHAPTER 10

My Philosophy of Religion

SINCE MOVING TO THE LOWER EAST SIDE, I HAD GIVEN MUCH thought to starting a place of worship. Through studying the philosophies of many traditional religions, I concluded that they can justify anything. There is such a tragic history attached to traditional religions that, at times, it has resulted in people judging and hating others simply because of their differing beliefs. It has even given rise to horrific wars. What hypocrisy!

I should mention that while at university, I became interested in the philosophy of free thought. After reading a great deal about the subject, and perhaps because of my scientific knowledge, I embraced the idea that precepts should be based on logic and rational thought.

When I arrived in America, I became acquainted with the philosophy of transcendentalism, which was espoused by Ralph Waldo Emerson. Emerson embraced the idea that each of us should have an authentic personal experience with the sacred, one that did not have room for ritual. He believed that all people have the potential to develop their own upright, decent, and benevolent characters by looking inward. I felt comfortable with that philosophy which coincides with my belief of free thought.

Later in life, I studied the writings of Felix Adler and embraced his perspective, which I include in my philosophy of belief. I had the pleasure of meeting Felix and we spoke about our positions and our families' displeasure with our philosophical choices. Felix Adler, as I, had attended the University of Heidelberg, but he attended much later. While there, he was influenced by neo-Kantian philosophy which espouses the idea that the development of morality can be accomplished outside the confines of theology. He also was outraged by the exploitation of women and children in the labor force in America. This led to his initiating a doctrine called Ethical Culture, in which the main tenet is that each of us should live according to ethical principles and support each other in the quest for good character. It would result in each person contributing positively to the world.

I understood Felix's plight in being expected to follow in his family's clerical tradition and yet not being able to accept those maxims of his religious upbringing. Felix was expected to be a rabbi, like his father Samuel Adler, who had been rabbi of the Reform Jewish Temple Emanu-El in New York City. As I mentioned previously, my grandfather was an Evangelical minister but I could not abide his beliefs or those of the Lutheran ministry.

Although Felix and I had both encouraged German immigrants to learn English to assimilate, there were times, such as in services and meetings that we used the German language. This allowed for a relaxing, meditative, meaningful environment for those not yet fluent in English. I was surprised to learn from Felix that his father agreed with this approach and had conducted his temple services in German, rather than the traditional Hebrew.

In 1851, I rented a building at 151 Christie Street and opened the Universal Church, a unique place of worship. I wanted to preach a message that had the precepts which I embraced and were unlike traditional, organizational religions.

In general, the religious makeup of the area in which we lived was a mix of Jews, Catholics, and Protestants. By the mid-1800s, on the Lower East Side, there were several traditional places of worship: two synagogues, two Roman Catholic churches, and five protestant churches of various denominations. Then, there were unique churches like the one I established. In general, the populace of the Lower East Side, no matter what religious affiliation, were not usually conscientious attendees. They mainly frequented places of worship for special religious events. Therefore, I was pleased that many came to my place of worship more frequently.

During the time I ministered my church, I introduced the doctrine of morality as a replacement for ritual theology and preached the dogmas of transcendentalism. At first those who attended were primarily intellectuals, but, as time went on, a range of Christians, Jews, Protestants, and people unsure of their beliefs began to join. Attendance increased substantially.

Although I understand those who follow ritualistic religions, to me the doctrines of free thought and transcendentalism embrace my philosophy. Later I was pleased to be part of the ethical culture society because it encompasses the belief that we should encourage each other to live meaningful lives, perform charitable works, and promote social actions for the betterment of humanity.

After six years of ministering the free thought church, I resigned. At that point, a friend who was my ministerial assistant assumed the leadership position. I should add that, although I did not continue regular ministerial services, I did perform special religious celebrations in individual homes or other places of worship upon request.

During the years that I led the church, Anna attended services only once. She could not understand my religious philosophy and continued to follow her traditional beliefs. We had discussed differences before marriage, but it now had become an unresolved issue. What was difficult to understand was that she could accept my following a different traditional religion, but not free thought. To her free thought and transcendentalism were excuses for religion. I asked the reason she had not mentioned her opinion when I previously spoke of free thought and she replied that she assumed it would never materialize. Discussing the topic became fruitless and her lack of tolerance was disappointing.

CHAPTER 11

Cocaine, Heroin, and Other Pharmaceuticals

BY THE 1850s, MY DRUGSTORE BUSINESS WAS SO SUCCESSFUL that I opened several others. I closed the one at 30 Grand Street and opened others at 393-395 Grand (a large property), 112 Houston, 43 Avenue B, and 208 Avenue A. My son Augustus was employed part time in one and my nephew Frederick Bechtel managed another (while he was establishing a music career). Several other relatives and friends were clerks in the other drugstores, all of which I oversaw.

I believe the success I had in maintaining so many drugstores resulted from several circumstances: I had a medical degree, always stocked the current remedies, and taught my clerks about the most up-to-date medical practices. Many also trusted me because of my reputation in the community. Thanks to my close relationship with Johann, I was able to remain apprised of developments in modern medicine. Many drugstore owners had no knowledge of chemistry or the contents of their products and were only in business for financial gain.

In the 1850s, Johann and I attended one of the first pharmaceutical conventions held in New York City, and two years later, we attended another in Philadelphia. An aim of these conventions was to draft a document of standards for the profession and determine a means of monitoring manufacturers of medicines. Eventually this resulted in the *American Journal of Pharmacy* being founded and the American Pharmaceutical Association being formed. The establishment of these was a beginning. Unfortunately, they have not had much influence during the 19th century, especially regarding monitoring of remedies.

Johann and I were advocates for stricter regulations of manufacturers of remedies. On numerous occasions, we proposed that all ingredients be divulged on the label of the medicine and that regulations be enforced by inspections from medical professionals. This has been an arduous struggle. During the 1870s some state laws were enacted to regulate the manufacturers of medicines, but none have yet been enforced.

In the 1860s and 1870s, there were at least seven colleges of pharmacy that had been established in the United States with an emphasis on the importance of chemical knowledge. They were modeled in a similar fashion to European pharmaceutical colleges. However, the U.S. pharmaceutical curricula only offered minimal educations.

Finally, an outstanding New York City Pharmaceutical College, The Arnold and Marie Schwartz College of Pharmacy and Health Sciences opened in Brooklyn, New York, in 1886 and offered an extensive and ambitious curriculum. I encouraged any of my employees who were interested in the profession to enroll and I would assist with the cost.

My clerks were required to know every item in the store, understand its use, and keep an inventory. I insisted that they never claim that our remedies cure diseases, but rather lessen discomfort. In this way, they could comment intelligently. They were also reminded that customers should be told that the items they purchase must be used cautiously and that patients must be monitored while taking them. I met with all the clerks weekly to review the products, discuss any new additions to the inventory, and review the sales for the week. They were diligent and I paid them fairly.

When time permitted, Johann and I instructed my clerks about the current state of medicine. My brother had a great power of cogitation and never perfunctorily accepted or employed the latest approaches in the field of medicine without much consideration. He and I often spoke about the fact that we didn't know if a patient's death resulted from illness or a reaction to a medicine being administered. We also were concerned that some medicines masked the progression of an illness and simply treated the symptoms.

I had a laboratory in one of my drugstores where Johann and I analyzed the contents of the popular remedies of the day before I included them in my inventory. New medicines awaiting patent and other items for experimentation such as healthy leeches, morphine, hemlock, opium, herbal roots, and others were available to medical colleges and pharmacies for purchase from chemistry shops. At times, we customized medications for specific customers using chemicals and herbs which I always kept in stock.

One of my pharmaceutical concerns was the realization that many of the remedies had ingredients that could be addictive. For that reason, I required my clerks to list the names of any customers who purchased those medicines and make note if they attempted to repeat the same purchase in too short an interval. Although my clerks informed each customer who purchased a remedy that contained an addictive substance, some still attempted to repeat the purchase. Some purchased the same addictive medicine in other drugstores but I had no control over that circumstance. That is why addictive drugs should only be available with a doctor's written approval. Legislation is needed to that effect.

Addiction was becoming a serious problem and doctors did not know how to address the situation. An example that comes to mind is the events that began as early as the 1830s. Some Boston million-aire merchants were part of an illegal opium trade. They purchased opium from Turkey and sold it in China in exchange for tea and silk, but retained some opium to sell in the United States. A percentage of the huge profits made from these ventures was donated to support Boston hospitals, schools, and libraries. Meanwhile, opium sales in Boston and other areas of the United States were unrestricted and no safe cure from addiction was available.

The heroic depletion theory which was popular until the mid 1800s was of concern because of the large amounts of mercury ingested. Many of us believe this could have resulted in numerous deaths.

By the 1860s, heroic treatments had substantially waned and others were replacing them. The concept of treating the whole body was also replaced by the philosophy of treating only the injured or affected body part.

Johann and I always read the latest medical views in journals from both Europe and here. By the 1870s and 1880s they were expounding the idea that no single medicine is appropriate treatment for all illnesses. Some should be used repeatedly for chronic illnesses, others for a deficiency of the body, and in all cases the patient should be monitored for any adverse effects.

A method that gained popularity after the decline of heroic treatment was homeopathic medications. The findings and law of Hahnemann ("like cures like") remained the basis for homeopathic cures throughout the 1800s.

Dr. Frederick Humphreys, a native New Yorker, was an advocate of homeopathy. Humphreys graduated from Pennsylvania Homeopathic College in the mid-1800s, had a large patient following, taught homeopathic methods, wrote scholarly papers (many regarding his research) and ultimately founded the Humphreys Homeopathic Medicine Company.

He also developed a system of homeopathic specifics, which was presented in manual form and distributed to interested doctors and pharmacists. The manuals were published in five languages and have circulations of millions throughout the world. In the 1890s, his countertop cabinets became popular and have been purchased by many pharmacists. They are a clever item. One side lists the specific illnesses, assigning each a number. The other side has numbered drawers to easily locate the specific homoeopathic remedy.

Humphreys' cabinets and manuals are a wonderful means of advertising, but many other manufacturers also published clever advertisements in newspapers, magazines, and almanacs, and displayed posters with their remedies. This offered additional information to the public, albeit at times exaggerated or inaccurate. I will describe some of the popular remedies during the 1800s.

Sarsaparilla was a very popular herbal medicine that I stocked from the time I opened my first drugstore. It was believed to cure numerous ailments, such as skin and blood disorders, cancers, and tonsillitis. I thought much of its effectiveness was exaggerated, but it did seem to have success in helping some ills. I sold sarsaparilla medicine manufactured by Old Doctor Jacob Townsend. He began producing it in 1806 and many of us saw virtue in the manufacturing process of his sarsaparilla.

Then along came Samuel P. Townsend, a young contractor who changed his focus to pharmaceutical manufacturing. Although not related, the two shared the same surname which was at first extremely confusing to the public. Samuel Townsend began his business in the late 1840s but claimed falsely to have preceded Old Doctor Jacob Townsend.

Sarsaparilla Townsend was the nickname given to Samuel P. Townsend. He was an incredible business promoter and, by the late 1840s, his company was manufacturing 5,000 bottles of sarsaparilla per day, which was not enough to cover his worldwide orders. Sarsaparilla Townsend spent an enormous amount on advertising. As an example, he paid $20,000 for an advertisement in the *Franklin Almanac*. In addition to advertising in the United States, he promoted the product in Europe, the West Indies, South America, and Canada, and his impressive advertisements resulted in a great amount of purchasing.

His claims were erroneous and his product poorly produced. Following are excerpts of a typical advertisement that Samuel P. Townsend placed in newspapers and other printed materials praising his product and criticizing others.

DR. TOWNSEND'S COMPOUND EXTRACT OF SARSAPARILLA.

Wonder and Blessing of the age.

The most Extraordinary Medicine in the World.
The great beauty and superiority of this Sarsaparilla
over all other medicines is, that while it eradi-
cates the disease, it invigorates the body. It is one of
the very best SPRING and SUMMER medicines
ever known; it not only purifies the whole system, and

strengthens the person, but it *creates new, pure and rich blood*; a power possessed by no other medicine. And in this lies the grand secret of the wonderful success. It has performed within the last five years, more than 100,000 cures of severe cases of disease, at least 15,000 were considered incurable. It has saved the lives of more than 5,000 children the two past seasons.

At a medical meeting, doctors and pharmacists discussed the two Townsend sarsaparilla brands; over 100 of us agreed that Old Doctor Jacob Townsend's was the only one that we could endorse. To educate the public, we distributed a signed card which explained our experiences, observations, analyses, and conclusions that Old Doc Townsend's sarsaparilla was superior.

Samuel P. Townsend nevertheless, through his claims of curing thousands worldwide, did continue to sell his product. I have thought about the reason for his success and am convinced it was totally due to his ingenious advertising based on some clever knowledge of the human mind. He knew that the frequency and size of his advertisements in popular publications, criticizing his competitors, and printing statistics, albeit false, would lead people to believe in his product's success.

There have been many other popular medicinal remedies during the 1800s, some of which I stocked, while others I did not because their claims were too outrageous. If I believed a product was helpful, but only addressed some of the claims, I would sell it with the proviso that my clerks or I make the shortcomings clear to customers. I will mention some of them.

Mrs. Winslow's Soothing Syrup was introduced in 1849 and the ingredients include sodium carbonate, aqua ammonia, and 65mg of morphine per fluid ounce. It is used to offer relief for children who are teething. Customers mentioned how effective it is in relieving pain and putting children to sleep.

Kimball White Pine and Tar Cough Syrup was introduced in the 1860s. It contains chloroform and is recommended for cold symptoms and bronchitis.

Laudanum was a medicine whose production began in the 1870s. The contents include tincture of opium and alcohol and are widely used for colds, insomnia, heart ailments, and meningitis. It was also given to babies to relieve teething pain and convulsions.

Cocaine Toothache Drops were also introduced in the 1880s and of course contain cocaine to alleviate painful teeth and gums.

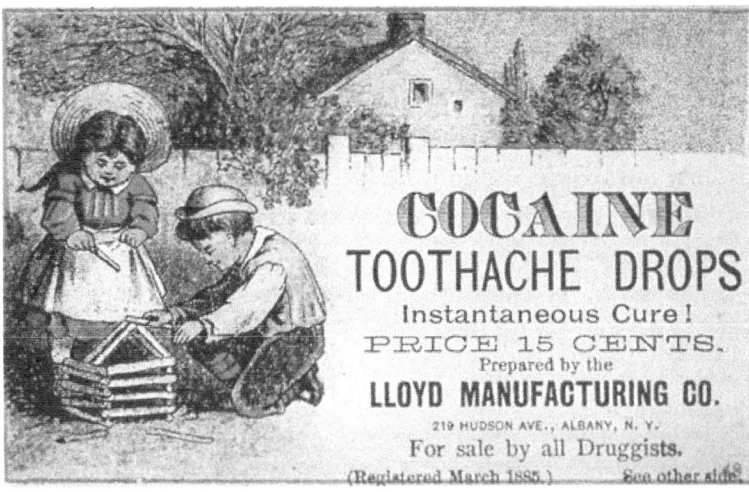

An Advertisement for Cocaine Toothache Drops

Dr. Batty's Asthma Cigarettes were introduced about 1890. They did not divulge the contents, and claimed to provide temporary relief of asthma, colds, canker sores, and bad breath.

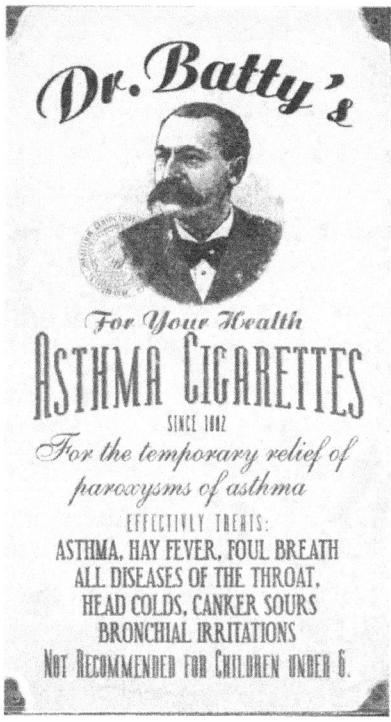

Advertisement for Asthma Cigarettes

My brother Johann and I were not in agreement with the claims of the smoking products and believed they irritated the throat and lungs rather than relaxing and soothing them. I never sold any smoking products, although many drugstores did. New smoking products continued to be produced, but Dr. Batty's Asthma Cigarettes remained one of the most popular.

Ayer's Cherry Pectoral became available during the 1890s and is very popular. It contains morphine and is touted as a cure for colds, coughs, and other diseases of the throat and lungs.

Scientists at the Bayern Pharmaceutical Company recently (circa 1896) invented a new medicine, heroine (named due to the heroic feeling it produces). They claim it is a miracle drug because it slows breathing, gives almost instant relief for diseases of the lungs, is a cough medicine, a cure for morphine addiction, and is non-addictive.

Not only are heroine products marketed by the Bayern's Pharmaceutical Company, but its modifications of salicylic acid show superior success in trials compared to any other pharmaceutical companies. The white powdery substance manufactured by the Bayern Company is patented and named Aspirin. The company has begun distribution as of March 1899. The demand from hospitals, clinics, and pharmacies has been incredible. I have used the product and it has provided relief for my joint pain. There are rumors that the company might eventually manufacture the powdery substance in pill form. That would be more convenient. I believe this medication is a valuable addition to the existent list of pharmaceuticals.

During the 1890s I reduced my drugstore ownership to two, which allows me to stay apprised of the latest medications, but work fewer hours. Johann also partially retired during the 1890s, but he too, remains informed and still volunteers at various medical clinics.

CHAPTER 12

Adultery, Bigamy, and the Law

MY BROTHER JOHANN RECEIVED A LETTER FROM HIS FRIEND Jacob with whom he graduated from medical school. Jacob explained that he had recently become a widower and had arranged for immigration to New York City with his daughter Marie. He sought my brother's assistance in finding lodging. In turn, Johann requested my help in accommodating them since I regularly offer that service through fraternal organizations and immigrant committees. My brother also requested that I introduce Jacob's daughter to some of my musician friends. Marie was 27 years of age and had studied music with the finest musicians in Germany and France. She was a talented pianist, vocalist, and proficient in several languages.

They arrived January 1856. When Marie disembarked the ship, her beauty was to behold. She had lovely long flowing brown hair, stunning brown eyes, an exquisite body, and a beautiful smile. I escorted them to a boarding house in which rooms had been rented for their use.

Anna suggested we invite them for dinner and they gladly accepted. She prepared a delicious meal: pot roast, carrots, and spaetzle with delicious gingersnap gravy. Then she served her delectable homemade apple strudel. Anna was a wonderful cook and baker. This meal, in particular, reminded me of the same one my mother frequently prepared before she became ill. After the visit, as they were leaving, they expressed their appreciation over and over for the delightful evening of conversation and for Anna's wonderful home cooked meal. After they departed, Anna agreed that they seemed to be refined, accomplished, and caring people.

Occasionally during the next month, I visited them and Jacob was not feeling well. Less than two months after arriving in America, he had contracted cholera and died shortly after. Marie was devastated; both her parents had died within a year.

After Jacob's death, I visited Marie several times a week. One day, when I arrived at the boarding house, she was in the parlor playing the piano and singing. How correct her father had been. What a talent she possessed. I arranged auditions with musician friends and they too were impressed and offered her several small vocal and piano parts. Her skill, technique, and artistic sensibility were superb. I never missed a performance.

She was so beautiful, soft spoken, intelligent, talented, and had such a delightful personality. We often spoke for hours about many topics of both serious and frivolous nature. I began finding any excuse to spend time with her.

In August 1856, as I was about to leave, we gazed at each for a moment and before any rational thought intervened, we tenderly embraced and passionately kissed for the first time. She pressed her magnificent statuesque body against mine and within minutes our beautiful friendship became intimate. It was more and more difficult for me to leave her and when I was not with her I longed for our wonderful dialogue and lusted for our lovemaking.

In December 1856, during a visit, we lovingly embraced and kissed as was our usual greeting, but then she whispered in my ear, "We are going to have a child." I was flummoxed, speechless, and remained motionless for a few moments, but then we exchanged words expressing our feelings of overwhelming joy.

We sat on the settee, she placed her head on my shoulder and looked up at me with her beautiful eyes and lovely smile. She seemed to have not a care and displayed a gaze of placid happiness. Meanwhile for me, joyful feelings were now replaced with reality as thoughts poured forth, What had I done? What will I tell Anna? I was 45 years of age and Marie only 27, but I did love her. Although Anna and I had become distant (no longer enjoying much in common) she was a kind and caring person and I didn't want to cause her distress.

I avoided discussing the situation with Anna, always finding it too stressful. She was accustomed to my being away a great deal of time because of work and organizational meetings so it wasn't too difficult to avoid the problem.

In June 1857, Marie gave birth and we had a healthy son we named Jacob. I provided lodging and other essentials for Marie and Jacob and visited them each day before returning home to my wife Anna. Other times, I made excuses to Anna so that I could spend Sundays with Marie and Jacob.

For the next three years, I believed Anna perhaps knew the situation, but never confronted me. When I was home, I found that she was even more distant and spent many hours quietly doing embroidery which she sold. My nephew Frederick continued living with us as did our adopted son Augustus.

On one occasion in 1860 when I visited Marie and our son, Marie relayed that she had been shopping in a local store where she unexpectedly came upon Anna. Marie remarked that it was awkward so, on the spur of the moment, she decided to offer a friendly greeting. Anna stared at Marie with a look of disdain, subjected her to a great deal of contumely, and then hurriedly walked away. Marie was very upset and insisted I discuss the situation with Anna.

The following evening, I spoke with Anna. She did not seem shocked. I do think someone had alerted her, but she never commented about it. People who knew (or I believed were aware) never broached the subject with me.

I definitely did not want a divorce and Anna who could have requested one did not either because of the stigma divorce implied and because according to law, she had to have a witness(s) to verify my infidelity. However, she reminded me that she could request one since the law allowed a woman to solicit one if she could prove infidelity. For me, I would have had to endure such ignominy. We agreed on a quiet separation without court intervention.

Anna was intelligent and civic-minded. She always followed the progress of the women's movements and took part when she could. Therefore, when we discussed property, she quoted parts of the 1848 Married Women's Property Act and reminded me that the law allowed women to own property which would no longer be subject to the disposal of their husbands.

Then she made demands. She wanted to move close to her extended family in Brooklyn and wished for me to purchase a house and property in her name in a place of her choosing. She requested all of our furniture and other household possessions except for our bed and I was expected to pay for all expenses incurred in moving to the new location. She demanded that the Greenwood Cemetery plot remain hers alone and that a monthly stipend for her expenses be paid (subject to renegotiation every year). I agreed to her demands. Because of her repeated threats to renegotiate, I did not put any assets in my name after our separation.

In the 1860s, Anna was listed in the New York City directories as "widow." This was commonplace when a woman is quietly separated from her spouse, even though there is no evidence of her husband's death. Throughout the 1800s, a woman admitting she was separated or divorced often evoked the belief that in some way she was inferior. If labeled as widow, the woman is in no way responsible for her station.

When I mentioned to Marie that I had finally told Anna, Marie requested I procure a divorce. I explained that according to the current New York State antiquated divorce laws, Anna would need to solicit the divorce since I was the one who had been unfaithful. Marie suggested I obtain a divorce out-of-state.

However, such a divorce would likely not be recognized in New York. Marie understood and agreed to continue as we were, although she began calling me her husband and I called her my wife.

Anna moved to Adelphi Street in Brooklyn with our son, Augustus, and my nephew Frederick. The home was certainly sufficient in size, but a few years later Anna purchased an even larger home on the same street. To this day, my nephew Frederick lives with Anna and although he and I no longer live in the same dwelling, we still have a close relationship. He visits Marie and me frequently, and at times we attend various events together.

I did see Augustus, at least once a week while he was working part-time in one of my drugstores. He was cordial to me and never spoke of my separation from his mother.

In 1860, I convinced Marie to pose for a portrait to give me as a birthday gift. She reluctantly agreed and we made an appointment to have the portrait photographed at the expansive nine-room Gurneys' exhibition gallery on Broadway.

Jeremiah Gurney and his son Benjamin, through advertising and displaying their work, became the chosen photographers of many celebrities. Benjamin was the one who photographed Marie and I was most pleased with the finished product. The lighting was perfect and the focus clearly showed the details of her beautiful face and clothing.

Portrait of my dear wife Marie

During a visit from my nephew Frederick in 1861, he mentioned that my wife Anna had accompanied Elizabeth Cady Stanton and others to Albany to protest the current divorce laws in New York State. Marie said that she had read about the efforts of Stanton and commended her, but feared progress would be slow. Frederick and I agreed.

There has been little revision in the legal code regarding divorce since colonial times. Prior to 1787, if a divorce was granted in New York State, neither party could remarry. Since colonial days, New York State's legal system viewed the sanctity of marriage as needing to be preserved no matter what the circumstances or how horrific the marriage. From the day of marriage, the couple was considered united for life. It was believed that this rationale preserved societal morality. If a divorce were granted to the aggrieved person, there was no enforceability of the conditions provided by law.

In 1787, revised legislation was passed involving dissolution of marriage. One could obtain a divorce, but only on the grounds of adultery. The plaintiff had to show proof (not an easy feat), but if the defendant could prove ill conduct on the part of the plaintiff (any specious reason would suffice), the case was dismissed. If the defendant were found guilty of adultery, that person could not remarry while the other was alive.

Showing proof was often impossible. In desperation, this led to collusion to substantiate the claims of the plaintiff by paying doctors, prostitutes, and others. If an attorney had been retained, he would sometimes find and pay people to help free his client from a horrific situation.

There was another revision of state law in 1813 when the New York State Legislature reaffirmed the same rules that existed previously, but added that if proof of extreme cruelty, abandonment, or adultery could be shown, it would warrant a mensa et thoro (a separation of the parties by act of law, rather than a dissolution of the marriage: literally divorce from bed and board). This again was difficult to prove on the part of the plaintiff. If a legal separation were granted, the couple was still considered married and neither could ever remarry while the other was alive. During the 1820s, the legislature added that only the guilty party could not remarry as long as the innocent one was still alive, but the rest of the legal code remained status quo.

Since divorce was equated with adultery, the public knowledge of such cases placed a stigma on the couple. That explains why people suffered in silence and, only under dire circumstances would consider applying for a divorce. The other option was that the couple agreed to a separation (sans court proceedings) in which the two established their own contract as did Anna and I. After separation, one or both sometimes remarried, ignoring the law, but if discovered, a criminal action of bigamy could be brought. New York State's stringent, unreasonable divorce laws inadvertently encouraged adultery.

An example of bigamy was the case of George Bookman which was reported in 1849 in the *New York Herald* as follows:

> Charge of bigamy — The police arrested, yesterday, a man by the name of George Bookman, on a charge of marrying one woman more than the law allows. It appears, from the evidence, that the accused was married on the 27th of May 1840 to Clarissa M. Corney, by the Rev. Leonard O. Marsh, residing at 21st Avenue. The second marriage took place on the 12th September last, to Catharine White, by the Rev. Philip Merkle, of Grand Street. The affidavits of both these ministers were taken, setting forth the facts, which made out a clear case of bigamy.

Both of George Bookman's wives had presented marriage documents signed by the clergy who performed each marriage. I was unaware of the previous marriage, but realized the ramifications for Bookman once the bigamy was revealed. He would be sentenced and incarcerated. Under the current laws, "Why would a person not rather commit adultery and live with the person of choice than be charged with bigamy and be incarcerated?" In New York State adultery is not illegal, but bigamy is. Perhaps Bookman was ignorant of the law.

The newspapers (especially *The New York Times* whose reports offered the most comprehensive accounts) frequently published court cases regarding separation and divorce. Unfortunately, most judges took a cavalier attitude in ruling on separation and divorce and when cases were heard, the courtrooms were usually filled with observers who often behaved like they were witnessing a comedic performance. To illustrate the application of the legal code regarding separation and divorce, I will mention the contents of a few cases.

Madame Eliza Jumel vs. Aaron Burr

This was an early case that began in 1834. Madame Jumel, who was married to Aaron Burr for four months, requested a divorce, claiming he was committing adultery with publicist Jane McManus. Burr was age 77 and Madame Jumel age 57.

Jumel's attorney was Alexander Hamilton's son. Burr tried to prevent the divorce but later decided he wanted it and realized he had to show his guilt. Therefore, he requested that his servant witness his act of adultery in order to testify. Before the judge, the servant gave details of having watched Burr remove his pantaloons and commit the act. The divorce was granted September 14, 1836 but Aaron Burr's jubilation was short-lived when later that day he suffered several strokes and died.

Elizabeth Dietz vs. Frederick Dietz

The particulars of the case were reported in *The New York Times*, January 19, 1861 entitled "Wives be Obedient Unto Your Husbands." The case involved a request for separation mensa et thoro and was brought on the grounds of alleged inhuman and cruel treatment of plaintiff Elizabeth Dietz by her husband, defendant Frederick Dietz.

The argument between plaintiff and defendant concerned her husband's cruel behavior. The plaintiff stated two causes of action: one, after returning from a walk, they found their dog on the bed. Frederick, angry, struck his wife on the nose and cheek causing her to fall insensible to the floor. On another occasion, he threatened to beat her with a wooden stick so severely that he would wind up in prison. She opened the door to make his threats heard and he dropped the stick.

The judge concluded that only two acts of such treatment could not be interpreted as sufficient cruelty to warrant separation. The cruelty would have to be continuous and the judge reminded the wife that the vows she was attempting to dissolve were taken for life, for better or worse. The judge dismissed the complaint.

Charlotte Smith vs. James Smith

This case was reported in *The New York Times* February 19, 1861 and was entitled "Another Outraged Wife, Is a Black Eye Sufficient Ground for Divorce?" It was heard in Supreme Court before Justice Wells. The case involved Charlotte Smith, plaintiff against her husband James Smith defendant.

The action was for the purpose of obtaining a separation a mensa et thoro on the grounds of cruelty. The plaintiff claimed the defendant used vulgar language, repeatedly used personal violence against her (at one point causing a black eye, another time seizing her by the hair and dragging her, and on another occasion grabbing her by the neck attempting to cut her throat with a knife). Fortunately, her screams brought the neighbors and she was saved. The judge dismissed the case on the basis of insufficient cruelty.

Throughout the 19th century, newspaper reports in New York State regarding separation and divorce (by and large), were biased and usually favored the defendant. They advocated the current laws of the state and thus supported the idea of marriage for life no matter what the circumstances.

As I complete this book (it is early 1899), and although it will no longer affect my personal situation, I hope that continued pressure on New York State lawmakers will ultimately cause wise legislation. Why should people not have the right to dissolve a marriage and why should it be illegal to want to be with someone else? Perhaps someday, these stringent antiquated laws will be drastically revised and couples will have the right to request a divorce without a long court procedure, a great deal of expense, public humiliation, and the refusal to have the right to remarry. This issue has been frustrating for many of us. Several attorneys have recently told me it is estimated that at least one in 16 marriages ends in disunion, so most of these cases are dissolved outside the law.

CHAPTER 13

About Augustus

OUR ADOPTED SON AUGUSTUS WAS AN INTELLIGENT PERSON, a caring person, and aware of the importance of service to mankind. After completing his education, he worked as a clerk for the Water Purveyor of the Croton Aqueduct Department and also as a part-time clerk in one of my drugstores. He always studied the inventory and the purpose of each medicine. At times, he submitted articles that were accepted for publication in the foremost pharmaceutical journal, the *American Druggists Circular and Chemical Gazette*. His first article appeared in 1858 and he received compliments for the information and thoroughness of his research.

In 1861, Augustus enlisted to support the Union cause during the Civil War and chose the 7th Regiment of the New York Militia volunteers, which in 1862 was renamed the 7th New York National Guard. The regiment was an old and prestigious one. Nevertheless, Anna was so upset and displeased that he wanted to serve because she realized she might lose her other child. I too had reservations and misgivings about his choice, but after speaking with him and discussing the issues surrounding the war, I realized he had a clear understanding of them. At that point, he deserved my support and good wishes.

On special request from Abraham Lincoln, the 7th Regiment (1,050 strong) left New York City for Washington, D.C., on April 19, 1861. The sendoff was impressive. Thousands of New Yorkers lined the streets of New York City to wish them well. It was a bitter-sweet moment to see them proudly marching, but to also realize what they might encounter.

The 7th Militia units continued to the ferry which would transport them across the Hudson. From there, they would travel by train to Washington, with a detour by boat transport through Baltimore. The detour was cautionary because Baltimore had been the scene of a previous battle in which Union soldiers traveling south were unexpectedly attacked by Confederate sympathizers. On April 23rd, it was reported that the 7th Regiment units arrived safely in Washington D.C.

While in Washington, the regiment was housed in the Capitol buildings and mustered into federal service to protect several camps and assist in the building of Fort Runyon. There was a second call of the 7th Regiment in 1862 and a third in 1863.

During the war, the Emancipation Proclamation was issued which became effective January 1, 1863. In preparation for its passage, I spoke at fraternity meetings, as did the leaders of B'nai B'rith, reinforcing the importance of freedom and equality for all. I was pleased that there were few incidents of bigotry or violent actions in our community and hoped that our actions helped defuse those possibilities.

However, although a long overdue action, the issuing of the proclamation resulted in problems and resentment against former slaves in many parts of our country. Segregation, and exclusion continued to exist in many venues, including hotels, restaurants, ferries, river steamers, railroad cars, and places of worship. Racial invective was commonly heard and often turned to violent acts.

However, I will focus on our adjacent neighborhood and the issues that arose on the Lower East Side Five Points area between the colored people and the Irish. I will explain the main reasons. Many prior slaves moved to the north and were willing to work for lesser wages than the white impoverished northerners causing discontent among them.

What further incited poor white men was the announcement of the new stricter conscription rules. They required married white male citizens between the ages of 20 and 35 and unmarried white males between the ages of 30 and 45 to be subject to a draft by lottery while colored males were exempt because they were not citizens. However, if a white male provided a substitute or paid $300 to the government, he would be exempt. Needless to say, most working-class men did not have the funds for exemption, but also resented that colored men were exempt. To exacerbate the situation, many Irish political leaders encouraged the already impoverished Irish to respond aggressively.

This ultimately resulted in acrimonious behavior between the impoverished white and colored men culminating in a violent insurrection in the summer of 1863. It lasted five days and is referred to as the New York City Draft Riots.

The rioters began by destroying government buildings, especially the draft office, but within a short time their anger shifted to the community of colored people. They tortured colored men, women, and children and any white persons who pleaded on their behalf. The colored men suffered the worst torture. Some were brutally beaten, others burned, and about a dozen lynched. What barbarity!

As part of the insurrection, the rioters proceeded to the Colored Orphan Asylum, where 233 colored orphans resided. The mob was reportedly temporarily distracted from entering the orphanage by a white man who shouted pleas for benevolence toward the children. The insurrectionists delayed the entrance and focused on the person who pleaded for compassion, by viciously beating him. Then they entered the orphanage, first looting anything of value. These diversions allowed the matrons time to get the children safely out a back exit. The orphanage was then burned to the ground. Fortunately, the orphans were escorted safely to a local police station.

When the New York City police department could not quell the rioters, the 7th Regiment, along with other militia totaling about 4,000 were called to assist. By the time the riots were completed, many colored people and their sympathizers had been viciously attacked or killed, and their homes destroyed. It was estimated that thousands of participants terrorized the city. During my lifetime, the draft riots have been the largest civil insurrection in America excluding the Civil War.

After Augustus was discharged from the 7th Regiment, he and I spoke about the draft riots that the 7th Regiment was called to quell. The riots made a lasting, unforgettable impression on him. He said that he witnessed such brutality between the groups, including several lynchings, but was unable to stop the acts. He also observed the burning of buildings, such as police stations, the mayor's home, the Colored Orphan Asylum, and several places of worship. Fire vehicles were destroyed, horses killed, and the police superintendent attacked, and badly beaten. Augustus told me that the disregard for human life, animal life, and the wanton destruction of property, were unfathomable. He would not soon be able to put those mental images out of his mind.

An illustration of the lynching of a colored man during the Draft Riots which appeared in *Frank Leslie's Illustrated Newspaper*, 1863.

An illustration of the burning of the colored asylum during the Draft Riots which appeared in *Frank Leslie's Illustrated Newspaper*, 1863.

Wherever he saw need, Augustus offered to help. With the change in conscription rules and the draft by lottery, many were confused and frightened about the process. I was proud that in his spare time, Augustus helped in this endeavor. There was an article printed in the *The New York World* acknowledging his outstanding command of languages, (he spoke four) and his ability in calming apprehension about the lottery.

On the Lower East Side, there was such need for doctors to treat the injured returning soldiers, that I reopened a medical clinic. The high level of trust and respect that had developed for me because of my medical and pharmaceutical knowledge and reputation, resulted in my practice increasing rapidly. I treated many soldiers, some of whom were amputees and others with serious wounds (often infected). However, there was a large percentage requesting medication to help them sleep, be free of nightmares, and/or suicidal feelings. I realized that they not only needed physical attention, but also emotional support.

Therefore, I arranged one evening per week for any who wanted to discuss their experiences during or after the war. At first few came, but eventually there were many attending and a dialogue ensued. I believe some were amazed to learn that others had the same difficulty adjusting to the aftermath. As I listened to the conversations among the soldiers, I realized, for this group, race, and ethnicity did not exist, just the common feelings from which they were suffering and now supporting each other. Augustus attended some of the meetings and shared his haunting remembrances. He mentioned after one of the meetings that it was an excellent idea having these weekly gatherings.

Augustus also informed me that he had become fond of a woman named Josephine Deppish, a native of Savannah, Georgia. She visited him in New York in late 1864. I was in her company several times during that period and found her to be a woman of good character.

She remained until February 1865, when she and Augustus left for Georgia to be married in Savannah on February 14th. They returned to New York on Friday, February 17th, and Anna had a lovely party in celebration of their marriage to which I was invited!

Augustus told me that he had been a bit concerned about the wedding reception in Savannah because Josephine's brother was a corporal in a Confederate unit and he and a few other Confederate soldiers were in attendance. Fortunately, it was a cordial event.

In June 1865, Augustus received an invitation from William Backhouse Astor and John Jacob Astor III to a reception for the 7th Regiment at the Astor house. Augustus was permitted to bring a guest and he invited me. The hosts spent time talking with each soldier and his guest and provided a wonderful afternoon.

William Backhouse Astor is the son of John Jacob Astor and John Jacob Astor III is the son of William Backhouse Astor. John Jacob Astor had the distinction of being the richest man in America and his son and grandson carried on that title.

John Jacob Astor III served in the Civil War and was promoted to brigadier general. In addition to the family business success, he was proud of his military service and that of others.

I learned that he had a special appreciation for the 7th New York Regiment in which Augustus served. The 7th was known for not only conducting themselves valiantly in the Civil War, but also for quelling many riots in New York City. That is probably the reason he had the reception for the regiment and made it an annual tradition. Astor III became a treasured friend with whom I met socially during other times of each year.

Another of Augustus' missions was improving safety on ships traversing the east coast and beyond. He had read about the sinking of the ship *Arctic* in the 1850s, which was bound for Liverpool, England from New York City. The ship had a capacity of approximately 400 and yet only about 80 survived: 20 male passengers, 50-60 crew members, and no women or children. It was learned that the *Arctic* had about half the number of lifeboats necessary for its passenger capacity.

In spite of several other ship disasters resulting in similar casualties, no improvements were made to safety requirements. Governmental agencies and ship owners (whose only concern was financial gain) showed little interest in safer seafaring ventures. There were some laws in place, but they were by no means sufficient to make much improvement in safety nor were there any requirements for inspecting the ships for compliance.

I supported Augustus in this endeavor, but took no active part in it, because I wanted it to be his crusade. He prepared crucial information, statistical analyses, and proposals to improve safety, presented them to state and federal agencies, but to no avail. After contacting ship owners, he was finally successful in being granted a meeting with one, but the owner was indifferent about Augustus' presentation. He curtly informed Augustus that he, along with other ship owners, were disinterested in such suggestions and warned against his interference. Some men even accosted Augustus as he walked to work, warning him to cease his activities. Not dissuaded, he continued his efforts. His work was not totally in vain; his campaign had piqued the interest of some newspaper owners who began reporting about the lack of safety on ships.

In December 1865, Augustus informed me that his wife was with child; the expected birth date was sometime in July 1866, and Josephine wished to return to Georgia. He said he would be resigning from his employment in New York and, fortunately, had the possibility of employment with a firm in Savannah. He also intended to pursue his crusade for ship safety while living there. I told him I was proud of his civic advocacy and wished him the best in this venture.

My nephew Frederick Bechtel and I went to the dock to bid them farewell. A month later, Augustus penned that he was employed as a bookkeeper with an excellent firm. In July 1866, we learned that the child had been born, a boy, who was named Augustus John Merkle.

Two months after the birth, Augustus had earned a week's vacation, and he, Josephine, and the child were going to visit us. But plans changed because he and Josephine believed the child was too young for a trip of that distance, so Augustus traveled alone.

We were pleased to have the opportunity to spend time with him. Not only was he enjoying his family in Georgia, but he had excellent employment there. At the end of September, he left New York to return to Savannah and had passage on the ship *Virgo*.

About a week later, we read that a steamship, the *Evening Star*, had left New York about the same time, on a similar route as the *Virgo*. It had encountered gale-force winds and had sunk. The vessel was carrying about 300 passengers, of which only 17 survived. After the sinking, reports indicated that the ship had approximately four lifeboats for the hundreds of passengers. Crew members had secured the lifeboats for themselves, beating passengers with oars as they tried to climb on board. We could not help but be grateful that Augustus did not travel on that ship and hoped that this latest tragedy would give him additional arguments to support his pleas for implementation of safety regulations.

We did not hear or read any news about the *Virgo* having difficulties, but waited anxiously to hear definitively. We were totally assured a few days later, when we read in a local newspaper, that except for the *Evening Star*, all ships (including the *Virgo*) that had traversed the eastern seaboard during that storm, had docked safely. We were so grateful and relieved.

Two weeks later, we received a letter from Augustus' wife Josephine which included two newspaper articles relaying the fact that the *Virgo* made it safely to the Savannah port and all passengers were accounted for except Augustus. It was assumed by authorities that during the gale-force winds and the rocking of the ship, he had fallen overboard. It was difficult to accept the horrible news, especially since Augustus was always cautious when sailing and advising others of the dangers. To this day, I question whether his advocacy resulted in his death. The following are the newspaper accounts which Josephine sent:

TRAGIC ACCIDENT----Mr. Augustus Merkle,
of Savannah, who
was a passenger on the ship *Virgo*, on a
late trip from New York was missed on
the late passage out and it is supposed

that he lost his footing during the heavy
gale, and fell overboard.

Augusta Chronicle, October 11, 1866

DROWNED AT SEA.---Augustus Merkle, a
passenger from New York to Savannah on
board the steamship *Virgo*, which arrived on
Saturday, was washed overboard Friday
morning, about three o'clock. The deceased
was a native of New York, a sober, steady
young man employed in this city as a bookkeeper in the wholesale establishment of
Unckles & Son. Mr. Merkle was united to a
young lady of this city about a year ago, and
was returning from a visit to his relatives at
the North when his untimely death occurred.

Macon Telegraph, October 11, 1866

When our relatives and friends learned of Augustus' death, there
was an outpouring of condolences in the form of cards, letters, flowers, and donations to charitable causes. The Astor family gave a generous donation in Augustus' memory to the 7th Regiment of the New
York National Guard.

After the visits and condolences, Anna and I spoke compassion-
ately to each other as we had many years ago. We reminisced about
our wonderful son, the grief we were feeling, and the difficulty in
accepting the loss of someone so vital and contributory. He had been
such a hard-working, intelligent, civic- minded, pleasant man of good
character and then was taken at such a young age. My only regret was
that I had never verbalized to Augustus the love and affection I had for
him and the pride I had for the person he had become.

Josephine never remarried and left the upbringing of my grandson to a well-to-do aunt and uncle. Augustus John Merkle, my grandson, attended a boarding school, seemingly received an excellent

education, and eventually began writing to me. He, like his father, became a bookkeeper for a prestigious firm and was well-received in Georgia's social circles.

When my grandson, Augustus John Merkle was 21, a photograph was taken of him and a copy sent to me. He looks so much like his father had looked.

My grandson, Augustus John Merkle Age 21.

Several years later, when he was in his late 20s, he wrote that he had been elected to the Board of Education in Savannah. Then in January 1899, he penned that he had met a lovely young woman and would be marrying in April. I explained that I did not travel any longer and wasn't in the best of health. He understood and after the marriage, sent me the following article about the wedding. The article, entitled "Women and Society," appeared in the *Augusta Chronicle*, April 5, 1899, the day after the marriage.

Women

and

Society

Merkle-Croake

At 8 o'clock yesterday morning at
St. Patrick's church occurred an Easter
marriage of much beauty and solemn
impressiveness. The nuptial mass that
followed the marriage ceremony was
celebrated by Rev. P. H. McMahon.
And the lives of Miss Nellie Croake and
Mr. Augustus Merkle were united.
The bride and groom entered unattended.
She wore an exquisite gown of white Liberty
silk over white satin, daintily trimmed in ribbon and
small ruffles of the silk. A white hat trimmed in
white plumes and roses completed the beautiful
toilette. She carried an armful of Nephetos rosebuds.
Mr. and Mrs. Merkle left immediately after the
ceremony for their home in Savannah, accompanied by the congratulations and best
wishes of their numerous friends here. The
bride is a woman of most lovable characteristics and is well qualified to make happy
the heart and home of the fortunate one
on whom she has bestowed her affection.
Mr. Merkle is a prominent young
gentleman in Savannah business and
social circles and has hosts of friends;
who will extend to his charming bride
a cordial greeting to her new home.

My grandson has developed into a wonderful adult of whom I am
so proud, as his father would have been. I couldn't help but think that
my son Augustus survived the Civil War and the New York City riots,
and then died in such a bizarre twist of fate.

Both my adopted children had passed far too soon. Julia was only 18 and Augustus was 25.

CHAPTER 14

Sorrow and Joy

SADNESS STRUCK AGAIN. OUR SON JACOB DIED. HE HAD BEEN a fine boy, with an inquisitive nature, and very intelligent. Marie and I were proud of him. Then in November 1866, (one month after the loss of Augustus) he contracted smallpox and, following a short struggle against the disease, he succumbed. He was only 9 years old. Marie and I were brokenhearted. What a terrible loss for us. Unlike my regretful lack of outward affection for Augustus, I did devote a great deal of time to Jacob and showed him love and affection on a daily basis. It did not make the loss easier, but it allowed closure with fewer regrets.

After Jacob's death, Marie was disinterested in most everything for a long period of time. My nephew Frederick and I finally convinced her to become more active which we hoped would somehow sooth the pain of the loss.

Marie loved animals so we adopted two dogs that were found wandering on the Lower East Side, emaciated, and having been abused. I thought caring for the animals might help her to heal. It was obvious they were not purebred but did resemble golden retrievers. Their personalities were quite different: one energetic and the other placid. Marie suggested we name them Presto and Largo based on their temperaments and of course, influenced by Marie's knowledge of music. When I had the opportunity to walk them, if anyone witnessed my calling their names, they looked at me incredulously.

Since Marie had always enjoyed attending music events, Frederick (who visited us frequently) was instrumental in encouraging her to engage in music discussions and finally convinced Marie to attend some functions. I noted such joy in her demeanor when we attended cultural events or met people involved in various aspects of music. Through Frederick we were introduced to some of them.

We made the acquaintance of Heinrich Steinwig (who later changed his name to Henry Steinway). He founded Steinway and Sons in New York City where he was producing and selling about 500 pianos a year by the late 1840s and early 1850s. During the next decade, sales increased to about 2,000 a year. He needed a larger facility and moved to a new location-a full city block at Park Avenue between 52nd and 53rd Streets. As a result of his flourishing business, I was pleased that he was able to constantly increase employment opportunities.

Over the years we continued following and learning about his amazing inventions and patents. His creativeness and innovativeness constantly improved the mechanisms of the piano, which, in turn, resulted in incredible financial gain.

Frederick and Marie were so enamored with the Steinway pianos that we visited the factory frequently so that they could perform and assess some of the instruments. Henry Steinway was in the showroom and impressed by their performances. We spoke for a long time and after several visits, I surprised Frederick with the news that I would gift him a piano of his choosing with the stipulation that he bequeath it to a talented musician and that the tradition be continued by each person who inherited the piano. He agreed, was so grateful, and treasured the instrument. On Marie's birthday, I surprised her with a visit to the Steinway factory, where I purchased a beautiful Steinway piano of her choosing with the same stipulation that I had requested of Frederick.

During the 1860s, Henry Steinway's son, William Steinway, (with whom Frederick, Marie, and I had become well- acquainted) planned and opened Steinway Hall on East 14th Street. It was the second largest concert hall in New York City and had a large showroom. The arrangement was such that to reach the concert hall one must walk through the showroom. The clever layout resulted in increased sales. It became one of New York City's most prominent cultural centers, housing the New York Philharmonic until Carnegie Hall opened a few years ago. At the same time, the Steinway's boasted that they employed the largest labor force in the city, (a wonderful boost to employment).

Another enjoyment of Marie was shopping for chapeaus. In the spring of 1867, for Marie's pleasure, I invited her to peruse the millinery shops on Broadway near the intersection of Fulton Street. From there we could see the newly constructed iron bridge. Marie was enamored with hats and on both sides of Broadway, there were millinery shops. The location at Broadway and Fulton had been one of the most dangerous intersections in lower Manhattan due to the many carriages, animals, and people attempting to cross. A pedestrian bridge seemed to be a solution.

Philip Genin, a hatter on the west side of Broadway, was responsible for convincing the New York City Council to have a bridge constructed for pedestrian use. It was approved and an iron bridge was erected. It was named Loew Bridge to honor the former county clerk Charles Loew.

The bridge seemed well-constructed and attractive. I was impressed by the ease with which we crossed Broadway and amazed by the number of millinery shops on either side. It was a boring day for me, but I did purchase a bonnet for Marie's enjoyment.

Sometime later, a problem arose between the hatter who convinced the New York City Council to have the bridge constructed and a rival hatter whose shop was on the opposite side of Broadway. It was reported that the bridge increased the clientele of the shops on the west side of Broadway (where the Genin shop was located), but placed a shadow over the east side, causing those stores to seem obscured and unappealing. The east side shops reportedly suffered a loss of business. The vendors on the east side went before the Council, demanded the bridge be removed, and they prevailed. Therefore, only a year after the construction, the bridge was removed and the dangers of crossing Broadway and Fulton Street among pigs, dogs, horses, carts, carriages, and pedestrians, returned.

The short-lived Loew Bridge located at Broadway and Fulton.

What a stupid decision! In essence, the council had reinstituted the former dangerous situation. If more time had been taken, the council might have convinced each side of the importance of safety at the intersection, rather than abiding their short-sighted and emotional arguments for its removal. It was a frustrating, but not unusual hasty decision made by a governmental agency with no thought of consequences. I knew that after erecting and then dismantling the bridge, there was little chance that the council would approve rebuilding.

Frederick continued searching for events that Marie might enjoy. He suggested we attend a service at the Plymouth Church on Orange Street in Brooklyn. Shortly after the Civil War, Frederick began attending services there, which is only about a mile from his residence on Adelphi Street. I assumed his motivation for attending was mainly to hear the organist perform on what Frederick described as an incredible instrument with a magnificent timbre. After hearing about the organ and organist, Marie became enthusiastic about attending a service there.

Although I had contemplated other ways to spend a warm, beautiful spring Sunday morning, at Marie's coaxing we traveled for over an hour from Manhattan to Brooklyn, met Frederick, and attended a service at Plymouth Church. As we entered the church, I was amazed by the large congregation of several thousand. The organ was impressive and, according to Frederick, had 4,000 pipes, which I could believe by feeling the instrument's vibrations. Both the choir and the organist performed exceptionally well.

I was aware that the church was established in the late 1840s by New England families that trace their lineage to the pilgrims of Plymouth Rock and that Rev. Henry Ward Beecher was the pastor. The sermon I anticipated hearing would be of anti-immigrant sentiment, but I was pleasantly surprised and impressed by Beecher's words. They conveyed the importance of social justice and the need to be active in seeking equality for all.

After the service, Beecher greeted members of the congregation along with other attendees. He had a pleasing personality and a charismatic nature. We also met Beecher's wife who stood next to him with their 10 children and who also greeted the congregants.

My anticipations for that day were totally in error. I admitted to Frederick that I had been impressed with Beecher's oration and Frederick retorted that the Board of Trustees obviously concurred since Beecher received a salary of $100,000 annually!

Frederick mentioned that at various times, notables such as Samuel Clemens, Walt Whitman, and Abraham Lincoln had attended the services and marveled at Beecher's energetic presentations. I also learned from Frederick that prior to the Civil War, preacher Beecher had established the lower level of the church as a stop on the Underground Railroad route and had even held mock auctions to emphasize the barbarity of slavery.

President Lincoln had requested that Beecher tour Europe during the Civil War to encourage support for the Union cause and at the end of the war to speak at the raising of the flag at Fort Sumter. I also learned that he was the brother of Harriet Beecher Stowe who, prior to the Civil War, had authored the book *Uncle Tom's Cabin* which deeply impacted those who read it by the descriptions of the horrors being withstood by those enslaved.

However, according to Frederick, there were rumors of Beecher's infidelities and affairs especially with women in the congregation. One was Elizabeth Tilton who confessed to her husband Theodore that she had an affair with Beecher.

Apparently, Theodore Tilton, an author, editor, lecturer, and friend of Beecher was shocked and felt betrayed. He and Beecher had edited the religious periodical, *Independent* and were reported to have a close personal relationship.

In 1874, Tilton brought suit against Beecher for criminal conversation with his wife and the alienation of affection. In January 1875, there was a civil court trial which drew local and national attention. Marie and I followed the details of the trial. From the beginning, as Marie read the daily newspaper accounts, I heard outbursts of, " Philip, listen to this." She would update me regarding the progress of the trial, commenting rightfully so, "How could his wife after learning of his many willing mistresses, not want to be rid of him?" "Why would his mistresses not be angry to hear of all the others when they thought they were the only one?"

Despite the supportive testimonies for Elizabeth Tilton by famous women activists, Susan B. Anthony, Victoria Woodhull, Elizabeth Cady Stanton together with other claims of infidelity against Beecher, he was acquitted! By the conclusion of the trial, the Tilton's had separated and both were excommunicated from the church. When Marie and I read the outcome, we exclaimed in tandem, "How could this happen?" I said to Marie, "Why were the Tilton's who were clearly wronged, punished?"

After the trial, Beecher responded to inquiries posed by an investigative committee of the church. He admitted during the trial that Elizabeth Tilton had sex with him, but he had not with her. As Marie rightfully asked, "How is this possible and why was it accepted as a cogent and truthful response?"

Beecher added, "It is perfectly all right to convey the exact opposite of the truth as long as your words, technically considered, did not lie." I have no idea what his response even meant and why it was accepted without question. I could not help but wonder, "Was the investigative committee lacking in the ability to hear or were they as immoral as Beecher?" To Marie and me, Beecher's responses are incomprehensible, but must have satisfied the committee because Beecher was exonerated and given a $100,000 bonus.

After pondering further, there is obviously another component that must be considered in the decision by the committee in ignoring the immorality of Beecher. They realized that there was such interest in the trial and subsequent curiosity, and intrigue by many that the number of congregants increased substantially. The increased financial result greatly pleased the church committee. Money was probably the bottom line.

A famous lithograph drawn by artist James Cook in 1875 depicts Elizabeth Tilton in the center holding a Bible sitting on Henry Beecher's lap with Mrs. Beecher crying in the background. The center sketch is surrounded by vignettes such as Tilton and Woodhull (swimming) at Long Branch with the caption," What are the wild waves saying?" A table of poisons with caption, "Beecher's Choice," a woman kissing Beecher identified as Mrs. Moulton (a church member) and Beecher on the edge of a ragged saw blade with the caption" I feel like one in a dream," as the devil is pictured next to him.

Marie and I agreed that the lithograph by Cook excellently captures the essence of Beecher. Nevertheless it had no influence on the church committee and little on public opinion.

Besides the details of this much-publicized case, the legal ramifications and public response were also of interest and amazement to me. I hoped the case would indicate the need for legal reform regarding marriage. Elizabeth Tilton could not testify due to the common-law rule of inter-spousal immunity which was believed to preserve the sacredness of the marriage and since the same applied to Theodore Tilton, his testimony could not mention any private admissions by his wife.

Although Tilton was suing for $100,000 claiming "distress in body and mind," his lawyer, in summation stated, "This is no ordinary case-it is more far-reaching in its consequences than any case ever tried in this country. This is a trial that involves not the right to property or liberty, but it is a trial the consequences of which reach to the very foundations of society. The home, the marriage relation, with all that is dear in that relation, is upon trial in this case. Upon the result of your verdict to a very large extent, also, will depend the integrity of the Christian religion." I was extremely disappointed that he was advocating the upholding of New York State's antiquated laws and equating the outcome as a reflection of Christian religion. What a short-sighted and anachronistic lawyer!

I read that the trial agitated the public to the extent that there were angry discussions between traditionalists and progressives (those who wanted change regarding the antiquated marital laws). Some gathering places had to forbid any debate about the trial because they feared violence would ensue. Overall, newspaper reports and the preference of the public favored remaining with the traditional, antiquated laws rather than the progressive idea of the right for dissolution of marriage.

Even many in New York State were reported to be content with the so-called sacredness of marriage and preferred the legal acceptance of committing adultery rather than separation or divorce. It is difficult for me to understand those who consent to traditional laws which condone spousal abuse, and the resistance to separation and divorce. I commented to Marie, "How long will it take society to become progressive in their thinking regarding this topic and advocate for implementation of reform?"

Needless to say, Marie and I never again frequented that church.

CHAPTER 15

The Development of New York City Libraries and Societal Rejection of Non-Traditional Relationships

A FEW MONTHS AFTER AUGUSTUS' DEATH, MY FRIEND JOHN Jacob Astor III invited me to lunch at Fraunces Tavern on Pearl Street. It was a place of historical interest and I recall learning of the events that took place during the time Samuel Fraunces was the proprietor. He purchased the building in the mid-1700s and sold it less than 25 years later, but during the time he owned it, many notables frequented the tavern. For example, in 1783, New York State Governor George Clinton held an Evacuation Day celebration in the tavern and a few weeks later, George Washington invited his Continental Army officers to meet there so that he could bid them farewell.

During lunch John Astor III expressed his deepest sympathy for the loss of Augustus. I was impressed by his sensitivity. Every so often, I hear from him, arrange a meeting, and enjoy some discussions about many subjects of the day.

A conversation at one of those luncheons was about the Astor Opera House, also called the Astor Place Theatre. It was built by the Astor family with the upper class in mind. The interior was elegant with upholstered seats available by subscription only. There was a dress code which was thought to discourage the rowdy behavior often observed in theaters frequented by the working class.

Unfortunately, there was a horrific riot at the theatre in 1849. To help the reader understand, there had been an ongoing rivalry between two Shakespearean actors, an American, Edwin Forrest who would be performing at a nearby Broadway theater and William Macready, a British actor who would be performing at the Astor Theatre. Some newspaper reporters and the public became incited over the rivalry. The public took sides: the working class and gangs that lived among them were in favor of the American actor and the upper class was supporting the British actor.

One night in May of that year, Forrest supporters filled the Astor Theatre so they could disrupt the performance of Macready with shouts, hisses, and pelting of items at the stage. Macready did not want to continue his performance the following night, but a petition signed by upstanding New Yorkers convinced him to return.

Fearing that more manpower was needed than presently available, the mayor called for the 7th Regiment to assist along with mounted troops and policemen totaling about 500. Their task was to protect the upper class and their lodgings.

Before the performance started, it was estimated that 10,000 had gathered outside the theatre, some of whom tried to set the theatre afire. When the militia arrived, they were attacked and responded by shooting into the crowd.

Approximately 30 rioters were killed, about 50 wounded, and 200 police and militia injured. John and I spoke about how a foolish competitiveness can escalate into such a terrible disaster.

The upper class was unanimous in praising the police and militia for quelling the rioters. The Astor Place Theatre was never used again as a theater. It was nicknamed the "Massacre Opera House at DisAstor Place."

John remarked that his family believed that such a theatre would fill a need for those wanting a quieter and more refined setting and yet, it became the site of a disaster. He added that it was such a sad chapter in his family's history.

I suggested that he focus on the many wonderful accomplishments and contributions his family had made. He agreed and mentioned a few. Among them, the monetary support of his grandfather, John Jacob Astor for the brilliant ornithologist John James Audubon and his grandfather's establishment of an orphanage in his town of birth, Walldorf, Germany. John Jacob Astor III's father, William Backhouse Astor was a generous benefactor of St. Luke's Hospital and John himself had donated monies to erect the first wing of the New York Cancer Hospital after learning from his wife that Women's Hospital would not accept cancer patients. He also mentioned that, in his will, he had directed that a generous bequest be given to St. Luke's Hospital and the Children's Aid Society.

New York Mercantile Library

At another luncheon meeting, we discussed the New York City Mercantile Library in which we held membership. The library was established by William Wood in the early 1820s before I settled in the city. He was a successful Bostonian merchant and realizing, the importance of reading and education to develop tradesmen, was instrumental in the establishment of mercantile libraries in many cities, including New York City. Benjamin Franklin's recommendation of lending libraries had impressed Wood and he included that service in the mercantile libraries.

The annual dues were two dollars and the purpose was to offer merchant clerks a worthwhile place to go during leisure hours to read current publications and literary classics. The mission of the library was to educate young merchants for success in their respective trades and, in that endeavor, to introduce them to nonfiction publications. Interestingly, the members often enjoyed the few fiction offerings, known as "works of fancy," more than the nonfiction. In the 1830s, pressure from membership resulted in the board of directors' acquiescence that works of fiction also provide "an inducement to seek for the acquirement of knowledge in the alluring fields of romance and the imagination." Works of fiction were henceforth considered educational publications.

As the library continued expanding, the membership and volumes increased. Besides publications, there were courses in languages, sciences, music, and art. In the 1850s, lectures were delivered by many notables, such as, Oliver Wendell Holmes Sr., Richard Henry Dana Jr., and William Makepeace Thackeray. I attended all of these lectures and the evenings were enlightening and entertaining.

In 1854, the need for a larger facility was recognized and the Astor Place Opera House was purchased. John Astor III commented that it was a bittersweet day for his family when they relinquished the building. I responded that they should be pleased that the building is being put to good use. The association revised the requirement for membership and voted for it to be opened to all people of good character, including women.

I watched in amazement as this institution grew. By the 1870s, the library was the fourth largest in the United States and the largest lending one with a daily circulation of over 1,000 books. Membership was about 13,000 and the library housed approximately 120,000 volumes besides hundreds of national and international periodicals. A home delivery service was even established through which one could purchase a blank mail-in form with postage at the library, then when a book was desired, the person completed the form and mailed it. The library delivered the orders by horse and wagon. During the 1870s, it was estimated that 11,000 books were delivered to homes.

Because lectures and readings continued to increase in popularity, beginning in the 1870s, the library association arranged for them to be presented at large venues such as Steinway Hall, which accommodated 2,000 people. Such notables as Frederick Douglass, Bret Harte, and Samuel Clemens were among those invited. The presenters always performed to a sold out audience. In fact, so many were turned away from the Clemens presentation that he agreed to return the following month for two additional orations.

During the 1890s, the library had again outgrown its space, so it was razed and rebuilt as an 11-story edifice. In the new building, the library occupied two floors which offered ample space to house a considerably more complete catalog of newspapers, magazine publications, journals, dictionaries, and literary classics. The other floors were rented, which resulted in revenue for the library.

"What a wonderful addition this library has been to the cultural growth of New York City!"

The Astor Library

I also reminded John Astor III that another extraordinary gift his family had given to New York City was the establishment of the Astor Library in the East Village. He acknowledged that he was extremely proud of that undertaking.

The Astor family had been fortunate in being introduced to Joseph Cogswell, a bibliographer who saw the need for a public library in Manhattan. Cogswell suggested the idea to John Jacob Astor and, in 1838, he and Cogswell began planning the establishment of the library. Astor would bequeath the necessary monies and land, and Cogswell would offer his expertise in establishing the library's volumes. Once the two agreed about the topics to be included in the library catalog, Astor gave permission and funds to Cogswell, who began purchasing books as opportunities arose.

Astor III remarked that it was fortunate that Cogswell was willing to organize and lend his expertise to this venture. He was a brilliant scholar, educated at the University of Gottingen and Harvard University, a lawyer, world traveler, professor, librarian at Harvard, and at one time, editor of the *New York Review*. Cogswell was indeed an exceptional person.

Although preparations and some purchases were made, the plans were not fully instituted until the elder Astor's will was executed following his death in 1848. At that point, Cogswell became superintendent and head librarian. A board of trustees was established, and it consisted of William Backhouse Astor, author Washington Irving, and poet Fitz-Greene Halleck, among others. As the library building progressed, it became clear that Astor had not bequeathed sufficient funds for the building or its interior necessities, so John Jacob Astor III and his father, William Backhouse Astor provided the necessary monies. They continued to give donations to the library throughout their lives, as expansion and additional volumes were needed.

The Astor Library opened to the public in 1854 (the same year the New York Mercantile Library purchased the Astor Opera Theatre). It had been decided that it would not be a circulation facility, but a research library containing over 100,000 books which Cogswell had purchased both in North America and abroad. There were also gifts of documents from historic societies, the federal government, and various states and individuals. Admission was not only free to United States' citizens, but to all people worldwide. This was a clever decision since it encouraged donations of volumes from foreign countries.

John Astor III told me about two of the original trustees of the library, Washington Irving and Fitz-Greene Halleck who had a positive impact and tremendous influence on the library. Irving was humorous and engaging, had travelled widely, was an ambassador to Spain, a lawyer, and an editor, but ultimately preferred writing literature, often satirical works. He also wrote many works while in Europe and some in collaboration with European authors. Of course, his works are housed in the Astor Library and I have read most. According to John Astor III, many authors have mentioned how grateful they are to Irving for his advocacy in encouraging improvement in copyright laws.

Halleck (often referred to as the American Byron) had a charming demeanor and was considered an excellent poet. His writings, similar to Irving's, were often satirical in nature. The subject matter was frequently 19th century politics and the habits of the upper class. Several New York City newspapers such as the *New York Evening Post* published his poems, some under the pseudonym Croaker. In spite of his satirical poetry which criticized the upper class, Halleck's works were popular with them. I believe many of them accepted his poems as playful teasing, while others understood the deeper meaning, but dismissed it. He and his works were so well-liked that he was always invited to upper class social functions.

It was reported that President Abraham Lincoln, enjoyed Halleck's poetry so much that he often read the poems to his friends at social gatherings. Halleck was bequeathed an annuity by John Jacob Astor which allowed him to retire to Guilford, Connecticut in 1849.

I have read many of Halleck's poems or attended events in which his poetry was read. The poems are meaningful, well- composed, and at times contain homosexual overtones. My friend John Astor III and I visited Halleck in the mid-1860s. At that time the poet was in his 70s, and, during those visits, Halleck divulged some personal thoughts.

He mentioned that over the years, he had observed the slow progress toward freedom and equality for the colored people, but he couldn't help wonder how long it would take for freedom, equality, and acceptance of non-traditional relationships to occur. He believed that, in this matter, no movement had occurred, although there was a definite culture that embraced those differences.

According to Halleck, some have addressed this issue (including notables), but many, fearing repercussions or societal stigma, suffered in silence. He pointed out that societies with their so-called moralistic precepts have gone so far as banning or imposing terrible punishments if such leanings were realized or admitted. Fortunately, some authors conveyed such conflicts through their writings. Halleck commented that one who came to immediate mind was Walt Whitman who had written the "Calamus" poems that address manly love. These poems were included in his revised *Leaves of Grass* which I believe was published the beginning of 1860. When Whitman referenced amativeness and adhesiveness, he was attempting to reveal that there existed differences which societies should acknowledge.

I don't recall if Halleck mentioned he had visited the Coleman House hotel and restaurant on Broadway in New York City or if he had simply spoken to friends about it. He revealed that it was frequented by journalists, authors, and artists, many of whom had different preferences in relationships than accepted ones.

Several American artists lived in Rome, Italy at various times during the 19th century. According to Halleck, this was because they found more artistic freedom and acceptance of non-traditional relationships than in the United States. Some are: Emma Stebbins, the American sculptor who designed the Bethesda Fountain for Central Park, New York City, Mary Edmonia Lewis and Harriet Hosmer, American sculptors, Charlotte Cushman, British-American actress, and Matilda Hays, journalist. Emily Dickinson, Louisa May Alcott, and Henry James, according to Halleck, also expressed through their letters or works, the issue of non-traditional relationships and might also have personally dealt with them.

Halleck commented that there were many more examples of personal struggles and lack of acceptance caused by the intolerance and narrow-mindedness of societies and this must be reversed. He stressed that strength and advocacy should replace fear and secrecy.

"Young America," Halleck's last poem, which blatantly deals with the theme of homosexuality, was published by the *New York Ledger*. He seemed to want to be sure before his death that his voice was heard regarding this topic. In 1867 John Astor III and I were saddened to hear from his sister that Halleck had died.

Halleck would have been encouraged by an action that took place in Munich, Germany about a year after his death. I read that an attorney, Karl Heinrich Ulrichs, went before a meeting of hundreds of German jurists to encourage the repeal of laws forbidding relationships between men. He advised that people were being persecuted for possessing a nature opposed to common custom. Most of the audience was not receptive except for a few liberal attendees, but he had found the courage to begin advocacy.

A year after Ulrichs' address, an Austrian author Karl-Maria Kertbeny, who was also opposed to the restrictive laws, espoused the belief that governments do not have the right to interfere in private affairs, unless the rights of others are infringed. To replace the existent pejorative terms in referencing non-traditional cultures, he is credited with coining the terms homosexual and heterosexual (circa 1868).

Progress was slow, but finally, about two years ago (1897), Dr. Magnus Hirschfeld, a German physician, formed a committee to organize aggressive events for acceptance of all deviations from so-called normal relationships. Strides are being made and I assume and hope that these progressive steps that are taken in Germany will continue and set an example for America. The energy exerted on negative endeavors boggles my mind. "Why can't members of societies accept difference rather than focusing on bias and intolerance?"

The Lenox Library

Besides the Astor Library, another outstanding one is the Lenox Library which was established by James Lenox, a philanthropist and bibliophile. I met James Lenox a few times at his library, but he did not enjoy socializing and therefore was not seen at public functions. After graduating from Columbia University, he practiced law until his father's death. At that point, Lenox was 39 years of age, inherited several million dollars, and a great deal of land. From then until his death, he devoted his life to collecting rare art and books. Among the books he treasured was a copy of the famous incunabula, the Gutenberg Bible.

The Lenox Library is quite different from the Astor and Mercantile Libraries, but equally impressive. James Lenox established a private collection of works that I understand is worth more than any other private collection in the United States. He had accumulated some of the rarest manuscripts, statues, and engravings in the world. In the late 1870s, he opened his library to the public and shared his wonderful collection. However, in order to gain access, tickets had to be requested in advance, and the use of the library materials was only available to scholars. His generosity also included dispensing the necessary funds for the establishment of Presbyterian Hospital in New York City. He is truly an admired contributor to the cultural growth of the city.

Tilden's dream

I was well-acquainted with Samuel Tilden, former governor of New York. We often spoke about the cultural growth of New York

City including the libraries that the Astor family and James Lenox had established. However, we agreed that a free public library should be founded in which books could circulate. Realizing the importance of this, Samuel Tilden left most of his estate to be used for that purpose.

Four years ago (1895), I read that the trustees of the Astor Library and the Lenox Library (both libraries were having financial difficulties) and the directors of the Tilden Foundation (who were arranging and overseeing the Tilden bequests for a free public circulating library) met and agreed to consolidate the three libraries to form the New York Public Library. The consolidated library would be open to all, no matter race, ethnicity, religious affiliation, or other differences. Although accomplished posthumously, I am sure the Astor's, James Lenox and Samuel Tilden would have approved. What an incredible gift my friends have given to the City of New York!

CHAPTER 16

The Local Political Scene

BEFORE I DISCUSS MY APPOINTED AND ELECTED GOVERNMEN-tal positions, I should convey some information about the political scene at the time. That way you will better understand my situation within that context.

My philosophical bent was with the Democratic Party. Therefore, at age 25, I joined the Society of St. Tammany, which had principles closest to mine and where I hoped to make a difference.

Over the years, I became more and more informed about the society. It was named for a legendary Indian chief, the head of the organization was referred to as the grand sachem, and the meeting place was the wigwam. Can you see the theme? What was shocking to me was that, at its inception, the Tammany organization limited its membership to males born in America. "How incongruous!" Of course by the time I joined, it was open to immigrants. However, the membership quickly learned that not only were they required to pay dues, but they must give stipends to seek protection for their businesses.

During the first decade that I was a member, I learned that the organization had been founded in the 1700s to discuss and plan for improvements in the city and to address charitable needs of the working class. Those proposals were impressive and in concert with my goals. But then I noticed that the charitable acts were not being met, I voiced my displeasure, and eventually with time and persistence, I made some inroads in procuring funding for the needy.

During my tenure in the organization, I was appalled to learn about the early leaders. Now as I reminisce, they obviously set the stage for those who followed. The first grand sachem was William

Mooney (1789), an upholsterer who began the tradition of stealing from the public coffers. He admitted to having filched $5,000 from the public almshouse, but in his own defense, claimed that the funds were needed to purchase trinkets for his wife in order to maintain a cordial relationship. He was replaced.

In 1798, the Tammany leader was Aaron Burr who continued performing corruptive acts. In 1799, Burr was successful in the passage of a bill through the state legislature which allowed for the creation of the Manhattan Company (a public waterworks company). It was supposed to offer clean water to the Lower East Side and Burr would oversee the project. However, the bill included a clause, hidden in the verbiage, that monies remaining after addressing the water project could be invested in any manner deemed appropriate. Burr and his associates carried out the provision for a waterworks project, but used inferior water pipes (mostly hollowed out logs) which allowed for sewage to be absorbed in them.

This probably increased the disease epidemics in the city. Meanwhile the excess money (about two million dollars) was used to establish banks, which were overseen by Burr and his friends in an unprincipled manner.

When I later analyzed the history of Tammany, I believe Burr's investment idea served as a model for the development of a strong political machine in New York City. It portended the potential for financial gain disguised as actions for the public good. Meanwhile, many in leadership positions continued the dishonest actions of Mooney and Burr.

By the time I joined, the majority of the Tammany leaders were rumored to be unscrupulous. Their leadership positions and programs were usually assured by enlisting members of the vicious gangs in the Five Points area to manipulate elections and protect the leaders.

The Republican Party was founded in the 1850s and supported Lincoln. I did vote for Lincoln and encouraged the German community to do likewise because he represented the ideals we had sought in Germany. Eventually, I returned to the Democratic Party because opposing parties or movements including the Republican Party had tenets that were anti-immigrant, favored the well-to-do, and had corrupt elements.

At one point, some friends and I founded a splinter group with democratic ideals and no corruption, but the Tammany organization was too strong to replace. I had to be content remaining in the Tammany Society, attempt to eliminate the corrupt elements within the group, and seek to make positive changes.

I will comment about a few Tammany leaders with whom I was acquainted during my tenure in the organization. Some remain in my memory for their positive contributions and others for their corruptive acts. Many were devious, unethical, disreputable, and Jack-Braggers. Introducing these people might give a better understanding of the powerful leadership of New York City during my lifetime and the difficulty in being successful in effecting change.

In the 1840s and 1850s, there were several grand sachems or influential members who were rumored, or proven, to be dishonest. One such leader was Isaac Fowler. He served as Postmaster of New York City during the 1850s until he was accused of embezzling funds. Before his arrest, he fled to Mexico, but in the mid-1860s, a New York City district attorney announced that Fowler was not going to be prosecuted for the monies he had stolen and he was able to return to the United States. Most likely there was a quid pro quo between the district attorney and some members of Tammany.

Another Tammany leader, William Frederick Havemeyer, was seemingly a trustworthy politician and businessman. He served as mayor of New York City three times, twice during the 1840s and again in the 1870s. During his tenure as mayor, he established the New York Police Department and attempted (albeit unsuccessfully) to reform the city charter so that many positions that were appointed would become elected ones. I believe an equally important contribution was the establishment of the Board of Emigration Commissioners to help eradicate the abuses that immigrants were encountering. Some of the

Tammany leaders were opposed to Havemeyer's reforms and to show their displeasure, after two mayoral terms, he was not endorsed.

Tammany member, Fernando Wood, another disreputable leader, was elected mayor of New York City for two terms. In 1857, during his mayoralty, two terrible riots occurred in the city: a police riot and a gang riot. The success of the latter was in part because of the lackadaisical attitude of the police after the police riot. I will explain.

The police corruption in New York City prior to and during 1857 resulted in the New York State Legislature (also reportedly corrupt) relieving Mayor Fernando Wood of his control of the New York City Municipal Police Department and police board, which were viewed as ineffective and inefficient. They were replaced with a newly formed Metropolitan State Police Department and board of commissioners instituted by the New York State Legislature.

Wood would not accept the newly formed Metropolitan State Police and he had the support of the Municipal Police. When the Metropolitan State Police attempted to carry out warrants against Wood and entered City Hall, they were ejected by the New York City Municipal Police, but not before Wood was captured and arrested. This resulted in a riot between the Municipal and Metropolitan Police in which the New York City Municipal Police were the victors.

FIGHT BETWEEN THE METROPOLITAN AND MUNICIPAL POLICE.

A sketch of the police riot that appeared in *Recollections of a New York Chief of Police*, a book by George W. Walling published in 1887

A civil court determined that the State had no right to interfere in the appointments within the City of New York and Wood was released shortly after his arrest. Arrests that had been made by the Metropolitan State Police were overturned. Eventually, about September or October of 1857, the New York Court of Appeals ruled that the New York City Municipal Police be disbanded.

During the time between the Police Riot and the court ruling, there was a lack of police order. This resulted in unrestricted and unrestrained looting and fighting by the criminal element in New York City as evidenced by the horrific, two-day gang fighting in July of 1857.

The notorious gangs of New York fought incessantly. As a matter of course, the Dead Rabbits fought against the Bowery Boys, but during the two-day altercation, the fights escalated into a citywide rampage of criminal activity. It was estimated that more than 1,000 gang members from all over the city joined in these activities. The property damage, human death, and injury were substantial. The gangs used guns and iron bars, and pelted paving blocks and stones from rooftops at any who tried to stop the violence. Fires were set and residences burned. Finally, two regiments of the New York State Militia (one, the excellent 7th Regiment) were called and they eventually subdued the situation.

An illustration that appeared in *Frank Leslie's Illustrated Newspaper*, July 18, 1857, showing the vicious fighting and men and women throwing brickbats at the police.

Wood also opposed the 13th Amendment and encouraged the New York Council to vote for the secession of New York City from the United States to become a free city. The motivation for the proposal was to continue substantial revenue (from which many northerners benefitted), gained as a result of the southern cotton industry.

When Wood was not re-elected mayor, he returned to Congress (where he had served in the early 1840s). There he served two more terms including a position on the Ways and Means Committee.

John Morrissey was another member of Tammany (during the 1850s) who was a bare knuckles boxer and a gang member of the Dead Rabbits. He had tenacity and an iron will when in physical conflict, so much so, that on one occasion during a gang fight, his back was pressed against hot coals burning his flesh, but he prevailed. He had come to America having had a criminal record in Ireland and quickly gained one here.

A boxing event between Morrissey and William Poole known as Bill the Butcher (who was a boxer and an enforcer for the Know-Nothing Party) ended with the defeat of Morrissey. Several months after, a friend of Morrissey shot Poole to death. Morrissey (thought to be the instigator) and the shooter were accused of murder. Three trials resulted in hung juries and the defendants were freed. Morrissey also successfully ran for the United States Congress and served two terms in the House of Representatives. Then in 1875, he returned to New York and was elected to the New York State Senate. Despite his past, many now viewed him as a respected politician.

Another political acquaintance, Charles Godfrey Gunther, was a member of Tammany and mayor of New York City during the Civil War. I recall that he had the support of some of the city's finest newspapers, such as, the *New York Times* and the *New York Staats-Zeitung* whose editorials commended his integrity and intelligence. He only served one term, probably because of his lack of influence over the many city offices that were corrupt.

Without a doubt, Gunther, like many of us, began realizing the increasing corruption in the Tammany organization. He decided to distance himself from political life and became more involved in charitable endeavors. He also had the foresight to envision Coney Island as a recreational resort. He partnered in business ventures to construct a steam railroad. The rail was named the Brooklyn, Bath and Coney Island Railroad and its route was from Greenwood Cemetery to Coney Island. It was so successful that Gunther ultimately had six locomotives with over 20 cars transporting about 300,000 to 400,000 passengers per year. It was such a convenient way to reach Coney Island and enabled New Yorkers, including my family, to enjoy the beach resort and its amenities.

In spite of the obvious corruption and embezzling, by 1867 the member body had become so large that a building of greater capacity was needed. It was constructed on West 14th Street between 3rd and Irving and was appropriately called Tammany Hall. Throughout my conflicted tenure in the society, it has become an ever-increasing, influential, and powerful machine.

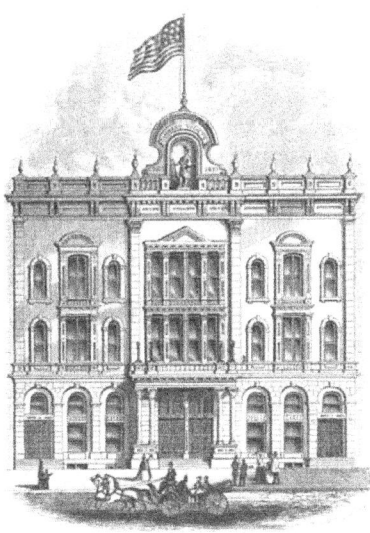

The design for the new Tammany Hall on 14th Street, which was included in the volume entitled, *Proceedings of the Tammany Society or Columbian Order: on the laying of the corner-stone of the new hall on Fourteenth Street.* It was published by New York Printing Company, Centre Street, in 1867 and distributed on July 4th of that year at the laying of the cornerstone.

I ask myself how such corrupt governments can prevail and for long periods of time. The reasons, most likely are, that they are often so powerful and feared by the constituency that change must come slowly. As a result, those of us active in seeking honest government must be cautious so that our work from within will not be in vein.

CHAPTER 17

Tammany, Tweed, and Acts of Charity

I WILL TELL A LITTLE ABOUT THE CORRUPTION, POWER, AND intimidation during the reign of Tammany leader, William Tweed (known as Boss Tweed) and his associates (known as the Tweed Ring). He and his Ring stole tremendous amounts of money through bribery and other dishonest means. I have so many notes in my diary about this man that I could compose a book. Ultimately, my friends and I assisted as much as we could in his downfall.

By the age of 30 (in the 1850s), Tweed had become influential, feared, and yet, revered especially in the Irish community of the Lower East Side. During that time, he was an alderman, held a position in the United States Congress, and in the New York State Senate where he was chairman of the finance committee. Simultaneously, he served as New York City School Commissioner, New York City Commissioner of Public Works, and was a member of the New York City Board of Supervisors. He used these positions to charge substantial fees to companies who wished to acquire contracts with the city.

Tweed's Ring was composed of those who held prestigious positions, or were given important assignments so that Tweed would be protected in his quest for illegal funds. One of his associates, Judge George Barnard certified Tweed as a lawyer, although he never completed elementary school. In the 1860s, Tweed had a lucrative (but fraudulent) law practice, was Chairman of Tammany's General Committee, and was elected grand sachem. The corruption became more and more evident.

Parts of his illegal gains were invested in New York City real estate and at the time of his downfall, it was learned that he was one of the largest landholders in the city. In the late 1860s, Tweed was instrumental (through bribes) in changing the City Charter to allow the Board of Audit (consisting of Tweed and two of his Ring), to control all city finances allowing more corruption and extortion.

There are many examples that were ultimately revealed, but one that comes to mind is the building of the New York County Courthouse. Tweed hired contractors to construct the building, whose cost was $13,000,000, of which $10,000,000 went into the Tweed coffers. I eventually learned that Tweed even controlled most of the newspaper reporters whose articles either detailed false news, or failed to report information of importance.

To illustrate the extent of the corruption during his reign, I will explain the interactions among Tweed and financiers Jay Gould and James Fisk. Tweed's position in the New York State Senate allowed manipulation and passage of laws to benefit his friends and him. For example, Gould and Fisk had issued counterfeit Erie Railroad bonds, inflating their share of the company, and deflating the price of the stock to gain control of the railroad from Cornelius Vanderbilt. Tweed agreed to legitimize the bonds by the passage of legislation and, in return, he received a large portion of the stock and became director of the company.

Another deception involving the three occurred when Gould and Fisk tried to corner the market on gold, causing the price to rise. United States President Ulysses Grant learned of the scheme and flooded the market with gold in order to deflate the price. This created a panic on Wall Street and forced the overall financial market into turmoil for several months. As a result of their relationship with Tweed, Gould and Fisk were not prosecuted because he arranged to have their cases heard before judges over whom Tweed had influence.

By the 1870s, Tweed lived in a mansion on Fifth Avenue and his control of New York City allowed him to continue pilfering large sums of money. The city debt rose during his governance to almost $150,000. City work was set at excessive amounts (about 75% over cost) so that the surplus could be retained by Tweed and his Ring. In addition to the Erie Railroad, he became director of the Brooklyn Bridge Company, and the Harlem Gas Light Company. To safely hide illegal money, Tweed and his Ring created a bank which protected their funds.

They were finally brought to justice during the 1870s. As with many corrupt leaders, what seemed an insignificant event, precipitated their collapse. In the case of Tweed, the impetus was a parade.

There was an annual parade arranged by Irish Protestants to celebrate the success of King William of Orange in defeating the Irish and bringing them under British rule. During the 1870 parade, there had been some violence by the actions of Irish Catholics, so Tweed decided to cancel the 1871 parade. When there was a backlash, he lifted the ban and ordered the presence of militia. Nevertheless, a riot (The Orange Riot of 1871) ensued which resulted in approximately 60 civilians being killed and over 150 wounded. Both the Irish Catholic constituents and the wealthy Protestant ones were distraught by the significant loss of life. They believed Tweed and his associates were losing control of the city. Although the corruption had been realized for some time, most of the populace didn't comment so long as it didn't affect them personally.

Reporters became less fearful and refused to be bribed by the Tweed Ring. The influential and wealthy citizenry offered their knowledge of some corruptive acts. When the news reached Europe, countries that had loaned money to New York City (assured of its solvency), now doubted its ability to repay the debts. This incident caused panic throughout Europe.

Meetings took place and committees were established (some by my circle of friends and me) to discuss means of bringing an honest government to New York City. At that point, many of Tweed's Ring resigned or left the country. Although some friends and I attended the meetings and served on committees to attempt to reverse the corruptive government, financial records had to be carefully examined and illegal acts investigated so that Tweed's attorneys could not circumvent the law.

Tweed and his Ring were finally brought to justice by a combination of committees, (in which I participated) newspaper articles, and most significantly, the satirical drawings of Thomas Nast and the investigative reporting of Samuel Tilden.

Nast so upset Tweed that he furiously said (regarding Nast's illustrations), "My constituents don't know how to read, but they can't help seeing them damned pictures!" He supposedly offered Nast $500,000 to leave the country. Nast refused.

A Thomas Nast cartoon which appeared *Harper's Weekly* September 23, 1871 is entitled, The Tammany Tiger Loose--- What Are You Going To Do About It?" depicting Tweed as emperor and the tiger representing Tammany.

A Thomas Nast cartoon which appeared in *Harper's Weekly* November 11, 1871 depicts a group of vultures waiting for the storm to blow over and is entitled "Let Us Prey."

Equally disturbing to Tweed was Samuel Tilden, a scrupulously ethical lawyer. On many occasions, Tilden and I discussed the necessity of removing Tweed and his Ring, but it was not an easy feat. For a decade, Tilden investigated and compiled the necessary legal documentation that would unquestionably divulge their corrupt acts. Tilden's findings contributed greatly to bringing them to justice.

As a result of Thomas Nast, Samuel Tilden, newspaper reports, and to a lesser extent my circle of friends and me, Tweed was arrested in 1873 and his Ring destroyed. His associates all began pointing fingers and placing blame on each other to try to avoid prosecution. Thomas Nast aptly portrayed this in one of his cartoons.

Thomas Nast's illustrated the pointing of fingers in the cartoon entitled, "Boss Tweed and the Tammany Ring," published in *Harper's Weekly*, August 19, 1871.

Tweed was imprisoned, escaped, and settled in Spain. He was captured and returned to the United States, again arrested, and this time died in prison.

Newspapers reported that the amount of revenue that Tweed and his Ring had pilfered from the electorate through required bribes and monies stolen from the city coffers was at least $50,000,000 and perhaps as much as $200,000,000.

John Kelly replaced Tweed as grand sachem. He had not been associated with Tammany for several years (including during the scandal) because he had left the country following the untimely death of his wife and children. As a result, he was known as "Honest Kelly" and even reduced the city debt in his position as comptroller. However, it was rumored that he, too, was corrupt since he was living too large for his income.

After Kelly's death in 1886, Richard Croker replaced him as grand sachem. Croker served in the 1880s as New York City Fire

Commissioner and later in the decade as New York City Chamberlain. As grand sachem, it is well known that his machine is reminiscent of Tweed's. It is thought the bribes he requires are supporting his interest in thoroughbred race horses and other expensive endeavors. In spite of several newspaper editors and other organizations attempting to have Croker's actions exposed, he remains grand sachem.

Acts of Charity

Every time I walked into Tammany Hall and saw so many self-satisfied, corrupt members, I felt overwhelmed and discouraged. Then I reminded myself of the apocryphal story of David and Goliath and David's victory. Perseverance can eventually cause positive change so I persisted. I will mention some positive accomplishments I and a few other members achieved.

I found that if I proposed a plan, exhibited its value, and tirelessly advocated for its inclusion, ultimately I was successful in its passage. The first item was convincing those in power to cease requiring payments from businesses on the Lower East Side (for protection). They were reticent but my determination eventually caused their acquiescence.

Other important projects reluctantly approved by the membership were humanitarian programs. I oversaw the establishment of a committee to meet immigrants when they arrived at the docks of New York. Even when the processing centers (Castle Garden in 1855 and Ellis Island in 1892) opened and the Board of Emigration Commissioners was established, the immigrants were still in need of direction and protection from the criminal element.

I established another committee to help immigrants find lodging and employment. To this end, I was successful in convincing Tammany leaders to establish a fund to offer temporary financial assistance to immigrants upon their arrival, if needed. In addition, I solicited the assistance of many business owners in offering employment when it became available, and was therefore successful in compiling a substantial list of potential employers.

A naturalization committee was established and overseen by me to assist immigrants in obtaining citizenship. We assisted them in completing paperwork, volunteered to be witnesses, and if needed, provided the fees, through a Tammany fund, for the citizenship costs.

There were few New York City social programs during the 1800s and as a result, we established another committee to distribute food and coal (in the winter) and ice (in the summer) to the needy.

We also convinced the leadership to set aside funds for the acquisition of land on which to build the Metropolitan Museum of Art, and Central Park.

I persuaded the leadership to set aside funds for humanitarian and cultural projects by convincing them that the relatively small amount of funds the programs entailed would be well spent for the good-will that would emerge. As a result, I and a few like-minded members made substantial changes from within. I was pleased that the proposed projects came to fruition.

I am no longer active in the political scene, but I keep apprised of the current activities. Throughout my tenure as a member of Tammany and the Democratic Party, I was never involved in any corrupt acts or illegal activities. I saw myself as a Simon-pure Democrat.

CHAPTER 18

The National Political Scene

FROM WHAT I HAVE READ AND OBSERVED DURING MY LIFETIME, corruption and bribery in the federal government surpassed the Tammany organization. That is hard to believe, but I have learned that few politicians in any party serving the federal government have moralistic and ethical motivations. They were, and continue to be in federal governmental positions to collect paychecks as reciprocity for nefarious agendas of their parties or to serve the desires of influential individuals.

In order to be successful in accomplishing their voting interests, they often employ extreme measures. Congressmen did not hesitate to resort to fisticuffs, caning, dueling, or the use of other weaponry to settle their disputes. The weaponry was carried into the Congressional chambers with no objection. Point in fact is the duel in the 1830s when Representative Jonathan Ciley of Maine angered Representative William Graves of Kentucky and the latter challenged Ciley to a duel. Ciley was killed.

Two decades later, Massachusetts Senator Charles Sumner, who favored anti-slavery, suffered the rage of southern legislators. Sumner gave a speech which insulted Representative Preston Brooks of South Carolina. As a result, Brooks so brutally caned Sumner, that Sumner had to be carried from the senate chamber and needed two years to recover. Brooks was censured by Congress for his unacceptable behavior, but nevertheless received many replacement canes as gifts from southern slavery proponents who encouraged continued use on abolitionists. Additionally Brooks was re-elected by a large margin.

A lithograph depicting Preston Brooks' attacking Charles Sumner in the United
States Senate Chamber by artist John L. Magee published December 31,
1855 in *Harper's Weekly*.

Reporters were also threatened if they communicated the information of select congressional events. With the onset of the telegraph, angry words, rather than destructive weapons, became the norm.

An example of an unscrupulous, immoral politician and lawyer who represented New York in the local, state, and national political scene was the infamous, Daniel Sickles. He served at the local level as Corporation Counsel of New York City in 1853 where his decisions always favored the interests of the Tammany leaders rather than the needs of the populace.

Much to the consternation of the organization, I mentioned at ratification meetings that Sickles was not worthy of the audience's votes. November 2, 1855, at a ratification meeting, I reiterated that votes should not be cast in Daniel Sickles' favor. My admonitions were reported in the *New York Daily Times* November 3, 1855. The following are excerpts from that article:

GRAND RATIFICATION MEETING

The meeting was called to order by Mr. MERKLE.
Mr. PHILIP MERKLE was the first speaker, and was
received with enthusiastic applause.
He then recommended the different
candidates but spoke against Senator, DANIEL E. SICKLES.

During other meetings, I continued my admonitions against electing Sickles as a representative to the New York State Legislature and later to the United States Congress. Although I had convinced enough people to vote against him, resulting in his defeat, nevertheless, the organization adjusted the election returns in his favor and he served in both venues.

In Washington D.C., where he served in congress from 1857-1861, he lived in a mansion with his wife Teresa Bagioli Sickles. He seldom attended meetings except if attendance benefited New York or one of its leaders. It was common knowledge that Sickles spent much time with a cross section of mistresses many from high society, but others who worked in brothels. Teresa was aware of his infidelity and decided to pursue her own love affair. Her lover was District Attorney of Washington D.C., Philip Barton Key II, (the son of Francis Scott Key, the poet/lyricist of the "Star-Spangled Banner"). Someone alerted Sickles of his wife's affair and he vowed to kill Key.

As was his custom, Key was in Lafayette Square across from the White House, awaiting Teresa, but instead, he was confronted by Daniel Sickles, who was in possession of several pistols. In the presence of many witnesses, Sickles shot Key several times at close range, killing him.

An illustration of Sickles murdering Key appeared in *Harper's Weekly*, March 12, 1859.

Sickles, although imprisoned, received many special privileges, including retaining his weapons and the use of the head jailer's apartment to receive his numerous and frequent guests. Among his visitors were congressmen, other high positioned politicians, and the social elite of Washington. He also received a supportive letter from President James Buchanan. All wished him success in his trial. Attorney Edwin Stanton and his associates were the legal representatives for Sickles and they pleaded, on Sickles behalf, temporary insanity. Sickles was acquitted. This was the first time in the United States that temporary insanity was successfully presented as a defense.

After the trial, Sickles returned to New York and organized regiments of volunteers for the Union cause. At the Battle of Gettysburg, he disobeyed orders and was responsible for the deaths of most of his corps. During the battle, a cannonball destroyed Sickles' right leg and it needed to be amputated. For his bravery, he was awarded the Medal of Honor. He donated his leg to the Army Medical Museum in Washington D.C., but never forgot his amputated leg and visited it every year on the anniversary of his loss.

His insubordinate actions were overlooked and he was appointed commander of the prestigious New York Excelsior Brigade. Treated as a hero, he had no difficulty procuring employment. He served as a diplomat, congressman, Military Governor of South Carolina, Sheriff of New York City, and was enlisted by Lincoln to analyze situations in the aftermath of the war and offer suggestions for Reconstruction.

Sickles and others always saw possibilities for manipulating the Electoral College through gerrymandering to assure election outcomes. This tradition continued and, in 1876, the election for United States president between candidates Rutherford B. Hayes and Samuel Tilden was thought to have been manipulated.

Samuel Tilden won the popular vote by a majority, but lost the electoral vote to Rutherford B. Hayes by one vote. Many of us believe that Samuel Tilden would have won the electoral vote, but a political deal had promised the presidency to Hayes and his followers if they opposed civil rights reforms. The 1876 election of Hayes over Tilden was reported in several newspapers as the stolen election. Since Tilden was such a dedicated public servant, I often think of the direction the country might have gone if he had been president.

Sickles was instrumental in preserving the Gettysburg Battlefield and encouraging the establishment of the Gettysburg National Military Park to honor the Union soldiers who had given their lives. It was finally established a few years ago, in 1895, with statues of the major officers who had contributed to the Union success. When Sickles was questioned regarding the fact that there was no statue honoring him, he supposedly retorted that the entire battlefield was a memorial to him.

Local members including me, who visited the United States Congress during the 1860s, 70s, and 80s witnessed the ultimate in government corruption and bribery.

During this period, many politicians in federal government gained their positions through financial purchase. I observed that many United States congressmen were disinterested in governmental matters except where it applied to the causes they were bribed to address. Legislation of substance that would be for the benefit of the populace was for the most part not considered during the past 25 to 35 years and only a handful of worthwhile bills were passed.

The lack of interest during this period on the part of federal government leaders in addressing the needs of the working people in America reached a peak. Congress continues to consist mostly of businessmen who buy their way into the position. Senate seats are commonly given to the highest bidder for specific favors. Wealthy businessmen, who are not directly involved in the political system, often give generously to support politicians who will protect their interests. Some who have been known to do this are: John D. Rockefeller, who had established Standard Oil in 1870 and which by the early 1880s controlled 90% of United States refineries and pipelines, J. P. Morgan, who controlled a great deal of corporate finance, Andrew Carnegie, who owned steel and other corporations, and Cornelius Vanderbilt, who was a railroad and shipping magnate.

Congress was, for the most part, equally divided between Republicans and Democrats, so quorums usually were not reached. When I observed Congress, during the 1860s, 1870s and again in the early 1880s, many Congressmen were inebriated, took frequent breaks to use tobacco, and spent more time doing non-Congressional activities than anything worthwhile.

In 1882 I read about a little known person, Grover Cleveland who was serving as mayor of Buffalo, N.Y. and acclaimed as a trustworthy leader. I followed his career and believed he was worthy of my support both in 1883 when I stumped through New York State to encourage endorsement of him as New York State governor and in 1884 for United States president. Many reporters interviewed me regarding my impression of Cleveland including a reporter from *The Brooklyn Daily Eagle* where an article appeared September 18, 1884 relating my appraisal of his potential success. I often spoke in his favor to audiences of over 20,000 in number who showed their enthusiasm for him. Both for governor and for United States president, my promoting him had successful outcomes.

Although I was in my 70s, I believed it was well worth the exhausting schedule to gain support for Cleveland. When I met with him on several occasions, both in Buffalo and Albany, he was refreshing, articulate, moralistic, seemingly of good character, and prioritized service to the needs of the populous. I believed he had the leadership potential to make positive change.

I was impressed that Cleveland remained seemingly honest and would not bend to the demands of Tammany and other unscrupulous organizations. His many assertions were profound and uplifting. However I was extremely disturbed by two of his pronouncements after election, as follows: "The lessons of paternalism ought to be unlearned and the better lesson taught that while people should patriotically and cheerfully support their Government its functions do not include the support of the people;" and "Sensible and responsible women do not want to vote. The relative positions to be assumed by men and women in the working out of our civilization were assigned long ago by a higher intelligence than ours." What was he thinking?

Through my entire affiliation with the political scene, I pondered how easily corrupt leaders can rise to power and how some moralistic ones can even change their colors. In addition the ability to buy votes and manipulate districts to gain power for desired outcomes is horrific. At the point that upstanding candidates have the opportunity to be chosen without exclusion by manipulation, maneuvering, and other illegal voting processes, we will have leadership which will serve the needs of the people. For now I must be content that my tenure in political organizations did allow me to guide citizens and cause positive change.

For distraction from the sometimes frustrating, depressing, dishonest, and corrupt political situations I encountered during my lifetime, I perused some of Mark Twain's' satirical and amusing governmental references which I have compiled from reading his books and attending his orations. They always caused temporary delight and profound contemplation. What a superb understanding of human nature he possesses.

Some of my favorite political Twain quotations are:

"Whiskey is carried into committee rooms in demijohns and carried out in demagogues." *Notebook*, 1868

"That's the difference between governments and individuals. Governments don't care, individuals do." *A Tramp Abroad* 1880

"It could probably be shown by facts and figures that there is no distinctly native American criminal class except Congress." *Pudd'nhead Wilson's New Calendar* 1897

CHAPTER 19

Drug Inspector, Interpreter, and Excise Commissioner

IN 1857, I BECAME SPECIAL EXAMINER OF DRUGS, A DIVISION OF the United States Treasury Department. I was more qualified than others who had been considered, but feared the corrupt political machines would prevent my election. The appointment was reported in local newspapers and beyond such as *The Washington Union*. Although a prestigious appointment, I did not divulge my motivation before election, which was to improve the situation at the New York City docks where it was rumored that there were tremendous amounts of pilfering taking place.

My assigned office was on Broome Street, close to the Port of New York, where I supervised inspections by examiners. There had been ongoing complaints by businesses, that there was a great deal of pilfering of products when they arrived or departed the Port of New York. The function of the examiners was to be sure that all imports and exports were labeled and contained the items that were indicated. I did note that some examiners were not inspecting the containers or only superficially surveying the contents while others were stealing objects. After warnings, if the lack of conscientiousness and dishonesty continued, I removed those examiners from the position. They thought they were protected by Tammany, but although unpopular, I was relentless in having the guilty examiners dismissed. The remaining examiners began working dutifully.

In 1873, I accepted a position as clerk and interpreter in Marine Court where immigrants received their citizenship. I certainly was qualified in that I am fluent in German, French, Hebrew, and English, but more importantly I was able to lessen the trepidation expressed by immigrants about the process. It was a rewarding experience and so many expressed their gratitude.

The naturalization books in Marine Court were in disarray. I was asked by the Board of Supervisors to do an extra service and index the many naturalization books for which I was promised a stipend of $1,000. The task required at least two hours per day after my usual workday and took about six months to complete. Upon conclusion of the service, I did not receive compensation and was told that, because I was already an employee of the city, I should not be paid extra. They added that there was no appropriation available to compensate me.

I decided to sue the city. The case went to trial January 1875 before Judge Lawrence. He directed a verdict in my favor in the amount of $1,231, but with the understanding that I would need to wait for a verdict in a similar case. My lawyer and friend Robert Strahan was persistent and I was compensated.

Following is a report regarding the case which was published in the *New York Herald* January 26, 1875.

> Philip Merkle, an interpreter in the Marine Court, was awarded $1,000 by the Board of Supervisors for extra services in indexing the naturalization books in that court. Failing to get the money he sued the city for it. The case came to trial yesterday before Judge Lawrence, in Supreme Court, Circuit. The defense was that there was no appropriation wherewith to pay this money; that the Supervisors had charged the payment to no specific fund, and that the plaintiff being an employee of the city, could not receive any extra compensation. As the same questions are involved in another suit now before the General Term on appeal Judge Lawrence directed a verdict for plaintiff for $1,231.

At the time I left Germany, had I questioned the government, I would have been jailed and certainly would never have been successful in a suit against them. The freedoms and ability to litigate injustice in my adopted country are phenomenal.

Another case that was also viewed as a test case was reported in *The New York Times*, April 17, 1879 regarding an excise law. The incident involved two detectives from the Society for the Prevention of Crime who went into a liquor store that did not have a license and obtained drinks of whiskey from the bartender, the brother of the owner. They reported the incident to the Commissioner of Charities and Correction who brought a suit against the barkeeper to recover the statutory penalty of $50 for the offense.

The lawsuit was brought before a judge and jury. Ex-judge Jesse Dittenhoefer, attorney for the defendant pointed out that the detectives entered with the purpose of inducing a violation of the law (knowing before they entered that the owner did not have a liquor license).

Testification by the bar owner indicated that the Excise Commissioner Owen Murphy had given him a receipt for $75 as earnest money so that he could continue serving liquor while awaiting the final determination of his liquor license application.

The attorney for the defendant moved to dismiss on the grounds that under the law, the action must be made against the bar owner (who wasn't there) and, since the sale was procured by decoys, the act was not within the meaning of the law. The case was dismissed by the judge based on the manner in which the evidence was acquired.

The reporter for *The New York Times* added that more than 100 suits of similar character brought by the Commissioner of Charities under the 1857 law were dependent on the final disposition of this case, which was viewed as a test case. The decision was a defeat for the Society for the Prevention of Crime, which was part of the temperance movement. The incident became known as Excise Commissioner Owen Murphy's Legacy.

Unfortunately, by the time the case was heard, Excise Commissioner Murphy's name had appeared in headlines for pilfering some New York City funds and taking refuge in Canada. The account of his actions was reported December 30, 1877, by *The New York Times* in an article entitled, "The Fugitive Commissioner."

Murphy was located in Toronto, Canada having absconded with a check he wrote to himself for $10,000. It was also discovered that he had taken $20,000 from another public fund.

As a result of his dishonest actions, he was fired, and the other excise commissioner was also removed. Although it was irrational thinking, for some reason, if one excise commissioner is shown to be dishonest, it was thought the other might be also. The public, including newspaper editors, advocated for honest commissioners, and awaited the mayor's choices. Finally, I was chosen to take Owen Murphy's place and Richard Morrison, another ethical person, was asked to replace the other excise commissioner. News of our appointments was reported during January 1878 in the *New York Evening Post*, *The New York Times*, the *Philadelphia Enquirer*, the *Albany Evening Times*, the *Utica New York Morning Herald*, and many others. The appointments were noteworthy because the Owen case had been so publicized.

It was a difficult time to be an excise commissioner because of the actions of the temperance movement in New York City. Those in the movement were advocating a ban on all distilled and fermented beverages, including beer and ale. They also wanted any establishments that served alcoholic beverages to be closed on Sundays and eventually closed completely.

The temperance movement was attempting to change the thinking of the long-time acceptance in America of drinking alcoholic beverages. As early as the 1600s and 1700s, many immigrants to America (both men and women) brewed ale in their homes. In the 1800s, German immigrants continued the tradition of ale and lager production in America.

Admittedly, imbibing excessively could cause problems in the workplace and in the home. But I believe that consumption of alcohol in moderation poses no problem.

Prior to our appointments, the temperance movement had established the Prohibition Party in 1869 to run in major elections, and also founded the Woman's Christian Temperance Union (WCTU) in 1873. Their efforts were definitely being noticed.

The absurdity of their actions was illustrated in the revision of a famous picture of George Washington. In the original, Washington bids farewell to his officers with a glass of liquor in his hand and a bottle of liquor displayed on the table behind him. In 1876, the temperance movement revised the image. In the revision, the glass in Washington's hand was removed and the liquor on the table was replaced by a hat. Ironically, president George Washington's preference in drink was low-alcohol ale for which he had even developed a recipe.

Through observation in lower Manhattan, Commissioner Morrison and I noted that there was definitely more consumption of beer and ale than whiskey. Saloons were meeting places of the working class, mostly on Sundays, their only day without required labor. And yet, the WCTU, the largest women's organization ever formed in America was often seen marching in large groups to the saloons and demanding their closure. They professed that any intake of distilled liquor was an evil occurrence. The movement also attempted to equate consumption of alcohol with crime and high child mortality rates.

During the time Morrison and I served as excise commissioners in New York City, there were over 7,000 establishments seeking licensing, all of which we were responsible to inspect. An incredible task for two people!

As we inspected the drinking establishments, there were some that we did not license because they were in basements or dark alleys and had a feckless element, but those were in the minority. The traditional gathering areas to enjoy a glass of beer were places where socializing could take place such as taverns, saloons, and especially beer gardens, many of which were beautifully landscaped. The beer gardens often offered games, entertainment, and the opportunity to sing and dance. The larger ones provided additional rooms for meetings of clubs and organizations. Some saloons, taverns, and beer gardens even welcomed families and served a delicious lunch. Why prevent such enjoyable socialization?

CHAPTER 20

Breweries and Temperance

BREWING AND SUPPLYING BEER WAS SUCH A LARGE BUSINESS that, by the time we assumed our positions as excise commissioners, New York City had 80 breweries, Brooklyn had over 40, and the nation-wide estimate was 4,000. During this time, New York State was the largest hops producer in the United States. I read last year (1898) that in spite of the temperance movement, the nationwide breweries were producing about 40 million barrels a year, with each barrel containing 31 gallons. As a result, I believe the temperance movement will not have any lasting impact on the industry.

Therefore those producing and serving alcoholic beverages offered employment to many. There were opportunities for jobs in saloons, taverns, beer gardens, and breweries.

Some Manhattan and Brooklyn brewery owners that I personally knew had the surnames Ruppert, Schaefer, Ehret, Liebmann, and Eppig. If I called on them to seek employment for a recently arrived immigrant, they would often be able to accommodate. But not only did they offer employment to many, they were also philanthropic and civic-minded. In fact several convened annually to have a Brewer's Ball from which the considerable proceeds were given to the needy.

Frequently I arranged meetings of clubs and organizations in beer gardens close to one of the breweries and the owners kindly provided the lager. The following is a little information about the outstanding brewery owners with whom I became well-acquainted.

Franz Ruppert was born the same year as I and emigrated from the same area of Germany. He was an early, if not the earliest malt dealer in New York City and had a small and profitable brewery, which he named the Turtle Bay Brewery. His son Jacob (with the permission of his father) established his own brewing company, Jacob Ruppert Brewing Company and later, Jacob's son, Jacob Jr., joined the business. The family was always generous to those in need and willing to support charities.

Another brewery friend was Maximilian Schaefer who emigrated in the 1830s, as did I. Within five years he and his brother Frederick bought a small brewery which they called the F&M Schaefer Brewing Company. Maximilian had brought with him a recipe for lager beer, which was so popular and financially successful that the brothers bought several large plots of land between 50th and 52nd Streets and built a huge brewery. The area since has become a desirable location, especially when the Grand Central Terminal opened in the 1870s. Maximilian told me that the brewery business had made them extremely wealthy and their land purchases were also worth a great deal. They, too, were civic-minded.

After the 1848 uprising in Germany, my friend, George Ehret immigrated to America when he was in his 20s. He already had an excellent knowledge of brewing and within a short time became a master brewer while working at a small brewery in Manhattan. After that experience, he founded his own brewery, which he named the Hell Gate Brewery after the Hell Gate Strait of the East River, where the brewery was located. It was an extremely successful endeavor. When I asked him to what he attributed his incredible profitability, he responded that besides using the best ingredients, he purchased the newest equipment, such as an artificial ice-making process and refrigeration system. By the late 1880s, his brewery had the largest output of beer in the country, but has now been surpassed, probably because he shipped only locally. I also learned his brewery and land investments were worth approximately $30,000,000 to $40,000,000. As a result, he generously donated to many charitable causes in New York City.

Another brewer friend was Samuel Liebmann. He emigrated in 1854 after the German government banned his business because of his sympathy with the German Revolutionaries. He had owned a successful brewery and inn in Germany, and, therefore, arrived in America with experience in the business. The family settled in the Bushwick section of Brooklyn where Samuel opened a brewery. His sons eventually joined the business, and like Samuel, were very involved with employee and community needs. Son Henry was held in such high esteem, that he was elected the first honorary president of the Workmen's Association of Brooklyn. Son Joseph was appointed the first president of the Bushwick Savings Bank, Director of Kings County Trust Company, and member of the Brooklyn Board of Education.

After Samuel Liebmann's death in the early 1870s, his sons continued the S. Liebmann & Sons Brewery Company, which has had ever increasing success. I knew Liebmann and his sons well, and was impressed not only by their business acumen, but their involvement in many cultural, educational, and charitable causes.

A few years ago, I met with Liebmann's sons for lunch, and, of course, with lunch, a glass of their excellent lager. They reminded me of an event about 15 years prior, which occurred after a performance at the Metropolitan Opera. That evening I, along with several other of Liebmann friends, were invited to have refreshments at Delmonico's Restaurant with Walter Damrosch, the conductor of the Metropolitan Opera. The beverage served was Liebmann's lager and Damrosch complimented the beverage, then held the glass to the light, and commented that it was the color of Das Rheingold (the Rhine River). At the time, I recall the brothers laughing and saying jokingly that someday they might give that name to a lager. Apparently they were presently considering the name Rheingold for one of their lagers. I like the idea and hope they do so.

Two other Brooklyn breweries of note were owned by Eppig family members. Older brother Leonhard Eppig came from Bavaria in 1854 learned the trade and eventually, in 1866, co-founded his own brewery. By 1879 he was sole owner of the tremendously profitable Eppig Germania Brewery. He was also philanthropic, made substantial donations to the improvement of his community, and gave charitable donations to all places of worship, especially St. Leonhard's Roman Catholic Church in Brooklyn. His younger brother Joseph who learned his trade working in Leonhard's brewery, co-founded another Brooklyn brewery in 1888 and by 1889 was sole owner. Joseph is credited with being one of the first brewers to recognize the importance of negotiating with labor unions.

Being apprised of the assets these men were to their communities, I think the reader can understand my frustration with the temperance movement.

However I accepted my job responsibilities as excise commissioner and enforced the licensing laws and other requirements for places that served alcoholic beverages. Nevertheless the extremism and impact of the temperance groups was bothersome.

Commissioner Morrison and I were constantly being harassed at our office by temperance representatives, demanding that we close all establishments that served alcoholic beverages. They were obnoxious and disruptive. Journalists were also frequently present to listen and report the results. It was a popular topic.

Before temperance representatives exited our office, they always left membership cards and pamphlets with their latest propaganda, for the purpose (I am sure) of taunting us.

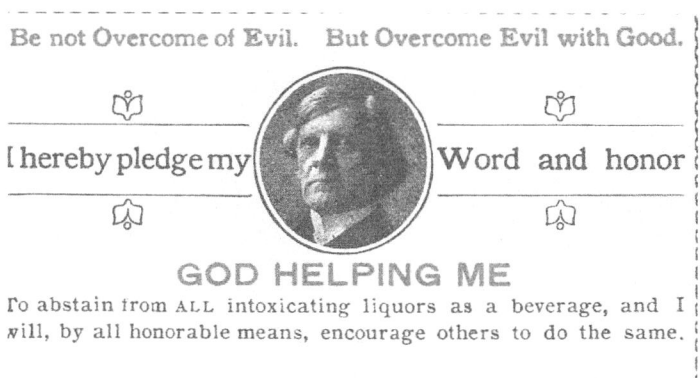

A membership card for a temperance organization. I found among my memorabilia. I don't know why I saved any of their materials, except perhaps to remind me of their intolerance.

I spoke at many functions during the time I was excise commissioner and whether or not the topic regarded temperance, members of the organizations were always present to cause a disturbance. One time in particular in September of 1880, I recall while presenting a speech (having no bearing on temperance), their groups distributed literature and chanted their beliefs inside and outside the hall where I was speaking. Journalists who attended these events reported my speeches in a complimentary manner, but refrained from any mention of the disturbances. I believe some newspapers avoided reporting about the temperance groups' inappropriate behavior because they did not want to be harassed by them.

As might be expected, the temperance movement members continued their vigilance about the work of the excise commissioners. On May 18, 1880 the *New York Herald* printed an article about the meeting of the WCTU in New York City at the Broadway Tabernacle, during which time they criticized and accused Richard Morrison and me of irregularities in granting licenses to liquor establishments.

With incessant criticism, they eventually were able to secure an indictment against us, charging that we had approved a license for an establishment that was simply a saloon, rather than a small hotel, as we had indicated on the document.

A trial (which was a waste of time and money) was held and Commissioner Morrison and I were acquitted. Meanwhile, because of the publicity regarding the case, those in charge of hiring decided to replace us. In December 1880, we completed our terms and were not reappointed. Quite frankly, I was not disappointed to be relieved of this employment, although I did not agree with the reason for replacing us.

It was appalling that the temperance groups wanted to remove employment, and the traditions of socializing in saloons, taverns, and beer gardens. If successful, their demands would result in approximately 50,000 men losing their jobs in the brewery business. Unfortunately, the influence of the temperance movement was increasingly feared.

During the hiatus between the completion of my excise commissioner term until my next employment, I was able to devote more

time to my flourishing drugstores and my association with fraternal organizations.

CHAPTER 21

Magnus Gross Association

I AND SEVERAL OTHERS WERE INVITED TO JOIN A SELECT LITER-
ary association founded by my friend Magnus Gross. The association
gathered fortnightly and the meetings were inspiring. Belonging to
the association placed me in the company of intelligent men of integrity and insightfulness. We were all leaders in our communities, who
through our writings, orations, and other actions, tried to guide those
with whom we interacted to make wise decisions. We were also instrumental in helping to build the educational, cultural, and charitable
metropolis of New York City. Besides Magnus, others in the association were Henry Alloway, George William Curtis, Frank Leslie, Oswald
Ottendorfer, Joseph Pulitzer, Carl Schurz, and Henry Villard. During
our meetings, we discussed literary topics, social issues, and political
subjects. Although at times we had different affiliations and opinions,
the discourse and debates among the group members were excellent
in providing other perspectives for consideration. I was particularly
pleased that several members were journalists so that I could suggest
content for articles. Our common goal was always equality for the
human race.

Magnus Gross was a brilliant man with an exceptional knowledge
of journalism. He came to America in the late 1840s and pursued
journalistic endeavors as an editor in several cities, finally settling in
New York.

He secured a meeting place for the Magnus Gross Association on
North 900 Third Avenue. It was a convenient location and the interior
of the dwelling was large with a parlor, dining hall, and other meeting
rooms. For the opening, Magnus hosted a social evening and arranged
for decorations of fresh flowers, a delightful orchestra playing popular
music from operas, and a sumptuous banquet.

The banquet was prepared by the chefs of the renowned Delmonico's Restaurant which was the reason there was such excitement about Gross's choice. It was by far the most praised restaurant in New York City.

I was invited to speak during the evening. A reporter from the *New York Evening Post* was there to document the occasion. His account appeared the day after the event in an article, May 12, 1871 as follows:

A Pleasant-Social Entertainment

The Magnus Gross Association, a social
and literary organization celebrated
the opening of the new and elegantly
furnished rooms at 900 Third Avenue
last evening. At the rear of the parlor
a large dining hall was splendidly
decorated with natural flowers, vines
and bunting,
The banquet served would have
reflected infinite credit upon Delmonico
himself. Embowered in a shelter of greenery
and flowers was a fine orchestra, which
performed during the evening airs from
the operas. A large number of prominent
gentlemen of the learned professions, with
a sprinkling of politicians were among
the guests. Coroner Hermann presided
and entertaining addresses were delivered
by Mr. Gross, Oswald Ottendorfer,
and Dr. Philip Merkle.

I will introduce the reader to members of the Magnus Gross Association.

George William Curtis was a journalist and wrote articles for the *New-York Tribune, Harper's Weekly,* (eventually becoming its editor)

Harper's Magazine, and helped found (with George Palmer Putnam) *Putnam's Magazine.*

In addition, he was recognized as an outstanding author and an impressive orator. Aware of his oratorical prowess, President Abraham Lincoln asked him to give a speech at Harvard University in defense of the Emancipation Proclamation and President Ulysses S. Grant requested he oversee civil service reform. In 1890, he became chancellor of the University of New York. As a columnist, critic, and editorial writer, it allowed him platforms to influence public awareness regarding political and social equality, public education, and civil rights.

Heinrich Gustav Hilgard arrived in the United States in the early 1850s after attending the Universities of Munich and Wurzburg. Shortly after arriving, he changed his name to Henry Villard so that his father (a conservative and supporter of the tyrannical Bavarian regime) could not locate him.

Villard was a war correspondent for the *Chicago Tribune* and was given an assignment to report on the Austro Prussian War. He later settled in New York City where he was a reporter for the *New-York Tribune and* asked to report the details of the Battle of the Potomac during the Civil War. As a result of his experiences as a war correspondent, he became a pacifist.

His outstanding journalistic writing resulted in articles published by the *New Yorker Staats-Zeitung*, the *New-York Tribune*, and *Frank Leslie's Illustrated Newspaper.* About 1880, he purchased *The Nation* and the *New York Evening Post.*

Another member, Carl Schurz was an extraordinary orator and journalist with whom I so enjoy discussing political ideas. He didn't join us until he moved to New York City in 1881.

Schurz emigrated after taking part in the 1848 uprising in Germany and first settled near relatives in Watertown, Wisconsin. After Lincoln's election, Schurz was appointed envoy to Spain. During his tenure, he influenced enough of Europe (especially Britain) to counteract aid for the Confederacy.

His journalistic acumen earned him positions as editor of newspapers in Detroit, Michigan, and St. Louis, Missouri. While in Missouri, he was elected United States senator and served from 1869 to 1875.

During the administrations of Rutherford B. Hayes and James A. Garfield, he was appointed Secretary of the Interior. In that position, he made contributions by promoting civil service reform, addressing the plight of the Indians, and advocating for conservation of our natural resources. After settling in New York City, he wrote free-lance editorials, articles, and books, and was editor of *The Nation* and the *New York Evening Post.*

Oswald Ottendorfer, who through his journalistic prowess, brilliantly created awareness of social injustice and political choices. Oswald had attended the University of Vienna and while there took part in the Vienna uprising in which he attempted to fight oppression. Fearing for his life, and realizing he could not do more for the cause of democracy, he immigrated to America and settled in New York City.

Although he had a jurisprudence degree and was a linguist (with a command of Latin, Greek, Hebrew, and several Slavic languages) he could not speak English. Therefore, he had to work menial jobs. Eventually, someone told him about employment opportunities at the *New Yorker Staats-Zeitung* where he was hired. After the owner Jacob Uhl died, his wife Anna successfully continued the publication and promoted Ottendorfer to editor. Meanwhile, he was spending more time socially with Anna and in 1860, they married.

After the marriage, Oswald found that the combination of editorial writing and newspaper management was overwhelming. As luck would have it, about that time, Magnus Gross came to New York looking for journalistic employment and was hired as editor-in-chief by the Ottendorfer's.

Oswald and I often spoke at the same venues. One such occasion was a mass Democratic meeting, in 1866 at which we were the featured speakers. The event and content of our speeches were reported in the *Brooklyn Eagle*, October 30 of that year.

In addition to Magnus Gross's journalistic skills, he was also an accomplished orator. He and I were often invited to speak at functions. One such event was held in 1870 at a Democratic committee meeting. An article appeared September 14, 1870 in the *New York Herald* regarding our presentations. It was an honor to be in his company and our proposals always included the importance of human equality.

After many discussions regarding the dishonesty in local government, Magnus Gross, Oswald Ottendorfer, and I, with several others started a political party whose purpose was to oppose other existent parties which had corrupt elements. The mission of our party was the betterment of mankind. We met with and had the support of many of the citizenry, but the new party and its tenets were not strong enough to effect change. I learned that we could have more influence from within political parties through journalistic reporting and spoken dialogue with the community.

At our meetings, we often spoke of needed reforms in the educational system. In 1869 Magnus became a member of the New York City Board of Education and a few years later served as New York City School Commissioner. After nine years as editor-in-chief of the *Staats*, he resigned to devote his full attention to the new position. Although Tweed and his Ring controlled the Board of Education, Magnus hoped he could make a difference as commissioner.

The Magnus Association members discussed and provided suggestions regarding curricular for academic and pedagogical training programs, requiring entrance exams for prospective teachers, regardless of ethnicity, race, religion, or social class, and providing equal pay for both men and women. We were all hopeful that positive change would occur.

At our following meeting, Magnus announced that one of the proposals was accepted, namely teacher training. It would include the acceptance of many first generation immigrants which the board members agreed would be helpful in classes where the children spoke little English.

Although he accomplished some positive change, so much corruption and resistance to improvement existed as a result of Tweed and his Ring that Magnus did not serve his full term. After leaving his position, he authored two books, *Languages and Popular Education* and *The American Crisis* which expounded his beliefs and attempted to expose the ills of city government. He returned to his editorial position at the *Staats* and by the 1880s, with the expert leadership of the Ottendorfer's, and his outstanding editorials, the circulation of the paper was comparable to *The New York Times*. I have always been impressed with both newspapers for their unbiased journalism.

Another member of the Magnus Gross Association was Joseph Pulitzer. After arriving in America, he worked many menial jobs in various cities, but finally settled in St. Louis, Missouri. There he made the acquaintance of Carl Schurz who became his mentor. Eventually Schurz provided him the opportunity to become a reporter. During his time in Missouri, Pulitzer was not only active in journalism, but also in politics, and became a member of the Missouri State Legislature.

I met Pulitzer for the first time in 1880 at a Democratic mass meeting in Albany, New York. We were two of the national selectees to address the meeting. The following is an excerpt from an article about the event which appeared October 21, 1880 in the *Albany Daily Evening Times*.

DEMOCRATIC
MASS MEETING
At TWEEDLE HALL
THE SPEAKERS ARE:
Hon. JOSEPH PULITZER of St. Louis,
Hon. FREDERICK DONNER of Rochester, and
Dr. PHILIP MERKLE of New York.

While in Albany, Pulitzer and I spoke at length and he told me about his background and the possibility of his moving to New York City. He was disturbed by the corruption in the Missouri Court System of which he became aware while he was in the Missouri State Legislature. While in the legislature, he proposed a bill that would remove the possibility of further corruption. He exposed, among others, a contractor who was being given favorable consideration and who was guilty of corruptive activities. The person so angered Pulitzer by publicly calling him a liar that Pulitzer told me he left the scene to get his army gun. When he returned, he gave the contractor the opportunity to apologize for the liar comment, but instead the man punched him. In return, Pulitzer, frustrated, shot the person in the leg. He was fined a great deal of money, but was so popular in Missouri that many people assisted in defraying the cost. He added that it was not a proud moment and one that he wished he could repeat with proper conduct.

During his time in St. Louis, he acquired the German newspaper the *St. Louis Staats-Zeitung* and the English language newspaper the *St. Louis Post-Dispatch*. Through his newspapers, he exposed fraud, monopolies, and other types of corruption.

His business success continued in St. Louis and then, two years after the Albany meeting, unfortunately, one of Pulitzer's chief editorial writers fatally shot a political opponent of the newspaper. After the shooting, Pulitzer decided to move to New York City. He did, however, retain ownership of the *St. Louis Post-Dispatch*.

Upon moving to New York City, Pulitzer purchased the *New York World*. He, like the rest of us in the Magnus Gross Association supported Grover Cleveland for president. Through orations and newspaper articles, our membership successfully promoted him.

Another newspaper that Pulitzer purchased was the *Evening World*. In his newspapers, he, through his principled reporting, exposed political corruption and the ills of the wealthy. For a few years, he was a representative from New York in the United States House of Representatives, but preferred his journalistic work and returned to New York City before his term had expired.

Henry Carter, another member used the pseudonym Frank Leslie. After immigrating to the United States in 1848, he worked briefly for Phineas Taylor Barnum (a politician, publisher, and showman) producing woodcuts for *P.T. Barnum's Illustrated News*.

Leslie founded several illustrated publications that addressed political issues, literature, and cultural topics. He had a social conscience and, for the purpose of public awareness and education, his illustrations often dealt with poverty, crime, and preventable horrific accidents. I was always impressed by Frank's publications: *Frank Leslie's Illustrated Newspaper* and *Frank Leslie's Weekly*.

The financial journalist Henry Alloway sporadically attended our Magnus Gross Association meetings. His financial articles in the *New York Times* were impressive. At one of the meetings, Adolf Ochs (who had been visiting Alloway) accompanied him to the meeting. Ochs informed us that he, too, was a journalist and hoped someday to continue his career in New York City writing for *The New York Times*.

We asked that he tell a little about himself and we learned he was born in Ohio, but after the Civil War moved with his family to Tennessee. There Ochs was mentored and employed by the editor of the *Knoxville Chronicle*, (the only pro-Construction newspaper in the city).

In the late 1870s, Ochs purchased a controlling interest in the failing *Chattanooga Times* and became its publisher. Alloway, in his travels through Chattanooga in the late 1880s, had met Ochs, complimented his objective reporting and invited him to visit in New York. Alloway was a cordial and astute journalist. We all enjoyed meeting him.

As I mentioned, one of the purposes of our meetings was to discuss pressing topics: women's rights, educational reform, acceptance of non-traditional relationships, religious and ethnic acceptance, and segregation.

I vividly recall one of our discussions about segregation. We had opposed it in spoken orations, journalistic editorials, and articles and followed, discussed, and supported the progress of a civil rights bill drafted in 1870, by Senator Charles Sumner of Massachusetts. Although it was not passed by the United States Senate for five years, we were delighted when, in 1875, the act was passed and became known as the Civil Rights Act of 1875 (also referenced as the Sumner Act). The act affirmed "equality of all men before the law" and provided for equal treatment in public accommodations and public transportation. Although it was limited to accommodations and transportation, we were pleased that the act included legal ramifications for non-compliance. It was a step in the right direction and we hoped that our advocacy had helped in this endeavor.

Then the unthinkable occurred in 1883. The United States Supreme Court declared the act unconstitutional based on their interpretation of part of the Fourteenth Amendment. According to their explanation, Congress had no control over private property or corporations under the Equal Protection Clause of the amendment. What a disappointment and another example of a political decision justified by spurious reasons and ignoring our country's tenet of equality for all.

On a chance meeting, (I believe in 1896), I met Alloway and Ochs, who were dining at a restaurant. Alloway informed me that it was a celebratory luncheon and invited me to join them. Ochs had earlier that day purchased the failing *New York Times*. I was not aware the *Times* was losing $1,000 per day as a result of the Panic of 1893. I was impressed by Ochs' philosophy and am hopeful that *The New York Times* can be saved. In 1897, he created the motto which appears on the masthead of the *Times* and states, "All the News That's Fit to Print." What an appropriate slogan for not only the *Times*, but all my journalistic friends' newspapers.

CHAPTER 22

Magnus Gross Guest Speakers

A FEW YEARS AFTER THE ASSOCIATION BEGAN, MAGNUS proposed that we invite guest speakers twice a year. He asked that I select them and arrange for the events. I did not want to unilaterally make the choices so I requested that the membership offer suggestions for consideration. There were many possibilities, but I chose one suggested by each member based on those I thought would be most engaging. Everyone always seemed pleased with my selections. I will introduce the reader to a few.

George Palmer Putnam, a friend of association member George William Curtis, spoke about his successful publishing firm, G. Putnam Broadway. But, what set him aside from other publishers was his advocacy for international copyright laws and his support of the arts. He was the foremost publisher of art works in the city. His dedication to the arts also resulted in his being a founder of the Metropolitan Museum of Art. Details he gave of all his endeavors made it an appealing presentation.

Another guest speaker was Albert Berghaus, who spoke about his experiences as an illustrator for Frank Leslie. He distributed copies of a few examples of his work, but one that I particularly recall, is the illustration of Lincoln on his deathbed. Berghaus sketched the scene after observing the actual event. Viewing and hearing about the works of this talented and innovative illustrator provided a delightful evening.

Businessmen Albrecht and Rudolf Pagenstecher (friends of Oswald Ottendorfer) informed us about their paper manufacturing business. They had purchased a patent and grinders from two German inventors which allowed a means of producing paper from wood instead of rags.

The brothers opened a paper mill and became the first in the United States to produce wood pulp for newsprint paper. The first purchaser was Oswald Ottendorfer who found the paper to be superior and less expensive. Because of Oswald's recommendation, owners of the *New York World*, the *Brooklyn Eagle*, the *New York Evening Express*, and *The New York Times* began purchasing the paper. As the Pagenstecher business flourished, they built more paper mills throughout the northeast United States and in Canada. What an incredible business idea and how interesting to learn the details of their extraordinary venture.

I learned recently from Oswald that the Pagenstecher's sold their business last year (1898) to a company named *International Paper* and the sale resulted in great profit.

Several of us were friends of the Steinway family. I invited William Steinway to address the group, not about his family's success in the music business, but rather his fascination and involvement with engines. Steinway and I had spoken on a few occasions about the great potential for the uses of engines. I believe I was as captivated by the idea as he and hoped the subject would be as exciting to the membership.

What was so intriguing to me was the possible implementation for alternate and faster means of transportation. I had thought about this every time I traveled to other cities.

Steinway explained that he had become acquainted with Wilhelm Maybach and his partner Gottlieb Daimler. Maybach and Daimler patented designs for engines and invented the first engine carburetor. Their engines were successful in converting bicycles to motorcycles and in motorizing boats.

Steinway and Daimler formed a partnership in the late 1880s, and Steinway agreed to open The Daimler Motor Company of New York in Astoria, Queens where they would sell engines for water and land travel.

He spoke enthusiastically about the possibility of automobiles. The idea was wonderful because the petroleum cost was about one cent per horsepower an hour which would make an automobile much less expensive than horsepower. Steinway was so high-spirited about the possibilities of automobile travel in the future and we members were equally eager about the prospects. It was indeed an evening of engrossing conversation.

A few years ago in 1896, I received a correspondence from William's family informing me of his untimely death. The excitement about automobiles had ended for William Steinway. Shortly after, his dream of the automobile engine introduction in the United States also ended when his heirs, disinterested in the automobile engine project, sold all of their inherited shares to a company called General Electric.

Another informative evening was provided by my friend Henry Bergh. His father had left a sizable estate to Bergh and he decided to devote his life to preventing inhumane treatment of animals.

He daily walked the streets of New York City and was appalled by brutish actions such as workhorses beaten, not given regular water, unprotected in extreme weather, and when no longer capable of service, released to wander the streets often resulting in death by starvation. He also witnessed many cats and dogs roaming the streets that were deprived of food, pets held for ransom by dogcatchers, dog and cock fights for amusement, and horrific practices in slaughterhouses.

This resulted in Bergh's founding the American Society for the Prevention of Cruelty to Animals (ASPCA) which was granted incorporation by the New York State Legislature. He was its president from 1866 until his death in 1888. In the early years of the organization, he donated the necessary funding to sustain the group.

Among Bergh's many accomplishments were the introduction of the first ambulance for injured horses in 1867 (two years before the first human ambulance) and the invention of a canvas sling to rescue horses. He was instrumental in having live pigeons replaced by clay ones for trap shooting, and in having legislation passed to ban cruelty to animals during interstate transport.

He also made us aware that the ASPCA was the first humane society in the Western Hemisphere. As a result he traveled throughout the country lecturing about his cause which resulted in organizations in other major cities being founded.

In concluding he expressed his gratitude to Frank Leslie for drawing The ASPCA's official seal. It depicts an angel of mercy protecting a fallen carthorse from a spoke-wielding abuser. Bergh gave each of us a copy of the seal.

The seal of the ASPCA

Another invitee was Elizabeth Jane Cochran who used the pen name Nellie Bly. She was an imaginative, investigative reporter who had been employed by Pulitzer.

Assignments she had preferred were those that would provide awareness of social ills in the hope that reform would take place. She told us the details of one such assignment. She inspected the asylum on Blackwell's Island where the city housed those considered insane or contagious. In order to observe the institution from within, she feigned insanity and after examination by several doctors, she was determined to indeed be insane, and was institutionalized.

After ten days, Pulitzer sent his attorneys who divulged the truth about Bly and she was released. Her observations and revelations were mind boggling. I recall some of the horrible details: the food was barely edible, water was contaminated, and because of overcrowding, many patients slept on the floor. Rats and human waste were seen throughout the asylum and inmates who were considered dangerous were tied together. There was no knowledge of the outside world and no opportunity to read or communicate with each other. They just sat on benches from morning until night. If found talking to each other, they were often beaten.

Bly also reported that suddenly several buckets of ice cold water were dumped over each patient. She did find opportunities to speak to some and was convinced they were falsely institutionalized. She informed us her investigation revealed that over 7,000 patients were housed in the asylum in those horrific conditions. I recall the membership being distressed and distraught and sitting silently in seeming disbelief.

Her report resulted in the convening of a grand jury to investigate conditions at Blackwell's Island (with her assistance). As a result of her observations and proposals for change, improvements were made, additional funds slated for the institution, and physicians' exams more thorough. The overcrowding also resulted in other institutions being opened in following years on Ward Island, Hart Island, and another to be built in Central Islip on Long Island. What a wonderful example of sacrificing for the betterment of mankind.

In 1890, I scheduled an evening with Samuel Clemens who of course uses the pen name Mark Twain. He presented his essay entitled, "The Awful German Language" and distributed copies for us to follow. (It is an appendix to his novel, *A Tramp Abroad* in which he describes his travels through parts of Europe.) Twain's reading of the essay offered a great deal of levity to our meeting. In a humorous way, he described the frustration he suffered in attempting to learn German as a second language.

The ten parts of speech in German, in his opinion, lack logic, are troublesome, and frustrating. When he finally had begun to understand the language, more exceptions appeared. According to Twain, "the inventor" of German must have taken pleasure in making it as convoluted as possible.

He explained some of the difficulties and exasperating inconsistencies. I will mention his vexation with the gender of nouns, and for which he believes one must "have a memory like a memorandum-book." He gave examples: "a young lady has no sex, while a turnip has. Think what overwrought reverence that shows for the turnip, and what callous disrespect for the girl; a tree is male, its buds are female, its leaves are neuter; horses are sexless, dogs are male, cats are female -- tomcats included, of course; a person's mouth, neck, bosom, elbows, fingers, nails, and feet are of the male sex, and one's head is male or neuter according to the word selected to signify it, and not according to the sex of the individual who wears it -- all women have either male heads or sexless ones; a person's nose, lips, shoulders, breasts, hands, and toes are of the female sex; and hair, ears, eyes, chin, legs, knees, heart, and conscience haven't any sex at all; a woman is a female; but a wife (Weib) is neuter -- which is unfortunate, and a fish is he, his scales are she, but a fishwife is neither."

After much arduous study, Twain confidently expressed his thoughts to the curator of Heidelberg Castle and proudly spoke in what he believed was flawless German. The curator listened intently before commenting that Twain's command of German was very rare and should be added to the museum's collection. Twain remarked that he wanted to tell the curator that what it had cost him to acquire this art of the German language would be far too costly for the curator or any other collector of rare art to purchase.

Since most of us in the Magnus Association had an excellent command of the German language, we understood his frustration and laughed heartily throughout his presentation.

That same year, after almost 20 years, the association disbanded following Magnus Gross's death. I am grateful to him for founding this group which was comprised of such insightful and caring individuals. I believe that our discussions during the tenure of the association caused awareness and positive change in the venues for which we advocated. And we developed such wonderful friendships which provided me with an outstanding circle of friends.

CHAPTER 23

More Tales of Two Cities

CORRESPONDENCES CONTINUED BETWEEN MY SISTER AND ME. From 1861 to 1865, our letters often focused on the events of the Civil War: the horrific battles, the tremendous loss of life, and the hatred between the north and south. My nephew Philip fought in the war and Friederike and I were so grateful he survived. Both New York and Missouri fought on the union side.

At the start of the war, Missouri was considered a slave state, but due to the tremendous immigrant population and their advocacy against slavery, Missouri voted to remain in the Union. There were some in New York, but many more in Missouri who were Confederate sympathizers, mainly because of the effect it would have on investments and businesses. Missouri received a great deal of goods from the South, but the most affected industry was cotton. I communicated to Friederike, that she must remember the United States produced the largest amount of cotton in the world, which therefore was a tremendously lucrative business for southern and border states. In large part, the profit-making was due to the use of over one million inexpensive, enslaved colored laborers who would no longer be available after emancipation.

A year after the war, some towns throughout the country commemorated those who had given their lives during the Civil War by decorating their graves and having ceremonies to honor them. However, Friederike and I noticed that unfortunately, in some towns, reports indicated that the ceremonies deteriorated into divisive words of prejudice similar to those that existed before and during the war. There was definitely still a divide in the country.

Hopefully in the future, the approximately 600,000 soldiers who lost their lives during the war, no matter on which side they served, will be remembered with an official commemorative holiday. And the country will reflect about the sadness of a war that perhaps could have been averted.

We discussed the establishment of professional police departments in both cities prior to the establishment of professional fire departments, but agreed there was as much need for the latter. My sister and I were elated reporting to each other that by the end of the war, both cities had founded professional fire departments.

In recalling happier times, Friederike penned that she and the children attended the first St. Louis Fair after the war. (The fair had been curtailed during the Civil War so that the grounds could be used as a training area for soldiers and a hospital for the injured or sick.) She was impressed by the many interesting educational products and displays in addition to a very well produced horse show and sulky race held in an amphitheater. In her subsequent writings, she indicated that the fair improved each year and attracted many notables from around the world.

In 1867, Friederike wrote that she had joined The Woman Suffrage Association of Missouri whose purpose was to gain the vote for women in equal status with men. The organization was unique in that it was the first group in the country whose mission had only one goal: suffrage for women. She believed that placing all their energies in one undertaking might result in greater impetus and strength.

Friederike was so anxious for us to visit that in 1867, I convinced Marie to travel with me to visit my family. While there, we toured many places that Friederike thought would be of interest. The first was their mercantile library which was established during the 1840s. At its founding, it was stocked with classic books, mostly having been brought from Germany and donated by German immigrants. Those interested would meet to share and discuss the books and other topics of the day.

Another purpose (similar to the New York City Mercantile Library) was to encourage young people to frequent a library so that their leisure time would be spent in a worthwhile manner. Within a year of its opening, it had well over 1,000 books and about 300 subscribers. The library's auditorium served many purposes over the years, such as the meeting place for the Missouri Constitutional Convention when they voted to remain in the Union, and again, in 1865, when they voted to abolish slavery. Friederike was extremely proud of the library as she should have been.

Another day, she arranged for a carriage ride to see some factories and shops. Because of Missouri's proximity to the south, cotton was easily accessible and therefore we saw several dry goods factories and stores. We passed several furniture stores and she explained that St. Louis boasted a large lumber industry resulting in the establishment of furniture factories and stores. Next we noticed the Liggett and Brothers Tobacco Company, a blacksmith factory, restaurants, bakeries and grocery stores. And then there was the incredible Keevil Hat Store. The store had a huge red top hat estimated to be 12 feet high, sitting atop the store's roof along with a United States flag. There is no way you would miss this display which was a wonderful means of advertising, but according to Friederike, William Henry Keevil, the proprietor gained even more publicity by promoting his hats in German and English newspapers in St. Louis. Of course it did not hurt business that hats were considered a necessary part of a man's attire in the 1800s which helped Keevil's success.

Compton and Dry Pictorial History of St. Louis drawing circa 1867 of the shop of William Henry Keevil. Courtesy of third great grandson Mike Keevil and the Missouri Historical Society.

After the tour, we had dinner at Tony Faust's Oyster House, the famous St. Louis restaurant. It was wonderful.

Before returning to New York, Friederike suggested that we take a carriage ride along the Missouri River to the City of Hermann, which is just west of St. Louis. There were about 500 acres that had been established for vineyards and wineries. As we rode, I couldn't help notice the clean air with the wonderful aroma of vineyard vegetation. Friederike and I looked at each other with tears in our eyes, realizing how reminiscent it was of the town of Freinsheim. Marie, Friederike and I had lunch in a small family establishment and sampled their wine. It was excellent. (Two decades later, I read Missouri was producing more wine than any other state!)

It had been a wonderful week and we promised to visit each other as often as possible. On the way home Marie agreed that it had been a pleasant visit which gave her the opportunity to get to know my delightful family.

Correspondences continued between Friederike and me. In 1872, I received the news that my nephew JF was to be married to Miss Sarah Stork of St. Louis, the daughter of a blacksmith. At the time, JF was working as a clerk in a grocery store. Then in 1874, I learned that he had started his own grocery business in a store attached to his home. I was proud of my nephew for his diligence and business acumen.

JF Conrad grocery store built in 1874.

In March 1874, Friederike communicated that JF, Sarah, and she attended a St. Patrick's Day Parade which was held in the Kerry Patch area of St. Louis. She commented that when they entered the area, it was a beautiful sea of green with huge crowds of people in attendance.

Watching the parade and other festivities made the day an enjoyable one. Friederike added that she read in the newspaper the following day that the St. Patrick's Day parade and celebrations had begun in 1820 in St. Louis when a few hundred Irish inhabitants gathered to honor the saint. The tradition has continued since, but with an ever-increasing attendance. The 1874 total numbered hundreds of thousands and the attendees came from many areas of Missouri and even other states.

When I responded, I told her that New York City's St. Patrick's Day celebrations began in 1762 and Marie and I attended two of the parades during the 1870s. They were well-organized with wonderful Irish music and many Irish groups represented.

Although it is important for all immigrants to assimilate and become citizens of their new country, I was impressed that the Irish realized the importance of preserving their heritage. I truly hope that other ethnicities will follow the example of the Irish, celebrate their heritage, and not allow their ancestry to be forgotten.

The same year (1874), I received the exciting news from Friederike that a rail bridge over the Mississippi had been built and would make a huge difference in railroad traffic to and from St. Louis. The bridge was named for its chief engineer, Captain James B Eads. After completion, it was the longest arch bridge in the world. It had been built with the strongest steel available and to test its strength, an elephant was paraded across. When that was successful, 14 locomotives traversed the bridge showing its stability. The bridge allowed for easier and faster transportation especially of goods between the East and St. Louis. It was wonderful hearing of more positive growth.

Unexpectedly, sad news arrived. My sister Friederike died in May of 1875. I immediately traveled to St. Louis for the funeral. I was so distressed by her passing; she was always dear to me and I will miss her deeply. She was obviously well-liked as evidenced by the many who attended her funeral and their kind words about her. My nephew Philip could not attend his mother's funeral due to illness. Philip had served in the Civil War, attained the rank of corporal, but within months after his release, he was diagnosed with nephritis. According to JF, the disease took its toll rapidly. Philip died in October, five months after his mother.

At the luncheon after Friederike's funeral, I met some of her friends. Susan Blow introduced herself and explained that she and Friederike recognized the need for improvement in St. Louis' public educational system and were advocates for their betterment. During the 1860s until 1875, Blow reminded me that Friederike had volunteered to teach reading and math in the public schools, which was where they had met.

Friederike had told me that Blow had visited Germany to observe their educational system and in particular was impressed by the kindergarten classes reflective of the methods of Friedrich Froebel. When she returned to America, with the approval of the superintendent of schools of St. Louis, she instituted a model for the first public kindergarten in America.

I mentioned that Carl Schurz (of course Susan Blow knew of his contributions in St. Louis), was most proud of his wife Margarethe for making use of her training with Friedrich Froebel. Margarethe had established a model kindergarten in their home in Watertown, Wisconsin (before moving to St. Louis). According to Carl, the children in her class were happy, and learning, which impressed their parents. At one of our Magnus meetings, Carl had told us that his wife had been credited with establishing the first private kindergarten in America.

During the luncheon, Susan Blow introduced me to William Torrey Harris who knew Friederike and praised her volunteer work. I learned that Harris had begun as a public school teacher in St. Louis presenting innovative ideas. Several years ago, he had become superintendant of schools. His foresighted ideas resulted in the improvement and expansion of the St. Louis public high school curricula to include the arts, sciences, and business training. He also was an advocate of the importance of establishing libraries in all public schools. Harris added that after observing Susan Blow's model kindergarten and being impressed by the physical and mental growth of the children, it convinced him to expand the number of kindergartens in St. Louis.

Another who attended Friederike's funeral was her friend Dr. Georg Engelmann. He emigrated from Germany about the same time as Friederike, eventually opened a medical practice in St. Louis, and became the physician to Friederike and her family. In addition to contributing research in the fields of medicine, meteorology, and botany, he was the founder of the St. Louis Academy of Science. A very intense, intelligent person!

Joseph Mersman, another attendee, spoke with me about his whiskey rectification business. He was a wholesale provider of whiskey and serviced 1,000 taverns in St. Louis including Friederike's restaurant. Mersman mentioned that during the Civil War, his business income increased substantially because he had signed a contract with the Union Army to supply the Union troops with whiskey.

I remained with my nephew JF and his family for a few days after Friederike's death and it was wonderful getting to know them better.

While I was in St. Louis, there were reports that on May 10, 1875 (a few days after my sister's funeral), the Whiskey Ring was exposed through simultaneous raids in various parts of the country. Many of us knew about the ring, but it was powerful and difficult to expose. JF was especially relieved to hear the news and hoped that his suppliers were not involved.

A day or two prior to the raid, JF and I had discussed the ring and hoped that its members would someday be brought to justice. If you are not familiar with this scandal, I will explain it briefly. The Whiskey Ring, with its hub in St. Louis, evolved during the presidency of Ulysses Grant. It involved many, from distillers of whiskey in major cities of the United States, to government officials on all levels. Instead of remitting the appropriate federal taxes, the distillers paid only half the amount that was mandated, and their products were stamped as having complied with tax law. The money collected from the distillers was instead distributed among the rest of the illegal ring. In essence, no tax was paid on the whiskey and the amounts paid by the distillers were shared by the rest of the ring.

It was a successful quid pro quo until United States Secretary of the Treasury, Benjamin Bristow found a way to destroy the ring. Aware that some of the ring's members were official federal government employees, Bristow, unbeknown to President Grant and his attorney general, gathered information through secret agents outside the government, and exposed the ring.

The trials took place in Jefferson City, Missouri beginning in October 1875. Much was written about them in New York City newspapers (and I am sure throughout the country).

From the time I returned home, JF corresponded with me and also sent St. Louis newspaper clippings as had his mother. It was of interest to read other newspapers' perspectives. One particular article he sent referenced William McKee, owner of the St. Louis Globe-Democrat who (according to JF) had been known to be an unscrupulous politician. It was estimated that McKee had benefited by over $100,000 in bribes from the Whiskey Ring and JF hoped he'd be convicted. Ultimately, over 100 people were convicted including Orville Babcock, private secretary to President Grant, along with others in various government positions, and, of course, many distillers. JF was pleased to inform me that William McKee was one of those convicted for conspiracy to defraud the government and was sentenced to two years in prison. Approximately $3,000,000 in owed taxes was recovered.

I read later that although Benjamin Bristow was praised by many for his accomplishments in dismantling the Whiskey Ring, he resigned from his governmental position because he was told that he had been an embarrassment to President Grant.

Correspondences with JF continued and a wonderful relationship developed.

CHAPTER 24

The 1876 International Centennial Exposition of the United States

THE 1876 INTERNATIONAL CENTENNIAL EXPOSITION OF THE United States was an exciting event. It was held on approximately 250 acres in Fairmont Park, Philadelphia, Pennsylvania to celebrate the 100 year anniversary of the signing of the United States *Declaration of Independence* and to show the tremendous progress our country had achieved in that time. The exposition lasted six months from May to November, and the total attendance was about 10,000,000 with over 30,000 exhibits. It was originally named the International Exhibition of Arts, Manufacturers, and Products of the Soil and Mine, but then became commonly known as The 1876 International Centennial Exposition of the United States. In addition to the United States, 35 or more nations, and about 20 colonies participated.

It was an amazing exposition, which offered international exposure for the exhibitors. As you entered the grounds, it was overwhelming. There were 250 buildings interspersed with 16 fountains for decoration. For convenience, there were 16 bridges, five and one half miles of railroad track, seven miles of walkways, elevators, wheelchairs, and a unique invention of a monorail to transport people 500 feet between buildings.

One of the buildings was Brewers' Hall. Prior to the event, I was invited by some of my brewer friends to be on a committee to plan the brewers' exhibition. National and international brewers participated and it was an amicable undertaking. The following excerpts regarding the brewers' exhibition appeared in the *New York Herald*, February 26, 1876, several months before the exposition. The reporter relayed the long period of time we had been organizing the event and those who would be implementing the plans. My name and the part I contributed are mentioned in the article.

BREWERS'CENTENNIAL EXHIBITION

Yesterday afternoon there was a
meeting held at the Brewers and Maltsters' Insurance
Company of the General and
Executive Committee of the brewers and maltsters'
trade organization.
Action of a harmonious nature is taking place
among the trade all over the Union in regard to the
representation of the brewing business at the Philadelphia Centennial Industrial Exhibition. Mr. H. H.
Rueter, of Boston, a prominent brewer, occupied the
chair. A resolution was offered that the work on the
proposed brewers and maltsters' buildings to be
erected in the vicinity of Agricultural Hall should be
given to the architect and the contractors.
The dimensions will be 260x80 feet, and it is estimated
that the cost will be about $40,000. The resolution
was adopted without dissent.
The entire cost of the proposed brewers' exhibition at
Philadelphia will be $70,000, and already $20,000 has
been subscribed by the trade but with very little solici-
tation...Letters have been received by the committee
from Austrian, Bohemian, German and English brewers, noti-
fying the association that they would send specimens
of their malty beverages for exhibition. The
work yesterday afternoon chiefly consisted in the
appointment of a sub-committee to further the work in
hand... Henry Clausen, Jacob Ahles and Philip Merkle
were appointed a committee.

My brewer friends and I traveled to Philadelphia in early May 1876 to
prepare our part of the brewery displays for the opening on May 10th.
Although Brewers' Hall was not one of the main exhibit halls, it was
an impressive separate building where brewers displayed the history
of the industry, their latest brewery machinery, and finished products.

Brewer's Hall from *Frank Leslie's Historical Register of the United States Centennial Exposition*, 1876.

In the hall, we arranged a display of a 100 year old brewery model where all labor was by hand in a shed under a thatched roof. Another display was a model of a current brewery, including many machines that would be used in a large factory. There was a great deal of interest by many of the visitors.

I remained a few days after the opening to help at the brewers' exhibition. Meanwhile I also attended the opening ceremonies for the entire centennial exhibition which were impressive. The first ceremony was the introduction of President Grant and his wife Julia Dent Grant, accompanied by the first reigning monarchs to visit the United States, Emperor Dom Pedro II and Empress Teresa of Brazil.

First Lady Julia Dent Grant, President Grant, Empress Teresa, and Emperor Dom Pedro II of Brazil observed the opening ceremonies. Illustration from *Frank Leslie's Illustrated Newspaper.*

Another opening ceremony I attended took place in Machinery Hall. There President Ulysses Grant and the Emperor of Brazil, Dom Pedro started the nearly 50-foot-tall, 650-ton Corliss two cylinder steam engine which produced 1,400 horsepower enough to power the 13 acres of exhibits in Machinery Hall.

A sketch of the Corliss cylinder from *Frank Leslie's Illustrated Newspaper.*

I returned home after assisting at Brewers' Hall and attending the opening ceremonies. Marie was anxious to attend so we returned in November for the final four days and invited JF and Sarah to join us. They gratefully accepted.

CHAPTER 25

Family Visit to the Centennial Exhibition

JF AND SARAH MET US AT THE TRANSCONTINENTAL HOTEL where I had made reservations. It was a relatively small hotel which accommodated only 500 people, but I chose it because of its convenience to the main entrance. We settled into the hotel and the rooms were small, but clean. Marie, JF, and Sarah were excited to be able to view the centennial grounds from the rooms. It was quite a sight! We freshened up from the journey and walked across the street to the exposition grounds.

We had to stand on a long line to pay our admission which was 50 cents per person. We finally had our tickets and entered the exposition. JF was the first to notice the arm and torch of the Statue of Liberty. It really did capture one's attention. Frederic Bartholdi and Gustave Eiffel had sent the completed arm and torch for display at the exposition in order to raise money to help defray the cost of the base which, as previously mentioned, was the responsibility of the United States. (This was nine years before Joseph Pulitzer's campaign for the remainder of funds needed for the base.) For a donation of 50 cents, a ladder could be climbed to reach the balcony around the torch. Of course, we all climbed the ladder. What a wonderful view.

The arm, torch, and ladder to the top of the Statue of Liberty to view the area. *Frank Leslie's historical register of the United States Centennial Exposition.*

One of the first buildings we noticed was a reception room. The following is a copy of the flyer regarding it.

CENTENNIAL
Department of Public Comfort,
RECEPTION ROOM,
Opposite Main Entrance Building,

*A convenient place, FREE OF CHARGE, where
parties may meet on entering the Grounds
and make their arrangements for
the day's pleasure.*

Satchels, Baskets and Bundles checked and taken care of for a moderate charge.

THIS BUILDING CONTAINS

General Parlor,	Coat and Baggage Room,
Ladies' Parlor,	Barber Shop,
Balcony for Refreshments,	Boot-Blacking Room,

Lavatories,   Theatre Ticket Office,

AND THE FAMOUS

AMERICAN LUNCH COUNTER

All charges are VERY MODERATE and under control of the
CENNTENIAL BOARD OF MANAGERS.

**Then we boarded the centennial railroad. What a wonderful
way to travel the grounds.**

The centennial passenger railroad. Sketch from *Harper's Weekly*, 1876.

Of the 250 buildings, there were five main ones: the Main Exhibit Hall, Art Hall (later called Memorial Hall), Machinery Hall, Agricultural Hall, and Horticultural Hall.

The Main Building was the closest to us so we explored it first. The poster near the building indicated that the edifice was enclosed by 21 ½ acres and was the largest known building in the world.

As we entered, Marie commented that she was amazed by the expanse of the interior. It was indicated on another poster that the building was 1,888 feet long and 463 feet wide!

Main Exhibition Building, from *Frank Leslie's Weekly*, 1876.

Machinery Hall was the second largest building and the next that we explored. According to the poster, it was 1,402 feet long and 340 feet wide. In addition, it had an annex area of 208 by 202 feet with another 1,900 exhibitors. The United States displays occupied about two thirds of the space!

Besides the amazing Corliss steam engine, there were many other creative machines, but the ones that drew the most attention were the wonderful Remington's capital letter typographic machine (that within two years after the centennial was able to produce upper and lower case letters), and a rubberized cloth portmanteau (similar to a suitcase) able to be converted into a bathtub. On a poster about it, was stated that its benefit was affording travelers the luxury and comfort of bodily ablution.

Another incredible invention, the telephone was demonstrated by Alexander Graham Bell. He had procured a patent for his invention a few months before the centennial. During one of his demonstrations, Bell spoke into the transmitter and requested that the Emperor of Brazil stand at a distance of 20 feet, holding the receiver to his ear. After hearing Bell's words through the receiver, the emperor reportedly exclaimed, "My God, it talks!" The scientist, Lord Kelvin also in attendance, expressed his amazement.

JF and I spoke with a young man, Thomas Edison, who was most enthusiastic to show his inventions of an electric pen and an automatic telegraph system. He has since become an acknowledged inventor.

Some other memorable aspects of the hall were the ability to borrow wheelchairs and have a lovely dinner within the hall for 50 cents.

Our next visit was to Memorial Hall (art gallery) with its many national and international displays of artists' works.

We were impressed by the beautiful paintings chosen for display and proud of the United States Gallery, which represented several schools and periods of art. They were all outstanding works, but one entitled *Under the Oaks* by Edward Mitchell Bannister was exceptional. It is an engrossing pastoral scene of such depth, and yet simplicity. The artist was obviously influenced by the Barbizon School and would probably be considered a tonal painter. It was so affecting, expressive, and impactful that we believed it would win first prize. Understandably, the composition was attracting a great deal of attention.

In another gallery there were 500 sculptures displayed (of which 152 were by American artists). One in particular attracted much attention. It was the *Death of Cleopatra* by artist Mary Edmonia Lewis, one of the artists I have already mentioned in another chapter who lived most of her time in Europe where her race, artistic preferences, and personal leanings were accepted. The sculpture is a marble work weighing over 2,000 pounds.

Although images and sculptures of Cleopatra have always been a popular subject for sculptors, this was a unique portrayal. Instead of glamorizing Cleopatra, Lewis portrayed her seated on her throne in a clumsy manner, at the moment of death after having been bitten by an asp.

Many critics believed the sculpture to be the most viewed and admired at the exhibit. A report in the *People's Advocate*, (a recently established newspaper published in Alexandria, Virginia) noted that Lewis' statue "excites more admiration and gathers larger crowds around it than any other work of art in the vast collection of Memorial Hall." We agreed that it was a phenomenal and imposing sculpture.

After the centennial ended, I read that Lewis was not having the sculpture transported to Rome, (where she was living) probably because of the transport cost and because she was hopeful it would be purchased by a museum either in the United States or somewhere else in the world. This did not occur, but instead it was placed in storage until 1878 when it was exhibited at the Chicago Interstate Industrial Exposition where it again was a popular attraction.

Following its display at The Chicago Exposition, the sculpture was returned to storage until 14 years later, when someone reportedly saw it in a Chicago saloon. Sometime after that showing, a race horse owner purchased it from the saloon owner to be used as a tombstone for one of his favorite horses, named Cleopatra. The horse is buried in front of the grandstand at the Chicago Harlem Racetrack. I do hope that this exceptional sculpture will be saved from its current location and appear in a permanent art venue.

Death of Cleopatra, *Frank Leslie's historical register of the United States Centennial Exposition,* 1876.

We saw so many wonderful exhibits and looked forward to more in the upcoming days.

CHAPTER 26

Exploration of the Centennial Exhibition continues

THE THIRD DAY BEGAN BY EXPLORING HORTICULTURAL HALL. The building was constructed with sections of glass enclosures to accommodate plants in need of extreme heat and light. The expanse of national and international flora displays was a sight to behold. The aromas and variations in color, and the manner in which they were displayed was outstanding.

Next we perused the exhibits in Agricultural Hall, (the last of the five main buildings). As we entered the building, there was an overwhelming aroma of tobacco. The exhibitors displayed tobacco for pipes and cigars, hand-rolled cigarettes, snuff, and green and powdered tobacco leaves. The medicinal benefit of the leaves was thought to give relief for pain by placing or rubbing them on the area of complaint. As we continued walking through the hall, Marie pointed to an interesting exhibit of wines from Germany and France. Even more exciting was when we noticed some from the Freinsheim area. There were also many exhibits and demonstrations of modern, innovative farm equipment.

Outside the building there were presentations of livestock and horses which were being judged. We enjoyed seeing the beautiful animals and the judging techniques.

Another exhibition we visited was the Women's Pavilion. We learned that they had anticipated having their displays in the main building, but were refused (it was assumed, due to their womanhood). Elizabeth Duane Gillespie (great-granddaughter of Benjamin Franklin) known to be an impressive leader, with the assistance of many other women, raised sufficient support to exhibit in their own pavilion. The interior was splendid, beautifully appointed, and visitors couldn't help but notice a spectacular fountain chandelier lighting the hall.

The contents of the displays were all developed by women with the purpose of showing that they had abilities equal to men and possessed the potential for contributions and profitability outside the home. Their exhibits were impressive in all areas: industry, fine arts, and literature: all achieved by women. There were about 80 patented inventions exhibited including a dishwasher, a self- heating iron, and a stove (all providing women more convenience and/or opportunities out of the house). To further illustrate their inventiveness and abilities, a woman was operating a steam engine that powered a printing press.

The women distributed copies of a printed newsletter entitled *The New Century for Women*. They also provided literature about the need for women's dress reform from the Victorian styles to more practical garments. Marie and Sarah were impressed, inspired, and totally concurred with the rationale. They couldn't seem to stop talking about the possibilities suggested for women. JF and I were equally impressed and enlightened realizing that beyond suffrage, there must be equality with men in all areas and endeavors.

During the time we were there, New York Day was celebrated and featured the New York Police Department and our governor, my friend Samuel Tilden. It was wonderful having the opportunity to introduce him to my family.

Next we stopped at our friend Henry Bergh's display and he was pleased to see us. While we perused his display, he distributed materials about the ASPCA, and relayed to visitors his observations and the need to stop abuse of animals. Many attendees of all ages were concerned and ready to help.

Henry Bergh and the display of the ASPCA, *Frank Leslie's Weekly,* 1876.

I haven't mentioned about restaurants at the centennial. There were so many that were recommended, many of which featured international cuisine. Those that we chose were excellent. The restaurants were always filled and in fact the first day of the centennial, it was reported that by the time President Grant and his party were ready to have dinner, there was no food left in his restaurant of choice.

There was a beautifully decorated German restaurant and beer garden which seated 1,000 customers and was always filled to capacity. This gave people who had not experienced the taste of lager to do so. Although offering excellent food and drink, we didn't eat there because we wanted to sample new or different cuisines. (I subsequently learned that after the event had ended, the popularity and sale of lager increased tremendously.)

I will mention some foods and drinks we enjoyed. We were being introduced to most for the first time. There was a product called popcorn which none of us had ever eaten. The popcorn pavilion was extremely popular and it was interesting to watch the product being created. A reporter for the *Philadelphia Record* learned that a merchant paid $3,000 for the right to sell popcorn at the centennial! The vendor made a considerable profit which indicates the extraordinary amount of this inexpensive product that was consumed.

Watching popcorn being prepared, *Frank Leslie's Illustrated Newspaper,* 1876.

Another item which was introduced was a yellow fruit called banana. I purchased one for each of us at a cost of 10 cents per banana. Each one was wrapped in foil and we were given a knife and fork with which to eat it. From watching others, we found that you peel and slice it before eating. JF, Sarah, Marie, and I agreed that the fruit was delicious. Since the exposition, JF stocks it in his store and when our grocery store has the fruit, we purchase it. According to JF, bananas are a popular item in St. Louis as we have noticed in New York City.

Another popular display was the Arctic soda fountain. James Tufts invented and patented the object in the 1860s according to the literature distributed. He not only had an exhibition at the centennial, but also purchased the rights to sell soda water at the event in all the main buildings and outside on the grounds. On the reverse of one of his trade cards, it mentions that inside the dome of his fountain, is an immense ice cavern, which is reached by stairs from the cellar. Workmen continuously supplied ice and fruit syrups into this cavern. The cost to erect the structure was $25,000. We stopped at his pavilions several times since the soda water was so thirst quenching especially during the hot weather we were encountering. Besides his successful sales at the centennial, I learned that since the event ended, the sales of his fountain equipment have increased substantially.

An illustration of the tall white marble design of Tufts Arctic Water Apparatus that displayed his countertop fountains. *Centennial Photographic Co.*

We read trade cards about the Fleischmann Company which had been founded in Ohio in the late 1860s by brothers Charles and Maximilian Fleischmann. The company produces compressed yeast, a byproduct of their distilled gin, and bakery products made with the yeast. At the centennial, the owners presented the Vienna Model Bakery to introduce the excellent quality of Austrian bread products made with yeast.

We went to the Vienna Model Bakery for a repast. What an impressive building and such wonderful bakery products and international coffees! There was also the option of sandwiches on their specially baked rolls. All the offerings were delicious.

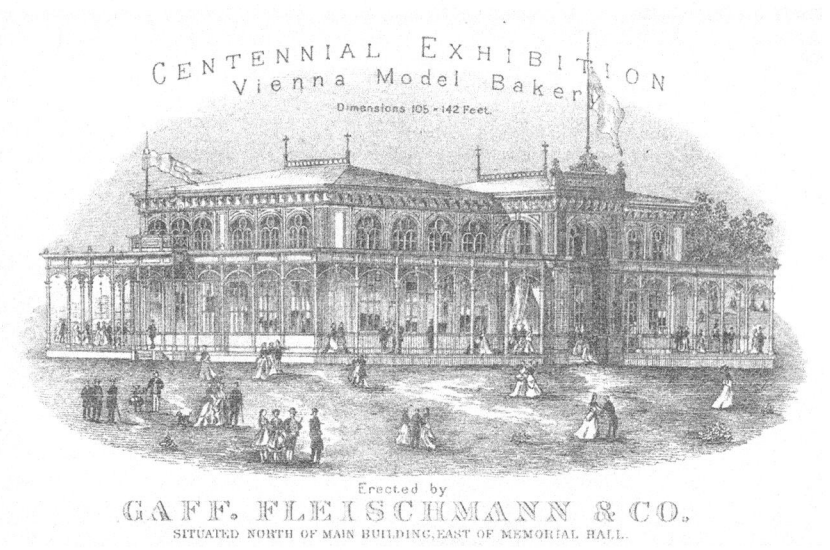

Fleischmann Building, Vienna Model Bakery. Trade card 1876.

We returned to Memorial Hall for the announcement of the winner for best painting. As we expected, Edward Mitchell Bannister's *Under the Oaks* was the winner and would receive the bronze medal. Then there was hesitation in presenting the award and we learned later that when the judges realized Bannister was a colored person, they reconsidered their decision. What prejudice and a disturbing example of discrimination! However, in a wonderful act of kindness, justice, and equality, the other contestants made their voices heard and insisted Bannister was deserving of the award. The decision was reconfirmed.

It always gives encouragement to realize that there are those who will look beyond racial difference.

Our last stop before returning home was at Brewers' Hall for the award ceremony. Henry Liebmann, (son of my friend Samuel Liebmann) received first prize for the family's excellent product and contributions. I was so pleased to be there to congratulate him and of course delighted that a New York brewer won.

On the walk back to the hotel, I mentioned to JF, Sarah, and Marie that it occurred to me during the event, that in spite of the Depression in the United States, surprisingly, many Americans attended the exposition. I wondered how so many could afford to do so. In addition, I indicated my extreme disappointment in learning the prejudice directed at women and colored people by some committees and judges. They agreed it was disturbing.

The visit to the centennial went by quickly. It was a wonderful four days which we enjoyed immensely. We bade JF and Sarah farewell and we promised to visit each other in the near future.

Since returning home, I have read several articles about the success of the centennial. For the United States, it served one of its main goals, a huge increase in exports and a decrease in imports. This was believed to be the result of the tens of thousands of exhibits, displays, and demonstrations.

The worldwide and United States attendees saw in one location, the tremendous strides that had been made in the past 100 years in our country. Many products were purchased or ordered, and a great deal of interest was shown in future product acquisitions. The United States had become a recognized and respected leader in all areas especially manufacturing and industry. In addition, probably because of the thousands of innovative ideas presented, others were inspired and applications for patents in the United States increased tremendously.

I am so proud of my adopted country. The exhibitions, contributions, and innovative ideas by United States citizens were heart-warming and gratifying.

CHAPTER 27

My New York City Coroner Journal, Part 1

I WAS NOMINATED FOR CORONER OF NEW YORK COUNTY IN 1881 and newspapers reported what they believed was the public confidence in my doing the job. The following appeared in the *New York Herald* November 7, 1881.

> Dr. Philip Merkle is admitted to be the best
> fitted for Coroner of all the candidates nomi-
> nated and if elected will administer the affairs
> of the office with integrity and ability.

That confidence was verified when I defeated my opponents by 5,000 votes. I was the only Democratic candidate on the ballot who won, which indicated to me that, although the Democratic Party was out of favor that year, people had trust in my ability. The following article appeared in the *New York Herald* Tuesday Dec 27, 1881, indicating that those elected were qualified.

> Dr. Philip Merkle will take Coroner
> Moritz Elilinger's place on Monday next. Mr. S.
> Berdett and Mr. Ernest Hall, both Republi-
> cans, who were elected Marine Court Judges, will
> also take office on the same day. There is little
> patronage connected with any of the positions.

There were four coroners and four deputies employed by New York County, but not all elected at the same time. When I began my employment, the other three coroners and deputies had previously been employed. Unfortunately, several of my colleagues were strictly beneficiaries of political patronage and their work was slipshod.

Our offices, inquest rooms, dead-house, and hospital museum were adjacent to the morgue on the grounds of Bellevue Hospital. Bodies could be brought to the morgue 24 hours a day and remain for no more than 72 hours under the watch of a warden. Removal of identified bodies required the written permission of a coroner. If the corpse was not claimed, it was taken to the dead- house. To allow for future identification of unclaimed bodies, a photograph of the corpse was taken, a grave registration number assigned, their clothing displayed for 30 days, and, if not identified, these items were retained for a year.

When a death was discovered, a coroner was required to be summoned to the scene for initial evaluation before the corpse was removed to the morgue. After autopsy, if an inquest was indicated (which was at the discretion of the coroner), the coroner was responsible to summon jurors orally or by correspondence. New York State law required they remain until a decision was rendered and required that interments not occur until inquests were complete.

After jury selection, the jurors were sworn in and taken to inspect the body. The coroner introduced the case and was judge and mediator throughout the procedure. Witnesses were subpoenaed and questioned and, if attorneys were representing either side, they could also question witnesses.

After deliberation, the jurors submitted their findings in writing to the coroner. If they determined that a crime had been committed and there was a suspect and/or accessory to the crime, the case was forwarded (with the coroner's and jurors' findings) to a criminal court for prosecution. If the jury determined that the cause was murder, assault, or some other heinous crime, the witnesses were retained until the completion of the criminal court proceeding. Of course, no inquest was needed if the evidence indicated no malevolent acts and that the person had died of a common malady, such as: cholera, malaria, typhoid fever, pneumonia, diphtheria, scarlet fever, meningitis, whooping cough, stillbirth, or dysentery.

Besides the many deaths that needed our attention, to abide the 1865 law passed by the Board of Health, all corpses that passed through

New York City needed to be registered to ascertain whether they were afflicted by a communicable disease. There were no exceptions. Even Abraham Lincoln's corpse had to be examined by the coroner when it was brought to New York City to lie in state at City Hall. Once the examination was completed, the New York City inspector, with the permission of the coroner, could issue a permit. The body would then be held pending arrangements for its removal to the next destination.

Since each coroner was permitted a deputy, I selected Michael Jean Baptiste Messemer, an outstanding physician, who had graduated from Bellevue Hospital Medical College with a specialty in surgery. His wonderful personality, medical knowledge, medical affiliations, and his beautiful townhouse made him popular with New York City society. He and I were diligent about our work and brought to the position not only medical knowledge, but an inquisitive nature, investigative skills, and scientific expertise in order to carefully assess each case.

I mentioned in a previous chapter about Rudolf Ludwig Virchow and his introduction and findings regarding cellular pathology, but I did not mention that a ramification of those findings resulted in his publishing a systematic methodology of autopsy. He advocated that all body parts be dissected and microscopically examined to analyze the cause of a deceased's death. Future study was encouraged by reserving some tissue so that further analysis could take place. During his autopsy and laboratory examinations, he was even able to describe and label many cancers, including leukemia, and identify deep vein pathologies of thrombosis and embolism. His findings also suggested the possibility that the body could provide identifying characteristics unique to each individual, which could be helpful as criminal evidence. His publications regarding autopsy were innovative and of great value to me.

I chose a few cases from my coroner's journal to illustrate the types of cases and places to which I, and sometimes my deputy, were called.

January 1882

I received communication that the *Atlantic Express* en route from Albany to Manhattan traveling the Hudson River Line had encountered an accident at Spuyten Duyvil. When I arrived at the scene, it was even worse than I anticipated. There were piles of snow hither and yon, and the rest of the visible ground was covered with blood. Lying on the ground, were charred bodies and injured people screaming in pain.

Before I arrived, the news of the accident had spread to those living in the surrounding areas. Many came to the scene and tried, as best they could, to help the injured by applying snow to their burns. Others attempted to extinguish the blazing fire by throwing buckets of water from the Hudson River on the flames.

Throughout my investigation, I learned that the *Atlantic Express* had stopped abruptly when someone pulled the emergency cord. The act resulted in the train being disabled.

The air brakes needed to be pumped for at least 15 minutes before the train could resume. Unfortunately, the train was in a precarious curve in the track where it was obscured from oncoming trains.

The engineer of the *Tarrytown Special* (an oncoming train) did not have sufficient time to stop and hit the *Atlantic Express* with such force that the two last cars of the *Atlantic Express* were totally destroyed. Most in those cars were killed or severely injured. The rear cars were the luxury ones, known as parlor cars, with stoves and lamps for added comfort. The impact set them ablaze, causing the woodwork and upholstery to quickly ignite. Many passengers in those cars were found wedged between seats and unable to dislodge themselves while the flames engulfed them.

I also learned that, because it was a Friday evening, among others on the train, were 10 state senators and 26 assemblymen returning for the weekend to their residences in the New York City area. According to the conductor, there was much jollification and they were excessively imbibing alcoholic beverages. It was surmised, that one probably pulled the emergency cord as an amusement. This information was only circumstantial and no one ever admitted to having pulled the emergency cord or having witnessed the act.

One of the senators was Webster Wagner who had been a popular representative since 1870 serving in both the state assembly and in the senate. He was also a member of the State Senate Railroad Committee.

It was well known that he had made a fortune having invented special sleeping cars and parlor cars equipped with many comfortable amenities and safety features, such as those in the last two luxury cars of the *Atlantic Express*. We didn't realize at first that he was a casualty because he had been crushed between two cars. By the time his body was discovered, it had been so charred that his legs were dismembered and his face not recognizable. Finally, one of the rescuers noticed his initialed watch and some political papers, specific to him, next to his body. It is ironic that the luxury amenities of his profitable parlor car invention contributed to his demise.

Among the dead were also Mr. and Mrs. Park Valentine, a young couple who had just married at a fashionable venue in Vermont and were on the train beginning their marriage tour. The conductor, George Hanford, told me that Mr. Valentine died as Hanford tried to save him, but his wife refused to be saved, choosing to stay in her husband's arms, and die with him. Such a sad incident.

Many others, unable to escape or not able to be rescued in time, were seriously burned or injured, including 12 fatalities.

Of course, this accident required that I compile the evidence and assemble a coroner's jury to begin an inquest as quickly as possible. I was not pleased with the haphazard manner in which juries were usually assembled with no opportunity to question the competence of them. Therefore, I specifically summoned men I knew were eminent engineers, and others who were competent in understanding the need for instituting railroad regulations. I told the jury that I trusted they would not only determine those responsible, but also offer recommendations to the New York State Legislature for rules and regulations to be immediately created to avert such a horrific incident from happening again.

During the inquest, there were several witnesses questioned by representatives of the district attorney's office, attorneys representing individual railroad employees, and, when needed, I interjected a judicious opinion. The most extensive employee testimony was by the rear brakeman, George Melius.

He was arrested and during the trial he was directly examined by his attorney and, at times, interrupted by a district attorney, or me. Melius testified that after the train suddenly stopped, he took two lanterns, one red and one white and examined the tracks and brakes on the rear car, which he claimed was his duty. This took about two minutes. During this time, he saw Conductor Hanford, his supervisor, go to the front of the rear car, but Hanford did not offer him any instruction. Melius explained that he waited about two more minutes and when no instructions were forthcoming, he took the responsibility of walking approximately 144 feet from the rear of the train, saw the flagman, and waved the red lantern. When the flagman started walking in the correct direction, Melius thought all was well. He further testified that when he heard the roar of an oncoming train, he started to run in the direction of the train and wave the red light, but the train passed him before slowing. He was questioned about his tenure with the railroad and replied that he had been working with Conductor Hanford for two and a half years and had been an employee of the railroad for 25 years.

In his own defense, he stated that it was his understanding that when a train stops between stations, it is one of the duties of the conductor to go to the rear car, and instruct the rear brakeman. Melius also pointed out that there had been three brakemen and safety tools: axes, crowbars, pails, hammers, and chisels, carried in the baggage car, until two years prior, when the Superintendent of the New York Central and Hudson River Railroad Company eliminated the position of one brakemen and replaced the safety tools with more passenger storage space to maximize profit.

After the completion of the inquest, I relayed my conclusions to the jury for their deliberation. The pulling of the air brake rope, either frivolously or accidentally, placed in jeopardy the safety of the train and its passengers which devolved on the railroad company through its employees. I suggested that the jury carefully consider the following questions:

Did the New York Central and Hudson River Railroad Company take needed precautions? And did employees understand and follow their duties?

The jury deliberated about an hour and returned a unanimous verdict. Following is a synopsis regarding the charges as reported in *The Railroad Gazette*, January 27, 1882, Volume 14:

UNANIMOUS VERDICT

In Spuyten Duyvil tragedy.
George Melius, the brakeman and his supervisor and
conductor George Hanford, Edward Stanford, engineman
of the leading locomotive of the Atlantic express,
Archibald Buchsnan, engineman of the locomotive
immediately attached to the express,
Francis Burr, engineman of the locomotive of the Tarrytown
special train, neglected their duties and are responsible
for the loss of life that followed such neglect of duty.
Also, John M. Toucey, Superintendent of the New York
Central & Hudson River Railroad Company neglected
to provide efficient safeguards against accidents and
that officers of the New York Central & Hudson River
Railroad Company neglected to provide suitable
instruments for the rescue of the passengers.
The jury further found that each and every person
named in the suit is responsible in his own
individuality, no one sharing the responsibility
with the other and that there seemed to be no
palliation whatever for the criminal carelessness
and disregard for human life exhibited by the railroad
company management and the employees
of the railroad. The jurors deemed it their duty to

urge the immediate and thorough protection
of the whole Spuyten Duyvil Branch railroad at
all the road and street crossings within the city limits.
In addition that the use of a cord attached to the
valve of the air brake in the passenger cars had
more elements of danger than safety. In summation
the jurors found that those named were negligent
by criminal means and had caused the deaths of those
who had lost their lives as a result of the accident.

I believe the jury returned a relatively fair verdict, but then the legal system deemed that a grand jury should re-examine the case. The grand jurors concluded that George Melius, the brakeman and his supervisor, conductor George Hanford, should be the only ones indicted. They received sentences of manslaughter in the fourth degree. The grand jury did make some excellent recommendations for improvements in safety on the trains. Unfortunately, there was no means of enforcing them.

In June 1882, there was yet another investigation by the New York Senate which included the members of the Railroad Committee. I, of course, had no part in this, but was curious to read their conclusions which were ambiguously written and, in my opinion, inconclusive. The senate was nevertheless explicit and adamant about two facts: first, that the only one to blame was brakeman George Melius and, second, that no blame was to be placed on railroad officials.

The outcome of the case was difficult for me to accept because the person who caused the accident by pulling the emergency brake was never found. After interviewing brakeman Melius, I thought it obvious that he did not know or had not been informed of the importance of walking a particular distance. He was shocked that, although he was energetically waving his red lamp, the oncoming train could not stop in time. He seemed sincere, but perhaps a bit lacking in intelligence. It was also learned that Melius was illiterate and the railroad had not checked or required that their employees be able to read any instruction manual or be tested about same.

I do think the railroad executives and owners should have had some blame since they were always trying to find ways of cutting costs. An example of the greed of the railroad owners and executives was the firing of the third flagman, which resulted in a saving of $30 per month. It demonstrated that they had no regard for the possible consequences.

After the conclusion of the case, and to the dismay of the railroad executives, I made it a point to include in my orations, what I believed to be the need for safety regulations on trains. I also encouraged newspaper owners to editorialize about the subject. In spite of those actions, and the persistence and advocacy that followed, little change has occurred.

An irony pointed out to me by those suffering from triskaidekaphobia was that this horror occurred on Friday the 13th, there were 13 cars on the *Atlantic Express* and the *Tarrytown Special* was 13 minutes behind the *Express*, which did not give it sufficient time to resume. I think the avoidance of the number 13 is foolish, but people point to the Babylonian Code of Hammurabi in which the number was deduced to be evil. I would view this as a coincidence in that the number 13 was simply found in three items that have application to the accident.

May 1882

I was summoned to the home of Maria Hogan, who while hanging clothes on her fire escape, fell to her death when the escape collapsed. After initial investigation of the site, it seemed evident that the fire escape had been in ill repair. I solicited testimony from a Bureau of Buildings' examiner who stated that he had inspected the escape a year prior when he received a complaint from the fire department. Further, he claimed that he had informed the woman that the fire escape encumbrances should be removed because they were not properly anchored.

He noted that he had not reported the fire escape problem because it was not required. As I continued questioning him, he curtly responded that to address all complaints would require a department of 100 men, and they only employed 18.

The coroner's jury verdict stated that the contractor, who had built the escape, was liable (unfortunately, there was no record of who had performed the work), and The Bureau of Buildings was equally responsible for certifying the work of the contractor.

May 1882

I oversaw the inquest concerning the death of Jacob Hoffman, killed when a rotted cable released in an elevator causing him to fall to his death. Witnesses, who were also on the elevator, but survived, testified that they saw the cable after it let go, and it was totally rotted.

The jury verdict was unanimous in that the proprietor of the elevator was responsible and should be censured. In addition, the Building Department must be compelled to inspect all city elevators frequently so that the constant accidents of this nature will cease.

June 1882

I was summoned to the Colwell Lead Company Works on Centre Street. Charles Roll had fallen through the floor to his death. I interviewed the owner of the building, representatives from the Bureau of Buildings, and representatives of the lead company and found all culpable.

I assembled a jury and they censured the owner of the building for criminal negligence, the company executives for not being vigilant regarding the weight the floor could sustain, and the Bureau of Buildings for not taking proper precautions for the workers.

The previous three cases within a month of each other are just a few examples of the negligence of the New York City Bureau of Buildings and the resultant deaths.

There needs to be pressure exerted on the Bureau of Buildings and others to make structures safer. In spite of juries suggesting improvements, to this point, they have been ignored. Therefore, I requested a grand jury trial so that there could be criminal charges brought against those the coroner's jury found responsible. After much deliberation, the grand jury did not bring any criminal charges. This was disturbing, but not shocking, because the employees of the building department were selected mostly through patronage and protected by the city's political machine. However, I believe the more injustices that are brought to the attention of the public, the greater chance there is for reform.

There were many other cases during 1882, but the aforementioned should give the reader an idea of some of the crimes, findings, and inquest verdicts that were delivered during my tenure.

CHAPTER 28

My New York City Coroner Journal, Part 2

THE FOLLOWING ARE A FEW OF THE CASES I WAS SUMMONED TO assess and determine cause of death during 1883 and 1884. Again, I chose a variety to illustrate the determinations of deaths.

January 1883

Gustave Aberle, a 40-year-old upholsterer, had committed suicide at his shop. I spoke with Aberle's widow who informed me that her husband had been upset and extremely unhappy the past year, since their neighbor, and business partner, had stolen a large amount of money from the business. His wife was convinced that was the cause of his action. I inspected the residence and found a diary in which Aberle had written that he wished for his neighbor (who had stolen the money) and his neighbor's wife to become blind and lame. While I was speaking with Mrs. Aberle, a man (who was introduced to me as Ferdinand Foster) apologetically interrupted to tell Aberle's wife that he had completed the funeral arrangements. When he left, Mrs. Aberle explained that Mr. Foster was her husband's best friend and lived on the opposite side from the disliked neighbors. According to her, Foster was a kind person and quite saddened by the death of her husband. He had offered to make the funeral arrangements to save her from the difficult chore.

As I was about to leave, a lad ran into the house saying that Mr. Foster had fallen down the stairs. I immediately went to the site and the man had indeed fallen, broken his neck, and died. I had both bodies removed to the morgue. The inquest results supported Dr. Messemer and my findings of suicide in the case of Mr. Aberle and accidental death in the case of Mr. Foster.

I couldn't help thinking about the unjust circumstances of this case. The kind, well-intentioned neighbor experienced the bad fate which had been wished upon the dishonest, swindling neighbor who escaped unscathed. What an incredible and unfair twist of fate!

February 1883

I was summoned to the site of a murder at Bellevue Hospital. It had taken place in the area set aside for treatment of patients suffering from delirium tremens (DTs). Those who witnessed the event reported that George Mahan, a powerfully strong man, was a patient in the alcoholic ward and, while suffering from DTs, beat to death Michael Kellaher, another patient in that ward.

Before committing the murder, he twice had attempted suicide by setting his bed afire and jumping out a window. In the latest incident, an orderly from another area, who happened to be nearby, supposedly attempted to intercede and George Mahan hit him on the head with a heavy object, fracturing his skull.

Mahan then turned his attention to the other patients, who managed to escape to the kitchen, pursued by Mahan. Two kitchen employees who had access to a rope transformed it into a lasso and restrained Mahan. By the time I arrived, Mahan was constrained. When questioned after his hallucinations had ceased, Mahan said that he believed the men in the ward had pistols and were about to attack him.

As part of the inquest, I insisted that a thorough investigation of the personnel involved with the alcoholic ward of the hospital be examined under oath. I added that it was a disgrace to our city that one of our most prestigious hospitals could have had such an occurrence. In my opinion, this murder could have been averted if the patients prone to insane behavior were properly guarded, and, if necessary, put into restraints if they became violent. I posed the questions, "Should George Mahan be accused of murder or temporary insanity?" and "How could this type of event be avoided in the future?"

It was my hope, that by subpoenaing knowledgeable, notable, influential men, they might, through dialogue during deliberation, not only decide a verdict for the accused, but also effect change at Bellevue Hospital to avoid any repetition of the event for which the jury was being assembled. There were hundreds of articles published throughout the country regarding my innovative idea and reason for summoning influential jurors. As such, I hoped that this action could be a prototype for any case in which reform was essential beyond deciding blame for the accused. The following excerpts are from articles in various New York newspapers:

New York Herald, February 8, 1883:

A NOTABLE JURY

Coroner Merkle yesterday summoned ex-mayors, ex-commissioners, ex-President Ulysses Grant, ex Senator Roscoe Conkling and other notable citizens to act as jurors on the inquest of Michael Kellaher.

New York Herald, February 9, 1883:

BIG GUNS TO BATTER BELLEVUE

If Coroner Merkle gets together the jury he has summoned to hold an inquest at Bellevue Hospital to-day perhaps the verdict will have more weight than verdicts in such cases usually do. If men of means, standing, ability, and character were to do their full duty as citizens there would soon be an utter lack of abuses needing investigation.

Brooklyn Union-Argus, February 10, 1883.

A HIGH-TONED CORONER'S JURY.

Coroner Merkle, of New York, caused a sensation in the Metropolis on Thursday

by summoning as a jury to hold the inquest
in the case of Michael Kellaher
such distinguished citizens as
.....ex-mayors William R. Grace,
Smith Ely, and William H. Wickham and
ex-County Clerk Charles E. Loew....
millionaire philanthropist F.B. Thurber
and journalist/social reformer Henry Villard.
At first it was supposed that the Coroner
had only summoned these well-known citizens by way of a joke, but, interrogated upon
the subject, he asserted that he was serious
in calling upon them to render services as jurymen. He further pointed, with some degree of ex-
haltation, to the law, which makes it obligatory
upon those gentlemen to obey the summons.

The jury that I summoned shocked even my closest friends and caused much conversation throughout the city and beyond. Journalists reported that it was the first time such a jury was ever proposed in this country and an innovative concept. I understood that most of the citizenry and newspaper reports were impressed by the bold step I had taken, but they did not believe any of those summoned would appear. I was vocal in reminding all that the statute regarding juror summonses stated that once a summons was received, it was obligatory to serve, unless a plausible reason to the contrary could be given.

According to law, if a summons was ignored, the penalty was a fine and imprisonment, and I intended to make sure the law was abided. I also mentioned, for public consumption, that these famous people had the same responsibility as all citizens, to serve on juries and perform their civic duty.

I, along with the public, awaited responses. Finally, I received replies which I relayed to them. The following are excerpts from an article that appeared in *The New York Times*, February 10, 1883, not only revealing the jurors, but the testimony of the witnesses.

CORONER'S GREAT JURY.

There was a buzz of expectation around the
Coroner's office yesterday afternoon, for many persons had gathered to stare at the great men whom
Coroner Merkle, full of esteem for the dignity of
office had summoned to serve as a jury to decide
the case of the death of Michael Kellaher.
There was withdrawal (with legitimate excuses
offered to Coroner Merkle) of some
important jurors such as General Grant who
sent word that he was a member of the
Mexican committee which was to
sit yesterday and therefore he could
not serve on the jury, though nothing would
have probably pleased him more.
At 2:30 o'clock, half an hour late, Coroner Merkle,
with spectacles on his nose and determination in
his eyes strode into the room. In a few moments
the jurymen were in their seats...they were:
Ex-Mayor William H. Wickham, ex-
Mayor W.R. Grace, ex-Mayor Smith Ely,
ex-County Clerk Charles Loew, ex-Commis-
sioner of Charities and Correction Town-
send Cox, Gen. Schwarzwelder of the Fifth Regiment, Dr. Balser,
Edward Haussor, and Edward Peyser.
The first witness, Dr. Henry Koplik, a house physician,
gave a description of what he had done
for the patient. The principal fact
brought out in his testimony was that, while he
did not consider Mahan dangerous, he feared that
he might be delirious in the night and ordered that
he should be closely watched.

Inquest, February 14, 1883 into the death of Michael Kellaher. Seated at the desk is Coroner Dr. Philip Merkle, facing and questioning witness Dr. Henry Koplik; to his right are jurors in order of their seating, ex- County Clerk Charles E. Loew, ex-mayors William H. Wickham, William R. Grace, and Smith Ely. The other jurors are out of picture range. The jurors are all looking towards George Mahan who has just entered the room accompanied by two guards. The other person seated at the desk with his back to the audience is a reporter writing the content of the witness's testimony. The others are giving information readying to testify.

The night orderly, who claimed to have been injured by George Mahan, did not appear for testimony, and was nowhere to be found. That seemed strange, and I considered that his injury might not have been caused by Mahan. The warden, in his testimony, stated that there was not a night orderly assigned specifically to the alcoholic ward and that the orderly who claimed to have been harmed by Mahan was just by chance passing the ward at the time of the incident.

The jury listened to testimony for two days and then, on the third day, issued their written verdict. Reporters, the public, the witnesses, and I eagerly awaited the reading of it. The verdict was published in newspapers throughout the country. It was even printed in such publications as the *Boston Medical and Surgical Journal.* The following are excerpts published in *The New York Times*, February 14, 1883:

CORONER MERKLE'S DISTINGUISHED JURY RENDER A VERDICT.

The jury retired to the end of the room,
arranging the chairs in a circle and talked the case over.
In half an hour they rendered the following verdict:
"We find that Michael Kellaher came to his death
by injuries inflicted by George E. Mahan. In view of
the evidence before us we believe that due care was
not exercised by the officers in charge of the alcoholic
ward, and in our opinion the system of management
is very defective. The wards at all times should, in
our opinion, be in charge of a responsible employee,
and we find that the orderlies are highly censurable for
leaving the ward without putting patients in charge
of a responsible person. We further recommend that
the furniture of the room-tables and windows-be of
such a character, and be so secured as to prevent the
possibility of their use as weapons of offense by patients."

Several weeks after the trial concluded, I toured the alcoholic ward of Bellevue Hospital and observed some positive change had already taken place. During the following year, I, and, often some members of the jury, made unannounced visits and observed that the ward was being administered properly. During the same year, not only had no other murders taken place, but no altercations (commonplace before the trial) had been reported. My goal had been attained.

May 1883

I was summoned to Bellevue Hospital by the police who had concluded that Edward Strong, a traveling salesman had died before reaching the hospital due to a self-inflicted gunshot wound to the head. Mrs. Clark, owner of the boarding house where Strong lived, and Minnie Edwards, another tenant at the house, had explained to the police that on the day of the event, Strong came home in an intoxicated state, had to be escorted up the stairs to his apartment, and fell on the bed. Edwards woke him several hours later, at which time he took a small pistol from his pocket, said that he may as well end it, and shot himself in the head. Found in his pocket was a letter from his employer stating that his expense account had been excessive and his employment was being terminated. His employer enclosed a check for his salary to the end of the following month so as to sever ties pleasantly. The police had a motive, a witness to the shooting, and the surgeon at Bellevue who confirmed the death as suicide.

I was not convinced by the testimonies of Edwards and Clark or the information in the police report. I had the body removed to the morgue where Dr. Messemer and I performed an autopsy to conclusively corroborate the findings of the police and the Bellevue surgeon.

We did not find any powder marks around the small bullet wound in the head. This was suspicious. In further examination, we found an extravasation of blood under the scalp over Strong's right eye, a fracture on the right side of the skull from the middle of the forehead to behind the right ear, and a fracture from the left temporal bone to the middle and anterior left side into the occipital bone an inch below the pistol-shot wound.

Messemer and I looked at each other in disbelief. These injuries in no way could have been self-inflicted. To further verify our findings, we checked the angle of the bullet wound and as we expected, it was not possible for Strong to have shot into his own head at that trajectory. Messemer and I concluded that it was not suicide, but murder.

The account of the two women was definitely erroneous, but why did they lie?

I immediately informed the police, but they had closed the case explaining they had enough evidence to call it a suicide. Why were they not anxious to rectify their findings? I kept insisting that they reopen the case, but to no avail. This practice was extremely upsetting, but frequent, and in definite need of reform. Someone had gotten away with murder and the police didn't care.

February 1884

I was summoned to the home of Dedrich Wenis, an engineer, who for the past three years, was employed by J. Rothschild. This young man, age 33, was reported to have killed himself. I interviewed some of his friends and employees of the engineering firm, and they divulged that he was a brilliant engineer who had a pleasant personality. Two of his friends explained that he was married for only a week to Pauline Reichter and he and his wife lived with her parents. Wenis had been frustrated because of the constant interference in their marriage by his father-in-law and the fact that his wife always agreed with her father's criticism of Wenis. As a result, he and his wife argued constantly.

He told his friends that he could not stand the situation much longer, but they never anticipated such a rash decision. He had been at work for about an hour, and then without saying anything to his coworkers or employer, left. His friends mentioned that this behavior was bizarre and unlike him. After work they went to his home to talk to him about the incident and learned from his wife that he had returned home, locked himself in his bedroom, and blown off his skull-cap with a bulldog revolver. The note he left explained the domestic troubles he could no longer tolerate with his wife and father-in-law.

Dr. Messemer and I determined that it was indeed a suicide. I could not help but think that if the marital laws allowed for separation or divorce, this might not have happened. But Wenis probably realized that according to the law, he had been joined for life, and obviously was unable to tolerate the abuse any longer. Legislators of societal law should take some of the blame for Dedrich's action. It also made me realize that there are not only instances of women being emotionally and physically abused, but the same abuses could be thrust upon men. Meanwhile, shockingly to me, the majority of people still embraced the antiquated marital vows: joined for better or for worse and for life. This raises my hackles.

April 1884

I was summoned to the Summit House, a poorly maintained hotel on Canal Street in the Bowery. The porter of the hotel had smelled gas as he passed one of the rooms, forced the door open, and found a man dead on the bed. The proprietor told us that the man had registered a few days prior as John Ford. We inspected the room and found no papers indicating his name, usual residence, or any other information about him. His body was removed to the morgue, was not claimed within 72 hours so the corpse was taken to the dead-house where it was stored until burial. At that point, I signed the death certificate and the man was interred in Potter's Field. He was about 35 years of age.

The following day I was summoned to the Brevoort Hotel, a luxurious establishment on the corner of Eighth Street and Fifth Avenue. I spoke with the proprietor, who escorted me to the room of the deceased and explained on the way that the man was found dead in bed. The proprietor mentioned that the man's name was George Ewing and that two rooms had been rented in his name by Henry Irving. He also commented that the previous day, Mr. Irving and a woman named Ellen Terry had visited Mr. Ewing.

I explained to the proprietor that Ewing was a renowned sculptor in Scotland and England and that Irving and Terry were famous British actors. Although I had never seen them perform, I had read critical reviews, which held them in the highest esteem, even proclaiming them, the best actors in England. According to other reports, they were often guests of high society and leaders of countries. In fact, a few years ago, I read that Irving was the first English actor on whom knighthood was bestowed.

When we finally entered the room, there was a strong odor of gas from a gasolier with three taps. The third tap, I ascertained, was where gas was escaping. It was possible, because of the way the gasolier was arranged, that Ewing had accidentally brushed against the third tap opening it fully. I went into the other room which was being used as Ewing's studio, and saw two partially completed medallion busts of Irving and Terry. I had Ewing removed to the morgue.

Deputy Coroner Messemer located Irving and Terry and they immediately came to the morgue and identified the body. During an interview, Irving explained that Ewing had been one of his best friends. He reminisced about Ewing's wonderful successes: sculpted marble busts of many notables of Scotland and England, four portrait medallions of Queen Victoria and Prince Albert, and a bronze statue of Robert Burns.

Irving had spoken to Ewing before he came to America and Ewing indicated that he intended to pursue his work in Philadelphia and then (at Irving's request) in New York, where he would sculpt medallions of Irving and Terry. He did mention that perhaps his health would improve while he was in America, but did not elaborate. Irving also mentioned that Ewing was not doing well financially so he had offered him a sizeable stipend to do the medallions and was paying for two rooms for his stay at the elegant Brevoort Hotel. Ewing accepted the offer and had been in New York about two weeks. The previous day, Irving and Terry had the first sitting for their medallion portraits.

I asked Irving if he believed Ewing could have been depressed and committed suicide. He said absolutely not. The previous day, he and Terry found him in good spirits and looking forward to their next sitting.

After Irving and Terry left, I conferred with Messemer and we agreed that we did not have sufficient evidence to report the cause as suicide, so I signed the death certificate as accidental. Irving arranged for services and the body was interred in Greenwood Cemetery. Ewing was 56 years of age.

In both cases, the deaths were caused by asphyxiation and registered as accidental. Having been to the two sites within a day of each other, I couldn't help but ponder the extremes I had seen: the first corpse in the poorly maintained Summit Hotel where the deceased was never identified and buried in Potter's Field, and the second, in the luxurious Brevoort Hotel, where the deceased was identified and buried in Greenwood Cemetery after a laudatory eulogy. What an explicit example of the diversity of life's outcomes.

The cases I mentioned are only a few of those that occurred on a daily basis. During my tenure, each day, at least three corpses were brought to the morgue.

But, there were occasions in which there were so many that it was difficult to attend to all in a timely fashion. This would especially occur when there was an epidemic or disaster.

Although I addressed each case with investigative skill and thoughtful analysis, I could not be totally dispassionate about the grief suffered by the families or deaths that could have been averted. Besides the instances of deaths by natural causes, the unnecessary deaths were most disturbing: numerous cases of infanticide, fires caused by negligence, and disreputable administrators of some hospitals, railroads, and other companies, all resulting in disasters.

In addition, there was the disconcerting trend of continuously increased suicides with little notice by the populous or concern in the medical field. I observed corpses of so many who must have been in such distress that they believed death to be their only option. This kind of despair was evident during the sessions I provided for civil war soldiers, but the gradual hope that appeared as they interacted with others suffering the same anguish saved lives. This convinced me that many who were brought to the morgue perhaps could have been saved if such venues were established.

Much more needs to be learned about the reasons for the constant increase in suicides in New York City (and most likely other cities) but throughout my lifetime, the popular explanation for the continuous increase is urban modernity. It is thought that rural family life was replaced by social and cultural disintegration as families moved to populated cities causing men, who were most susceptible to succumb to suicide.

To me, that explanation is too simplistic. I believe there are several possible causes: economics (especially during panics), marital strife, and inability to cope after a traumatic event. The lack of compassion by many for those who believed there was no other solution but suicide, bothered me tremendously. I pondered and internalized these situations to the extent that, after several years, I decided to resign from my position as coroner to advocate for changes which might lessen the death rate.

CHAPTER 29

Life After the Morgue

AFTER RETIRING FROM MY CORONER POSITION IN 1885, MY ENER-
gies were even more relentless in advocating for reforms in city and
state agencies. I have been successful in creating greater awareness
through dialogues with city administrators and by encouraging my
newspaper owner friends to publish articles in support of reform. I
will mention a few areas of concern that I addressed.

There was need for reform in the coroner's office. During my
tenure, because coroners and deputies often gained their employment
through patronage, they did not possess proper qualifications or were
not conscientious. I suggested the following changes: coroners should
be educated doctors and/or surgeons possessing medical degrees,
before election to the office, the person should take a written test,
be observed doing an autopsy, required to write his/her conclusions
to ascertain reporting skills, obliged to choose a jury, and administer
an inquest. In addition, coroners were not only paid an annual salary,
but also given a stipend per inquest, the need for which the coroners,
themselves, determined. As a result, there were many instances of
unnecessary inquests. Regulations for justification and approval of
inquests were needed.

Jury selection also must be revamped. More than the required
number of jurors should be summoned in case any are not acceptable
due to certain criteria: the person is biased towards the subject, does
not comprehend the language, or the content of the case. At present, it
is not required that any interaction between those summoned and the
coroner take place before a case is heard, or any provision for dismissal
of those thought to be unqualified. That is particularly important
when the case goes beyond the person being tried and there is need
for reform of an institution or agency. That is the reason I suggested

the selection process be changed to include the continuation of my innovative idea in summoning notables who had the understanding and influence to cause institutional reform.

In addition, the jurors should have a place away from the public to deliberate so there will be no undue influence. I do attempt to clear the jury room and leave the jurors to interact in private, but often, this is not possible because another inquest is scheduled.

Another area in which I became involved was reform in the Bureau of Buildings. There must be more inspectors, frequent inspections, and rulings instituted to force compliance of structural safety. If rulings are ignored, I believe the negligence on the part of the Bureau of Buildings should be viewed as criminal and penalties imposed.

Stricter rules and regulations should be imposed on railroad owners in order to increase passenger safety and avert horrific accidents. This is a difficult area in which to cause improvement because of the power and influence the railroad owners have on all levels of government. I encouraged my journalist friends to publish articles about the need for safety regulations.

Another area, difficult to combat, was the temperance movement. I was constantly amazed by their momentum and influence. Although I confronted them, along with many members of organizations, and journalists, their influence in the political arena was incredible. For example, in 1887, the United States Supreme Court decision in the case of *Mugler v. Kansas 123 U.S. 523 (1887)* upheld a Kansas law prohibiting business owners from using their properties for the purpose of manufacturing or producing intoxicating beverages, even if they had been licensed previously for that purpose.

The case involved Peter Mugler, a brewery owner, who had purchased his business 10 years prior to the enactment of the statute at a cost of $10,000. In addition, he had been authorized by the state to operate it. As a result of the enactment of the new statute, Mugler found that because the property could no longer be used as a brewery, its value had decreased to $2,500.

His attorney argued that he had been denied due process because the state had no right to prohibit alcohol production, in essence, having taken his property without just compensation. The Supreme Court upheld the statute, claiming that the state had the right to restrict owners from using their properties for injurious purposes, such as health and safety concerns, and therefore restricting their use could not be considered a taking! This example definitely illustrates the influence and impact the temperance movement has exerted in the political arena. In spite of constant opposition to the temperance movement, I don't believe organizations, journalists, or I made much progress in combating their ridiculous arguments.

A final area of concern regarded some methods of the police and hospital doctors. The police often had bodies removed to police stations or hospitals before the coroner's arrival. Hospital doctors, who were summoned, often quickly and superficially determined cause of death without proper examination. This allowed the police to close cases quickly.

I advocated for cases being reopened by the police if new evidence is found. Police and coroners have a responsibility to find the truth by following all possible clues in order to pursue justice for the victim. The deceased should be treated with respect and their families receive, as complete as possible, explanations of the cause of death and any circumstances surrounding it.

Although I had been meticulous in examinations and reports, unfortunately conclusions that had been hastily and incorrectly reported by the police often remained. A ruling must be established and cases not closed until the coroners' reports are presented. Many in the police department were angered by my outspokenness regarding this subject and preferred to continue their careless and lackadaisical investigative work.

I also advocated for the election or appointment of a director of the New York City Police Department, rather than having a captain of each precinct. At police headquarters, I had noted that those in charge often did not bother to request that their detectives and other officers conscientiously pursue leads, but instead were anxious to finalize cases. This can result in criminals going unpunished and others falsely accused.

A few years ago, I was introduced to Theodore (Teddy) Roosevelt, a New Yorker from a family of wealth and good morals. I was impressed by his ideas, intense nature, and vigor. He was insightful and had observed the need for reform in the police department.

He and I met on several occasions and he was impressed by my suggestions. We recently discussed the importance of physical and mental testing as criteria for hiring New York City police, and that hiring must be open to all ethnic groups and women. I explained that when I was a coroner, I had been outspoken about inconclusive investigative procedures and leisurely response time to calls, especially in the tenement areas. He agreed this needed to be addressed.

The opportunity to make substantial changes in the New York City police department occurred in 1895 when Roosevelt was appointed president of the New York City Board of Police Commissioners. In this position, he was able to accomplish reform expeditiously. He was, of course, unpopular with the police, but cared only about the final goal.

I spoke to the public and encouraged my journalist friends to advocate for the reforms. During the following two years, to meet the ever-increasing population and crime in the city, 1,600 recruits were trained and all police were required to follow stringent disciplinary rules.

I was pleased when Roosevelt addressed the lackadaisical attitude on the part of the detective bureau by reorganizing it with a system that required the constant inspection of their work. The aim was to be sure cases were thoroughly investigated before being closed.

The reported increase in police brutality, especially in the tenement areas was also of great concern. Roosevelt decided to walk precincts at various hours of the day and night, to ascertain if the police were in their designated areas and performing their duties conscientiously. Finally, the results of my advocacy were coming to fruition.

During 1895, I was invited to accompany Roosevelt and Jacob Riis (a Danish immigrant who was an advocate of reform for the downtrodden) on an unannounced morning walk to observe New York City's 21st Police Precinct. The 21st Precinct was known as the Gas House District, so named because gas tanks built in the area often leaked producing a horrible odor. It was a neighborhood of the extremely poor (mostly Irish, Germans, and Italians) living in deteriorating tenements. There had been previously notorious gang activity and reports of police indifference and brutality. At about 7 A.M., Roosevelt, Riis, and I inspected the officers of the 21st Precinct and found one sleeping, but the rest doing their expected tasks. When we returned to the police station, Roosevelt indicated our findings and informed the captain that we would be returning. After the inspection, on July 9, 1895, in the 21st Police Newsletter, the following appeared:

(l-r) ex-coroner Dr. Philip Merkle, Police Commissioner Theodore Roosevelt, and journalist Jacob Riis. (1895 near police headquarters).

THREE NOTABLES PAY UNEXPECTED VISIT

Last week, Theodore Roosevelt, President of the Board of Police
Commissioners, Dr. Philip Merkle, former coroner, and Jacob Riis, newspaper journalist reviewed our precinct. It was an unannounced inspection
of our patrol area and station house. After the inspection, President of the
Board Roosevelt gave his evaluation and except for one officer who was
sleeping, he was pleased with our officers. He will be returning for another
unannounced visit in the future. We were pleased to have a
visit from such notables.

After we completed our walk, we spoke informally about our ongoing observations and advocacy regarding the suffering of the downtrodden. Riis, in his position as police reporter assigned to the Lower
East Side, was responsible for numerous articles about the horren-
dous conditions in that area. In 1890, he had authored a book, *How
the Other Half Lives*. It is a compendium of photographs displaying the
conditions on the Lower East Side. I complimented Riis' outstanding
photography, and he replied that he credits some of his success to the
recent availability of flash photography, especially for night scenes.
The presentation of his work in a photographic medium made it even
more distressing and disquieting than the written word. Riis captured
the attention of some in the middle and upper classes and they began
advocating for change.

Like so many others, after having viewed the poignant and disturbing photographic content of his book, I understood its impact, but
unlike others, I was not quite as shocked because of my experiences
and observations for so many years on the Lower East Side. Through
his photography and commentary, he became a noted social reformer.
He is another example of an immigrant who contributed so greatly to
the need for change in New York City.

Roosevelt extended an invitation for us to again walk with him
and offer our opinions. I thanked him and responded that I would be
delighted to accompany him, but he must remember that he is in his
30's, Riis in his 40's, while I am in my 80's. I said, "When we walk again,

perhaps the pace could be slower to accommodate this old man." They laughed and agreed.

Although we remained friends, Roosevelt and I disagreed philosophically when he attempted to enforce a Blue Law for New York City. This law included closing beer gardens and saloons on Sundays. As I mentioned earlier, Sunday was the only day many workers had time to socialize and this law would prevent that pleasure. Not only politicians, but much of the public, who had supported his reforms, disagreed with him. After only two years of great strides in police system reform, he resigned because of the negative reaction of the public.

At one point I recall his telling me that when he was leaving for Harvard College, his father's words of wisdom were that he should take care of his morals first, his health next, and then his studies. I imagine after college, his father would have assumed studies would be replaced with worthwhile causes. His father and mine had similar philosophies. I do respect Teddy Roosevelt's moralistic qualities, insight, vigor, and passion for positive change, and hope that he will return to a leadership position in some governmental capacity in which I would again concur with his thinking. In that circumstance, I would gladly support him.

I continue to encourage the public to be vocal about the need for reform in the previous areas and my journalist friends to address the problems that need to be corrected. This helps greatly in bringing these ills to the forefront of awareness, advocacy, and reform.

CHAPTER 30

Artists and Patrons

AFTER COMPLETING MOST OF THE CHAPTERS, MARIE ASKED HOW many I had devoted to the arts and patrons of the arts. She reminded me of so many who resided in New York City during the century and contributed to its cultural growth. I told her it would involve enough chapters to write a book specifically about that topic. She insisted that introducing a few would give the reader a flavor of the cultural growth of the city. I decided to give Marie the task of making the selections. Of course her choices were people affiliated with music since that was her special love. Therefore, jokingly, I told her that I will dedicate the chapter to her so that if the reader is critical of her decisions or omissions, I can perhaps avoid responsibility. I do agree that her selections are exemplary of some of the best performers and patrons.

An artist of whom she and I are particularly proud is my nephew Frederick Bechtel who has become known in music circles for his outstanding performances and compositions. He is a professor of music (with many private talented students), an extraordinary pianist, and a prolific composer. His published opera, vocal, and piano works have been very successful. Marie has purchased all of Frederick's compositions and often sings some of them. Her favorite is "The Homeward March."

"Homeward March" music by F. Bechtel.

His opera, *Alfred the Great* required about five years to complete, and although it is a wonderful and notable piece, it is so immense in scope that he has never been able to find an opera company to produce it in its entirety. Excerpts from it have been performed and well-received. Frederick, Marie, and I attended the debut concert of excerpts from the opera at the Brooklyn Athenaeum.

Brooklyn Athenaeum, November 20, 1880.

Tonight's performance will feature excerpts from the opera Alfred the Great by Composer Frederick Bechtel.

Poster advertising the performance of *Alfred the Great*.

What an exciting evening, after which Marie and I gave a reception for Frederick. His guest list included 50 invitees. At the reception were many music notables and they were extremely encouraging and complimentary about his work.

Despite the exciting evening, I noticed that Frederick and Marie were greeting the guests as I stood to the side. For some reason, I began thinking that perhaps an affair between them had been taking place, especially while I was traveling for speaking engagements. They were the same age, had similar interests, and always were happy to share time. I had been told by friends that the two were seen together at concerts, publishing houses (perusing copies of music) and expressing immense joviality.

Those thoughts distressed me to the point that I asked Marie to join me in a private area of the hall. I outright asked her if she and Frederick were having an affair. It was one of the very few times that she became angry with me, and adamantly denied the accusation. We returned to the reception festivities and I smiled at the guests as if nothing were wrong, but sadly, I could never totally keep the possibility from my mind. We never spoke of the subject again.

Marie and I knew a few of the attendees. I will inform the readers about them in case they are not familiar with their accomplishments.

Patrick Gilmore was an excellent cornet player, bandmaster, composer, and lyricist. He represented the Union side in the Civil War and was named Bandmaster-general whose position was organizing and overseeing the Civil War bands. He was also the lyricist for the famous Union song, "When Johnny Comes Marching Home."

GIlmore had requested that Frederick compose some marches for his band. He had also invited Frederick to attend a festival in 1872 which took place in Boston where he was living at the time. Frederick invited Marie and me to accompany him and we attended the 18 day event named the World's Peace Jubilee and International Musical Festival. The instrumental and choral groups were large and spectacular. Some of the most renowned performers had been assembled such as the famous Johann Strauss II known as the Waltz King. That was the only time he ever came to America.

We only remained for three days, but during that time Marie and I had the pleasure of meeting Patrick Gilmore. We complimented him for the outstanding festival events and especially his band's wonderful performances.

About a year after the event, he moved to New York City. His reputation preceded him and he quickly became a popular celebrity in music circles.

In the late 1870s, Gilmore leased an open-air arena in Manhattan and named it Gilmore's Concert Garden. We were surprised that he did not exclusively use it for music events, but in addition rented it to others for flower shows, walking marathons, and the first New York Bench Show of Dogs.

Marie and I attended a wonderful evening band concert, the dog show (which the following year was renamed the Westminster Kennel Club Dog Show), and a flower show. The dog show was especially enjoyable. There were over 1,000 dogs shown and I don't remember how many people attended, but it seemed like thousands.

We heard from Frederick that Patrick Gilmore was financially successful with his concert garden events although the owners (The Vanderbilt family) did not renew his lease. They decided to personally oversee events in the arena (which they renamed Madison Square Garden).

Frederick, Marie and I often attended Gilmore's superb band concerts, and we were thrilled to hear Frederick's marches performed. After the events, we always had the pleasure of meeting with Patrick.

Another guest at Frederick's premier performance was Oscar Hammerstein I who had attended the opera and indicated his enjoyment of it. We were introduced and spoke briefly. I didn't realize how enamored Hammerstein was with opera. I learned that his vision was to revitalize opera in America and make it available to everyone, not just the upper class.

We were constantly updated regarding the progress of Hammerstein's endeavors from Frederick. Oscar first embarked on real estate projects that would include opera houses. He had 50 residences and an opera house constructed in Harlem on 125th Street in New York City. This area of Harlem was mostly undeveloped, but he believed the residences would encourage movement from downtown New York City.

I remember what a fiasco the building of the Harlem Opera House was. The cost of constructing the theater was estimated to be $175,000. Hammerstein wanted the construction to begin immediately. It was November of 1887 and the architect suggested that he wait until late spring or summer of 1888, but Hammerstein insisted it be started promptly.

The foundation for the opera house was half completed when the blizzard of 1888 descended on New York City. The storm approached with 35-40 mile per hour winds and the three days of uninterrupted snowfall reached seven to eight feet high. People froze to death in their homes, police and firemen could not respond and about 400 people died. After the storm, the estimate to complete the theater project tripled and the Harlem Theater opening was delayed until 1889!

During the time that Oscar owned the Harlem Opera House, he hired well-known actors with superb reputations. However, the actors often demanded up to 90% of the receipts in salary which resulted in Oscar being constantly in debt.

He solved the problem by having another opera house (the Columbus Theater) constructed on the same street as the Harlem Opera House. The Columbus would offer lighter venues and attract larger audiences while the Harlem Opera House would continue to offer upscale opera performances. He believed correctly that although the Harlem Opera House was constantly operating at a financial loss, the Columbus Theater would keep him financially solvent.

Marie, Frederick and I attended several of the performances at the Harlem Opera House and had the pleasure of meeting many well-known performers back stage or at social events.

Although not in attendance at my nephew's reception, there are other patrons and supporters of the arts that deserve mention. Andrew Carnegie realized the need for a concert hall suited for both choral and orchestral music concerts. The site he chose was an apple orchard in midtown about two blocks south of Central Park. What a perfect location. The cost to convert the site into a concert hall was about $1,000,000 which Carnegie donated. He named the building Music Hall, but the board members governing it persuaded Carnegie to allow the use of his name and the hall became known as Carnegie Hall.

Elkan Naumburg was always seeking ways to promote the arts and help support and sustain artists. He was instrumental in establishing a pension fund for the New York Philharmonic Orchestra members and his latest vision (which he discusses often) is offering free outdoor concerts in Central Park. He has been speaking with architects about designs for a bandstand in the park and I am confident that someday this will come to fruition.

Another person I must mention is Jeannette Meyers Thurber, an innovator and patron of the arts. In the mid-1880s, during an intermission at a concert that Frederick, Marie and I attended, we had the pleasure of meeting Thurber. She invited us to tour The National Conservatory of Music of America (located at 47-49 West 25th Street in New York City) which she had founded in 1885. The invitation was gratefully accepted and Marie, Frederick and I toured the school the following day.

We were impressed by Thurber's musical talent, but especially her innovative ideas. She had studied at the Paris Conservatory and while there realized that the United States was the only industrialized nation in which federal funding was not provided for the arts. When she returned to New York, she embarked on a mission to open a music school in New York City with federal monies. To this point, her attempts for federal funding have not materialized, but undaunted, she became the main patron of the school (with the generous financial assistance of her millionaire husband) in addition to contributions from other donors such as Andrew Carnegie.

We learned that her other goals for the school were not only to prepare students for careers as professional musicians, but, to make the program available to all races, ethnicities, non-traditional preferences, and handicapped persons so long as the entrant had musical potential. She also assisted those who could not afford the tuition by offering scholarships.

Another innovation was her desire to have the focus of music composition in the school on the development of an American music genre. To this point, music performed in America was imported from Europe.

A great appeal of the school is the impressive faculty that Thurber has gathered. Faculty member Max Spicker had studied at the renowned Leipzig Conservatory and was recognized here as an excellent organist and composer. He is not only a faculty member at The National Conservatory, but also serves as music director at Temple Emanu-El on Fifth Avenue.

Rubin Goldmark, another faculty member had studied at the renowned Vienna Conservatory and was recognized by Thurber as a superb pianist, music theorist, and composer.

Undoubtedly the most outstanding faculty member is the renowned composer Antonin Dvorak who served as director of the school and taught composition. His works were influenced by the developing American music genre which is evident in his wonderful compositions the *New World Symphony* and his *Cello Concerto in B Minor*.

The most talented student was Harry Burleigh. He had a wonderful baritone voice and after hearing him in concert, Frederick, Marie and I couldn't stop praising his talent. Burleigh was born in Erie, Pennsylvania and was a colored person who had been taught by his maternal grandfather to sing spirituals. While in high school, his outstanding baritone voice was recognized and he was often invited to be a soloist for Erie community events, several churches, and the Jewish synagogue. Erie should be commended for setting an example of tolerance and acceptance for racial differences.

After Thurber accepted Harry Burleigh to The National Conservatory of Music on scholarship, Dvorak recognized his talent, requested that he serve as his amanuensis and even used some of Harry's spirituals in his compositions. In addition to singing, Harry played double bass in the Conservatory orchestra, composed, arranged, and transformed spirituals into classical forms, all while retaining an American flavor in the compositions. Another accomplishment of Burleigh was being appointed soloist of St. George's Episcopal Church in New York City. I heard from church members that this was not without opposition from some congregants when they learned Harry was a colored person. Other more influential members were successful in his being hired. Recently the congregation of Temple Emanu-El in New York City is considering appointing him as a soloist.

The school has been successful, having started with fewer than 100 students in the mid-1880s, to the current enrollment (about a decade later) of several thousand. Jeannette Meyers Thurber's generosity, ingenuity, and imagination so impressed Marie, Frederick and me that we have become advocates and donors.

Oscar Hammerstein, Andrew Carnegie, Elkan Naumburg, Jeanette Thurber, and many others deserve credit for supporting, and financially promoting the arts during the 19th century in New York City.

As a result of many creative and talented artists and the assistance of patrons of the arts in New York City, I am pleased that I have been part of the amazing progress that has taken place in the arts during the 1800s.

CHAPTER 31

A Voyage to Germany and Return to New York

MARIE AND I HAD SPOKEN ABOUT VISITING GERMANY ONE LAST time, but there were always other priorities. In 1890, I was finally convinced by her to do so as a way of celebrating my upcoming 80th birthday.

Copy of my passport application.

I had mixed feelings about visiting. There were few people we had known who were still alive and domiciled there. But, seeing my village of birth and recalling some wonderful events with my family and friends, would bring forth happy memories.

In May 1890, we embarked on the North German Lloyd Steamer *TRAVE* which was an express ship that took less than six days to cross the Atlantic! I could only imagine a century from now, how quickly the Atlantic could be traversed.

An advertisement of the Trave.

We remained in Germany for about five months before returning to New York. I decided as a special gift to Marie, that I would arrange first class cabin accommodations which included all the amenities that were offered. The tickets were about $75 dollars each, but worth the joy the extra service and accommodations provided.

Throughout the first class cabin areas, everything was spacious and luxurious including the smoking and state rooms and according to Marie, the ladies' boudoir. There were lovely paintings hung tastefully throughout the first class area, seating that was comfortably uphol-stered, lovely tablecloths, beautiful draperies, and the best lighting for each room's purpose.

A picture of Marie taken by the cruise photographer during a concert performance.

The cuisine was prepared by the finest culinary chefs as found in the best restaurants of Europe and the elegant fare was served in a splendidly furnished salon. Because of the triple expansion engine, and in spite of the speed at which we traveled, the first class cabin salon felt no motion while we ate. The express steamers are amazing.

The first class cabin promenade section was on the top deck of the ship with awnings so that we wouldn't be bothered by hot weather and yet could enjoy the ocean breezes. The deck also served as a place for sports during the day and concerts at night. Decorous electric lighting adorned the deck in the evening.

We introduced ourselves to the others in our first class cabin section, but I will just mention those who were on either side of our cabin. One was occupied by William Butler, an interesting and talented man with such a wonderful sense of humor. Besides his achievements as a lawyer, he was an acclaimed author. One evening after dinner he agreed to recite his famous poem *Nothing to Wear* which I had read previously but which never fails to amuse me. The poem is satirical in nature and ridicules the frivolousness of an upper class woman, "Miss Flora McFlimsey of Madison Square who makes three trips to Paris in search of something to wear." He recited the entire poem which had us laughing uproariously.

The occupant of the cabin on the other side of us was Mrs. Austin Corbin. I knew nothing about her philosophies, but was pleased her husband did not accompany her. I consider him a despicable person. In addition to his reported unscrupulous business dealings regarding his railroad and resort ownership, he was anti-Semitic. He banned Jews from his Coney Island Resort as had Judge Henry Hilton from his Saratoga Hotel. In the late 1870s, the two joined to form the American Society for the Suppression of Jews. I had read that during a gathering of the society in Saratoga Springs with about 100 members in attendance, Corbin made comments such as "If we are a free country, why can't we be free of Jews?" and stated, "Jews are a nasty and vulgar race." What a contemptible person!

Shortly before we left for Europe, a friend purchased a portable film camera and loaned it to Marie and me for use during our trip. Fortunately, this photographic advancement occurred in the late 1880s before our venture. It was sold by George Eastman who resided in upstate New York and whose ingenuity resulted in his purchasing and patenting film in rolls and inventing a handheld portable camera for its use. It was simple to operate whereby one merely pressed a button to record the picture. As I recall, it allowed for about 100 exposures after which the camera was sent to the George Eastman factory. There, the film was developed, a new film inserted, and prints and camera returned. Shortly after we returned to New York, we sent the camera and anxiously awaited its return. The prints were wonderful and reminders of our memorable vacation.

The street of my family's homestead.

The homes on Breite Strasse one of which was where I was born and where my family lived.

Freinsheim nestled among beautiful orchards and vineyards.

The visit to Germany was bitter-sweet for Marie and me. There were a few descendants of relatives and friends who welcomed us and I also enjoyed seeing Freinsheim, my village of birth. It was as beautiful as when I left and I reminisced with many of its current, hospitable townspeople. But I couldn't help recalling my incarceration and the suffering of many others caused by the oppressive government.

During our return trip, I recalled having traveled the same route 55 years ago, but having taken seven weeks in rough waters, unsanitary, and uncomfortable conditions, unacceptable rations, and witnessing people becoming ill and dying on board. What an incredible contrast to what we had now experienced. When we returned to New York, we were surprised to read a short reference to us and the other cabin voyagers in *The New York Times*, October 18, 1890 as follows:

ARRIVALS FROM EUROPE

The North German Lloyds steamer Trave arrived from Bremen last evening. Her cabin passengers included William Allen Butler, Mrs. T.D. Boardman, Mrs. Austin Corbin, C.D. Dickey, Jr., H.E. Muller, Dr. and Mrs. Philip Merkle, Dr. and Mrs. Julius Schleppegrell, Prof. Gustave Windlsch, and Mrs. F.B. White.

CHAPTER 32

Change

IN 1892, I ARRANGED FOR MARIE TO PURCHASE A COZY HOME IN the Bronx, an area next to Manhattan. The Bronx is divided into two sections by the Bronx River: there is flat land on the east side of the river and hilly terrain on the west. Within the Bronx is a conglomerate of 50 villages, rural in nature. The west side had been annexed to New York City in 1874 and the rest in 1895. I had seen the area several times when I attended meetings, and told Marie that in my old age, I would like to live there.

The home we purchased is on the west of the river because it offers a more picturesque landscape. We were impressed that about 1/4 of the Bronx is comprised of undeveloped land due to cemeteries and parks. In fact, we visited the parks before moving there and enjoyed delightful picnics and concerts. Marie and I also enjoyed strolling through the New York botanical garden which is near our home. The fragrant aromas, diverse landscapes, and the splendid collections of plants and flowers are a sight to behold. It is indeed an impressive garden.

The area of our new house is quite dissimilar to the densely populated and polluted areas in which we had lived. Our home is of medium size, but many of the homes were more spacious because much of the land is inexpensive. An important aspect for us is that the area offers clean air which we enjoy as we sit on our front porch. The neighborhood homes are built with many comforts: electricity, steam, and plumbing allowing for a nice washroom. Marie has planted flowers in boxes on the porch, and together, we have planted a vegetable garden in the yard.

Stores are not easily accessible, but if we need an item that we cannot purchase nearby, we travel by rail or carriage to locations where the product is available. This is quite a contrast to the Lower East Side where shops were within walking distance.

Since we moved to the Bronx, I have become involved in civic pursuits in order to protect the area from overpopulation, allowing it to remain salubrious. I have been speaking at public meetings emphasizing that while there is a need for commercial buildings including shops, we must be cautious to maintain the flavor of the area and prevent excessive expansion.

So far, we are very happy in our new location. We still travel to Manhattan including the Lower East Side to visit friends and to shop.

Marie had befriended, Miriam, the widow of my journalist friend Frank Leslie. In 1896, Miriam contacted Marie, invited her to lunch, and an afternoon of shopping. She knew Marie had not been feeling well and told her that a day's outing would be invigorating. The following information about their meeting and travels is partially from my memory of Marie's account of the day, and from Marie's diary. It will give the reader a mental image of a changing area of the city.

Miriam arrived the following day with carriage and driver to escort them to the Ladies' Mile, an area where the well-to-do shopped and where ladies need not have male companions for safety. It spans 28 blocks between 15th and 24th streets from Sixth Avenue to Park Avenue South. Marie had never been there and was amazed to see carriages lining the streets, four deep. The stores accommodated, not only the increased population in those areas, but catered to the middle and especially upper classes.

When Marie returned home, she reported enthusiastically that it had been a lovely day and eagerly described the day's itinerary with great exhilaration. Miriam and she perused the merchandise in the newly opened Siegel Cooper Department Store, the largest department store in the world. It claimed to be the only steel framed store in the city offering safety from fire throughout. The store was located on 6th Avenue between West 18th and 19th Streets in Manhattan on 18 acres. This allowed for what seemed endless interior space. Marie said that as they entered the main floor there was a beautiful fountain enclosed in marble and a copy of the statue *The Republic* by sculptor David Chester French.

She estimated that there were over 100 departments and everything was displayed beautifully. As they walked through the store, it seemed more like stores within a store, rather than departments. Besides all the dry goods, there was a wonderful area with a grocery store, barber shop, theater, telegraph office, art gallery, studio for portrait sittings, a bank, a conservatory (where you could purchase beautiful and unique plants), a pet department, and a dental office! When they commented to one of the sales ladies that the store was incredible and what more could there be, she replied that it had its own power plant in the basement. She added that there were over 3,000 Siegel Cooper employees who were treated well with fair wages, proper hours, and a gymnasium for their use. Friends of Miriam who had seen the store previously, told her the slogan which has evolved to describe it, is that it contains, "Everything Under the Sun."

Miriam had heard that the restaurant within the Siegel Cooper store was excellent and it was there that they had a wonderful lunch. The restaurant was quite large, and the waiter told them that it seats 350 people!

Marie did not intend to purchase anything, but she remarked that there were so many lovely accessories that she couldn't resist. She and Miriam tried bonnets in the millinery department, and after trying many, Marie purchased one imported from Milan which she was sure would match one of her favorite dresses. Miriam purchased several exquisite dresses and accessories. I was surprised about Marie's purchase because she was usually frugal, but perhaps the company caused her extravagance.

They passed department stores: B. Altman, Lord and Taylor, and Best & Co., all of which had lovely display windows. Another store they passed was Arnold Constable and Miriam mentioned that she had seen many notable personages there, such as, the wives of Grover Cleveland and Andrew Carnegie. Apparently Arnold Constable was the most popular dry goods store of the elite, and was called by its patrons, "the Palace of Trade." They didn't stop at any of those stores because Miriam had other shops on her agenda.

Finally Miriam requested the carriage driver stop near W. and J. Sloane because she wanted to discuss delivery of a rug she had ordered. The furniture, carpets, and oriental rugs (apparently the first ever imported in the United States) were exquisite and the company had even decorated parts of the White House.

After Miriam established a delivery date for her rug, they stopped at Gorham Manufacturing Company where Miriam purchased a wedding gift for a friend. According to Marie, the sterling and silver plate items were beautiful. On display was a silver tea and flatware service which had a sign next to it describing it as similar to the one Mary Todd Lincoln (wife of Abraham Lincoln) had commissioned for the White House. Another display showed a sterling silver vase reminiscent of the one commissioned by Julia Boggs Dent Grant (wife of Ulysses Grant) for the 100th Anniversary of the United States.

Miriam told Marie that in 1873 when the country was in a depression and mercantile businesses were losing their customers, Gorham Company owners were concerned. Then the president of Universal Life Insurance Company of New York, Henry Jewett Furber commissioned the largest ever purchase of an almost 800 piece silver service, such as dishes, utensils, and matching epergne which was so beautiful that it was displayed at the 1876 International Centennial Exposition. It took Gorham seven years to complete the request and the purchase cost over $1,000,000. The owner of Gorham no longer had concerns.

Before they returned home, Marie asked Miriam if they might stop at the Fleischmann Vienna Bakery so that Marie could purchase some bakery products for me. Apparently Miriam commented that Marie was a very good wife.

Miriam had never been to the bakery so it was (for a change) something about which Marie could inform her. She explained to Miriam that after the success of the Fleischmann Vienna Model Bakery at the centennial exhibition, not only did yeast sales rise tremendously, but the popularity of Vienna Bakery products soared to the point that the

Fleischmann family opened cafes in many major cities throughout the United States. One of the Fleischmann brothers, Louis Fleischmann, established one in New York City, in November 1876, the month that the centennial closed. It was located at the corner of Tenth and Broadway. The chosen location was excellent, not only because it was near the Ladies' Mile, but also the beautiful and fashionable Grace Episcopal Church where many of the elite worshipped.

Marie explained to Miriam that European immigrants had been unhappy with the inferior quality of American bakery products which resulted in the success of the Vienna Bakeries. Louis Fleischmann had made the building appealing for those who wished to eat there by installing a large awning and decorative planters near the tables of the outside cafe, and adding a room on the second floor for a small restaurant.

As I had previously mentioned to Marie (which she relayed to Miriam) the bread products were so popular in the New York area that Louis Fleischmann offered delivery of breads via wagons to New York and Brooklyn destinations. Drivers in about 40 wagons or more delivered the ordered products and the area of delivery and profitability continued to increase.

Marie informed me that when the carriage stopped near the store, Miriam and she noticed that outside the bakery, a great deal of foot traffic was seen, mostly women wearing the latest fashions, and viewing the delicious breads and sweets displayed in the windows. The bakery goods were so appealing and the aroma so delightful that most decided to enter the store and purchase products. After doing the same, Miriam and she entered and purchased loaves of bread and some Vienna (hard) rolls.

That evening we had homemade soup for dinner with some delicious Fleischmann bread. The following morning Marie and I enjoyed some hard rolls with our coffee. Just as the bread is crispy, but light, so are the rolls. They are such an improvement over the seemingly half-baked, soft products that we previously purchased here.

On several occasions, I had met Oswald Ottendorfer for lunch at the bakery restaurant. The seating was comfortable, American and international newspapers were available, and not only were the bakery products superb, but the European coffees that were offered were equally acclaimed. After lunch, we always stopped for a short visit with Louis Fleischmann (whose family were long-time friends of Oswald) and of course we purchased some bakery products. According to Louis, the hard rolls were one of the most popular items, and were regularly purchased by German and Eastern European Jews because they served as a dairy meal in accordance with kosher law.

I never met Louis' brothers Charles and Maximilian, but in hearing about them, whenever we visited with Louis, I felt well-acquainted. His brothers were the ones who created the commercially produced yeast (which revolutionized baking in America) and then formed the Fleischmann Yeast Company with headquarters in Cincinnati, Ohio. They also produced the first American distilled gin which was well-received here.

At one point, Oswald told me that Louis was a charitable person which was demonstrated when late one evening, he saw some men standing outside his bakery over a grate from which the aroma of bread could be detected. Louis gave bread to the hungry men and began the tradition of giving bread to any hungry man that came late at night and stood outside his store.

It was reported recently that often over 500 people form a line before the bakery closes, and patiently wait (sometimes as long as four hours) for bread. After the bakery closes, Louis and his employees distribute bread and add cups of coffee during the winter weather. People began speaking of the incredible breadline at Fleischman's bakery. However, Louis was criticized by some for giving something for nothing. He ignored the criticism, believing that anyone who would wait for hours was genuinely hungry and nothing should be expected in return. In fact, if Louis Fleischmann saw an individual leave without eating his loaf, he presumed he was saving it for his family, would have the man followed, and later assist the man's family.

When I penned about the bakery in a letter to my family in St. Louis, they responded that they were enjoying baked goods and coffee at a Fleischmann cafe in St. Louis. In fact, the original cafe was so popular that larger quarters had to be located. The Fleishmann brothers certainly made an impact on America and brother Louis on New York City with his wonderful cafe, restaurant, baked goods, and coffee. But he will especially be remembered for his kindness to hungry and needy New Yorkers. Another contributory immigrant family!

CHAPTER 33

Concerns and Sadness

THE 19TH CENTURY IS COMING TO A CLOSE. DURING THIS LAST decade, in addition to our trip to Germany, our move to the Bronx and my fortunate acquaintance with Teddy Roosevelt, there is further news to share.

At times during my life, I have read medical reports about invalidism and tried to understand Mother's five-year affliction. Finally, during the 1890s, possible reasons have been published in medical journals which offer two possible reasons for the state of invalidism (where no physical cause is found). One is that an invalid appreciates the state of powerlessness that the sickroom provides because it offers a place to repose, meditate, and reflect while others fulfill the patient's usual duties. The other possibility is that an invalid enjoys the opportunity for authoritarianism gained from observing others perform unwanted chores. Either way it provides invalids with a method of escaping from their daily lives. In Mother's case, I wonder which explanation might have caused her condition and what repressed feelings would have effectuated its inception.

An unexpected event of the 1890s was meeting Susan Blow in New York City. She told me that she had moved east to lecture about kindergartens and establish them here. She added that St. Louis now had over 50 kindergartens. I am concerned that Blow will not be as successful in the east, especially New York City, in convincing those in leadership positions (many of whom are thought to be corrupt), to fund her outstanding programs.

The other news she conveyed was that William Torrey Harris, the innovative educator and superintendant of the St. Louis schools (to whom I was introduced after Friederike's funeral), had accepted the position of United States Commissioner of Education. What an excellent choice!

During the 1890s, we are continuing to witness the impact of the temperance organizers and support for the movement. In 1893, yet another temperance group was founded in New York: The New York Society for the Suppression of Vice. In 1895, the temperance groups boycotted root beer. Three years later, they admitted their error, but meanwhile, this action caused the manufacturers of the beverage a great deal of financial loss. And the WCTU has increased its membership from approximately 27,000 at its inception to currently (1899), over 175,000.

Wayne Wheeler, an attorney and supporter of the temperance movement, was well-known for his affiliation with the Anti-Saloon League (ASL), another group within the movement. He has been successful in exerting undue pressure, including intimidation of national candidates so that they would vote for prohibition. Then, through clever advertising, he convinces voters (no matter what their party affiliation) to support the candidates of the major parties that have prohibition platforms. He brags of the success of his "pressure" politics. This epitomizes the possibilities of inordinate amounts of power that a person can possess in influencing governmental agencies.

The national elections have shown increasing support for the Prohibition Party and a surprisingly successful response from the popular vote. This ever-increasing power of temperance groups boggles my mind.

However, their unreasonable threat that someday they will convince the United States government to include a constitutional amendment prohibiting the consumption of alcoholic beverages and declare the production illegal, will certainly never occur. What absurdity!

In both New York City and St. Louis (reported by JF), there are problems associated with electric lighting which often results in fires. The difficulty stems from the fact that poles carry all three wires: telegraph, telephone, and electric. During ice storms or blizzards, poles easily fall, caused by the weight of precipitation. When on the ground current continues through the wires and causes a tremendous danger to the populace. Hopefully the defects will be corrected and excellent means of communication will remain.

Another disturbing situation that exists in New York City and St. Louis is the increase in pollution. Factories producing various products such as paint, bricks, beer, liquor, and coal cause fumes and pollutants to be emitted. Legislation is needed, but meanwhile factories are concentrated in populated and poorer areas regardless of the health hazards they may cause. Conversely, wealthy areas are protected by politicians from having any polluting institutions built in their communities. To seek legal intervention has been unsuccessful because those in power want to maintain or increase the economy of the city while protecting the wealthy.

During this last decade of the 19th century, we also witnessed a depression known as the Panic of 1893 which resulted, by 1894, in a 19% unemployment rate and salaries reduced, at least 50%, for those employed. During the same year, there were at least 1,000 strikes (often accompanied by violence) involving approximately 700,000 workers. The depression lasted until two years ago, (1897) but we have not yet completely recovered.

This economic debacle began after the Civil War and has resulted in recessions, depressions, unemployment, and poor wages. The two major depressions were from 1873-1879 and from 1893-1897. In large part, I blame their causes on the tremendous growth in industrial capitalism and the resultant power of the capitalists. Appropriately, they have become known as robber barons because most of their riches have been gained by dishonest means. They control political parties, and for the most part rule the country.

During most of the 1800s, both New York City and St. Louis struggled to seek solutions for waste removal. I shared the news with JF that great strides had recently been accomplished in New York City after Civil War Colonel George Waring Jr. was appointed Sanitation Commissioner in 1895. Prior to the Civil War, he was an engineer who specialized in design and implementation of sewer systems and had successfully established a drainage system for Central Park.

His first acts in New York City were having a law passed which required horses to be stabled over night and mandating a white uniformed street cleaning department that he treated like a military unit. Employees were disenthralled with his regimental work ethic, but they adjusted and the needed tasks were completed.

He initiated an innovative method to dispose of waste. Solid waste was boiled for greases, fertilizers, and some used for land fill. Paper and metal containers were separately collected by scavengers. The successful sorting of garbage for various useful purposes and his insistence on employees working diligently, greatly improved the sanitation system in New York City to the extent that streets were totally clean. Waring remained in the position for three years until President McKinley requested that he be the advisor regarding sanitation in Cuba. Shortly after his arrival there, he contracted yellow fever and returned to New York City where he died in 1898. His contributions to waste disposal in New York City are amazing. When JF learned of the wonderful work of Waring, he regretted that Waring could not have established a similar plan for St. Louis.

The beginning of June 1896 was a tense time for me. The New York newspapers reported that a severe tornado had touched down on St. Louis the end of May. I immediately wrote to my nephew and was hopeful that I would hear from him presently. It was a few weeks before I received the following letter.

June 14, 1896
St. Louis, Missouri
Dearest Uncle Philip,

I apologize for not writing sooner, but correspondence was difficult which I will explain. You probably have read by now that tornados followed by a super tornado now called the "Great Cyclone" landed on St. Louis May 27th and in only twenty minutes caused great havoc. Thankfully the tornados did not injure any of my family or me and the damage to our home and stores was minimal. But the loss of life and destruction of property in our city is difficult to comprehend. The storm is reported to be the worst ever encountered in the United States.

The tornados came quickly changing a warm, humid day with stormy looking clouds to thick, low swirling clouds which turned to a green hue. The black funnels rolled along destroying anything in their path. But then an incredibly strong storm followed which did unfathomable damage making a ten mile path of destruction that was described as slicing through St. Louis like a turbine. Winds were measured up to one hundred ninety nine miles per hour. The Cyclone destroyed about twelve thousand buildings, (among them hospitals, places of worship, businesses and blocks of residential homes), uprooted numerous old well established trees that were thrown several blocks, tore trains from the tracks and into pieces, sank boats and destroyed part of the steel Eads Bridge that was thought to be storm proof. Heavy stone and steel parts of the bridge weighing several tons were tossed more than one hundred feet.

Fires broke out, but fortunately were extinguished by about three inches of rain that fell that evening accompanied by lightning which was the only light the rescuers had to locate bodies. During the Cyclone, electric wires, telephone, and telegraph poles were destroyed by the high speed winds leaving the city in the dark. Some live wires covered the ground causing rescue to be even more dangerous.

For most, there was insufficient time to take cover. Approximately 255 people died, 1,000 or more injured and in excess of 5,000 people left homeless having lost everything they possessed. The property damage is estimated to be between 20 and 25 million dollars.

Uncle Philip, you might recall Liggett Tobacco Company which (since your visit) became Liggett and Myers. The company was in the process of constructing a larger factory at the time of the Cyclone. Although the workers made it to the basement, the building's iron framework fell, crashing through the first floor to the basement and killing 13 of them.

Sarah and I alternate giving assistance wherever we are able. We offer food and shelter in our store and when I remain home with the *children, Sarah helps at the makeshift hospital. I think it will be a long time before our city is rebuilt and recovers from this horrific storm. I will conclude by saying that my thoughts are with you and Marie. I hope her health is improving.*

Yours respectfully,
Your Nephew, John Ferdinand Conrad

I was grateful and relieved to receive the correspondence and penned an immediate response. I was both gladdened by the news that my family survived, but extremely sad to learn of the suffering and destruction that took place.

1897 was a difficult year for me. Marie had not been feeling well and we had learned in 1896 that she had stomach cancer. There was little I could do but make her comfortable with medication to ease the pain along with a stomachic.

My nephew Frederick visited everyday for the last two weeks of her life which allowed me time to do necessary chores. Then on August 10, 1897 when I returned from making a few purchases for Marie at a local drugstore, and opened the front door, Frederick, with quivering voice, called to me, saying, "Come quickly." I knew my beloved Marie had succumbed. I dropped everything and rushed to the bedroom where Frederick was holding her motionless hand. They did have a special bond. He left the room and I held my dear Marie in my arms and with tears streaming down my face, I spoke to her as if she were still alive, telling her how much I loved her and how fortunate I was to have her in my life for over 40 years. I miss her dearly and will to my dying day.

The outpouring of sympathy from my family and friends was incredible and somewhat comforting. I was shocked and grateful that even JF and Sarah travelled from Missouri to New York for the services and remained with me for a week in case I needed help or companionship. The diversion was a medicine for me.

The last picture I have of Marie taken in 1897.

CHAPTER 34

Pleasant Conversations, New York City Sites and a Baseball Game

THE WEEK WITH JF AND SARAH WENT BY QUICKLY. WE conversed about many topics. I was updated about their children. They now have nine! The anecdotes they shared about the children indicated how delightful and intelligent they are.

During one evening of conversation, I asked JF if his grocery stores (he now has two) were financially successful and he told me they are thriving. The business was now incorporated, he was serving as president and his son Ferdinand E. Conrad was secretary. He also had items made for his store which displayed the label, Laurel Springs. Sarah added that the Laurel Springs brand products are extremely popular. The first item sold under the label was a bourbon, but now dairy products, meats, spices, and other items are also sold. The motto for his stores is, "It tastes like it costs more." People obviously appreciate that he sells quality merchandise at a fair price.

Ultimately, he was planning to go into the wholesale grocery business while continuing his retail stores. During his visit, he asked if I would show him possible areas for a branch office in New York City and introduce him to some store owners to ascertain if there would be interest. Those to whom he spoke were interested and impressed by his prices. We searched various locations and I suggested the area of Worth Street. He said he learned that you must move slowly in adding other facilities and would probably not add the New York branch until 1898 or 1899.

Since it was their first time in New York City, I offered to show them some sites. We toured Morris-Jumel Mansion, Trinity Church, St. Patrick's Old Cathedral, Grace Church, Beth Hamedrash Hagadol, and Tompkins Square. Then we had lunch at Fraunces Tavern and after strolled through Central Park. The following day, we perused the shops on Broadway, and the Metropolitan Museum of Art. I then treated them to dinner at Delmonico's Restaurant. They were impressed and enjoyed the tours. When the waiter learned that JF and Sarah were from St. Louis, he asked how they would compare Delmonico's to Tony Faust's Restaurant. We laughed because people in New York City who traveled to St. Louis commented that Faust's was the best restaurant west of New York City and those from St. Louis who had eaten in both believed Delmonico's second to Faust's. Quite a restaurant rivalry! I mentioned how much Marie would have enjoyed the day and JF and Sarah concurred.

During an evening of conversation JF and I discussed the breweries in St. Louis and the concern about the temperance movement. He spoke of three of the outstanding ones. The Adam Lemp brewery produced the first lager beer in St. Louis. Apparently, before refrigeration, Lemp had cleverly built his brewery on natural caves to keep the lager cold, and took large pieces of ice from the Mississippi, to be moved by conveyor belts to ice houses he had built along the river. Then when needed, they were moved to the caves helping to maintain cold temperatures.

The Chouteau Avenue Brewery founded by Joseph Maximilian Schnaider was the first in St. Louis to build a beer garden next to his brewery. The beer garden accommodated 1,000 people. While enjoying beer and food, they could watch shows and musical entertainment.

Then he spoke of the very successful Anheuser-Busch brewery founded by Eberhard Anheuser (who was now deceased). JF told me that it was interesting that Anheuser's family had owned vineyards in Germany since the 17th century, yet in the United States he was a soap manufacturer until he had the opportunity to purchase a bankrupt St. Louis brewery. Apparently, Anheuser always preferred wine to beer calling beer "slop."

JF knew a great deal about the family. Adolphus Busch (born two decades after Anheuser), a brewery supply salesman, settled in St. Louis and married Elise Anheuser (daughter of Eberhard Anheuser). Busch had been a partner of his father-in-law until the death of

Anheuser at which time Adolphus Busch became president of the company. With his innovative and savvy business sense, he established ownership of all aspects of the business including the hops farms in upstate New York near Cooperstown. By the 1870s, Busch was able to surpass his competitors by pasteurizing his beer and using refrigerated rail cars to transport his products. His customer base expanded to the point that he was thought to be the most successful brewer in the country. Many of my brewer friends in New York spoke of the competition from that company. JF commented as had I many times, that if the temperance movement were successful, vast numbers of people would be unemployed.

Another evening, JF and I conversed about baseball, a favorite pastime of ours. We discussed some game changes over the past few decades: bare hands replaced by protective gloves which greatly minimizes finger and hand breaks, unprotected faces and heads of catchers succeeded by masks to prevent head injuries, various sizes and materials of baseballs replaced by a standard size and material, various sizes of bats and styles to an agreed upon 42 inches long with no flat bats or sawed off ones permissible, underhand pitching replaced by overhand throwing, and the distance from home plate to the pitching mound increased from 50 feet to 60 feet 6 inches. Although not accepted by many, some catchers are crouching behind home plate rather than standing. In the future, I wonder if the crouching position will be adopted by more catchers.

We spoke about rule changes. Some rules have been revised such as: batters are no longer permitted to request where they want a pitch thrown (previous requests were from knee to belt or belt to shoulder), and foul balls are no longer permitted to be caught off a bounce. I assume the decisions were well-thought, but rules are continually being re-evaluated and thus fans have to learn the new ones. Although JF and I agreed that these changes were most likely positive ones, it has been difficult adjusting to some of them.

I told JF that if my sight were better, I would like to occasionally umpire games. I am recognized as a community leader, and as is tradition, the umpire is selected from the spectators at each game and often a known person is chosen from the crowd. I will tell the reader why I would like that task. The umpire is supplied with a comfortable easy chair and a fan to keep him cool. He sits behind home plate or near it. That makes it the best seat in the park for viewing and comfort. In addition, the umpire is treated with respect and never contradicted by the players or managers. Accepting this assignment certainly surpasses sitting with the cranks (now usually called fans) on the hard bleacher boards.

There were two popular New York teams, the New York Gothams (later called the New York Giants), and the Brooklyn Club (nicknamed the Brooklyn Bridegrooms) because several members were married during the 1889 offseason.

They were the team that I preferred and were thrilling to watch. In addition, they won pennants in 1889 and 1890 which were exciting events.

JF was a fan of the St. Louis Browns and although a compelling team, they were overtaken in the 1889 championship by the Bridegrooms. I always tease JF about the Grooms' superiority after that championship.

We spoke of some of our favorites associated with the teams.

JF mentioned a few people affiliated with the St. Louis Browns. He said that without a doubt, Ed Cartwright, a first baseman for the team was an amazing player. Probably Cartwright's most remembered game was when he hit a grand slam and a three-run home run (seven RBI's) in one inning. That is impressive.

He also mentioned his all time favorite player/manager with the Browns, Charles Comiskey. He began his career with them in the early 1880s. (At the time they were called the St. Louis Brown Stockings, and a few years later, the St. Louis Browns.) Comiskey was an outstanding pitcher, and excellent first basemen, and knowledgeable manager. He then became full-time manager and during his managerial years, his team's winning percentages were outstanding. From what JF observed,

Comiskey was well-liked by the players and because of his playing career could better make insightful decisions for the team.

With great disgust, JF spoke of the team owner Christian von der Ahe. He described him as egomaniacal, arrogant, and vindictive. JF mentioned that he heard newcomers to the game, as they approached the ballpark, noticing an imposing statue which they assumed was of a great Browns' player, but upon closer look, learned it was one commissioned by von der Ahe of himself.

JF continued that If the players didn't perform well, von der Ahe threatened to withhold pay. On one occasion, he criticized a player in view of the game spectators and as a result, the rest of the team was so appalled that it was suspected they started losing intentionally. Von der Ahe began having financial problems and to raise funds, sold some of his best players which culminated in the team statistics dropping rapidly. Then in 1892, Comiskey could no longer withstand von der Ahe's behavior and resigned. JF said they will need some extensive revisions to ever have a winning team again.

In terms of the Bridegrooms, I was pleased with the ownership, especially Charles Byrne and Charles Ebbets who are willing to fund the purchase of good players. For example, when von der Ahe was in need of funds, he sold three of his best players to the Bridegrooms for the incredible sum of $19,000: Bob Caruthers, Joe Bushong, and David Foutz. What a boost to the Bridegrooms.

A Bridegroom manager that impressed me was William McGunnigle. He had been an outstanding player, but sadly sustained a fractured skull while playing with a New England team which ended his playing career. He was hired in 1888 by the Bridegrooms as their manager. It was amusing to watch him blow his tin whistle to alert the players, but they seemed to respect him, and work diligently. He is to a large extent responsible for the pennant wins in 1889 and 1890.

There was one day left before Sarah and JF returned to St. Louis. JF suggested that we attend a baseball game and Sarah offered to clean and make dinner while we attended. I reluctantly agreed always having the loss of Marie foremost on my mind.

We went to Eastern Park in Brownsville (eastern Brooklyn), where the team was playing. The park held 12,000 people, and when we arrived, it was almost filled to capacity. The game was exciting and it was a diversion for me. At the park, we had a hot dog, and lager for lunch, and then watched an exciting game. When we arrived home, Sarah had done some laundry, cleaned some rooms, and had prepared dinner which was delicious. What wonderful gestures.

JF and I mentioned to Sarah that fans seemed to enjoy the game immensely, and for many, it is an excellent diversion from their difficult daily lives. We are convinced the enthusiasm and interest in the game will continue.

The following morning, before they left for St. Louis, I took the opportunity to tell Sarah and JF that our home and property were bequeathed to them. I explained that Marie's will left the house and property to them (as I previously mentioned, no property is in my name because of the marital situation) with the stipulation that I enjoy the remainder of my life in the house. Therefore, the sale of the house and property could not take place until after my death. They thanked me profusely and commented that it was a most generous offer.

When they returned home, JF penned that he had added a third store and his son Oscar J. Conrad had joined the business in charge of cigars and bourbon. According to JF, with Oscar's innate business sense, he has been successful in expanding the Laurel Springs brands. He also informed me that he now oversees his stores and products while others manage them. Meanwhile JF has become vice president and director of the Jefferson Bank of St. Louis, Missouri. He has not only established a successful business, but is involved in charitable causes. I am proud of his accomplishments as my sister would have been.

CHAPTER 35

Celebrations of Note

BESIDES MY DIARY NOTATIONS, MARIE KEPT A BOX OF NEWSPA-
per articles that referenced me. Some of a serious nature I have
mentioned in previous chapters, but as I perused others, they discuss
lighter, celebratory occasions of note. I will mention a few.

On September 17, 1866, (about a year and five months since the
end of the Civil War) there was an event in Union Square, New York
City (with the themes "Unity and Peace" and "Peace and Reunion")
to celebrate the September 17, 1787 adoption of the United States
Constitution. I was an invited speaker for the occasion.

The day after the event, many newspapers reported the details.
The following are a few excerpts from the 24 page recounting of the
occasion which appeared in The *New York Herald* September 18, 1866
as follows:

"Yesterday was a day to be remembered by every lover of his native
land; long to be remembered as the anniversary of that day on which
the Federal Constitution was adopted and made a safeguard of republican liberty by our fathers; long to be remembered of that eventful
struggle through which we have just passed, and from which we have
not yet entirely recovered."

In the words of the *Herald* reporters, "New York, the brain and
centre of this nation, speaks in thunder tones by this monster
mass-meeting silencing the discordant voices of Maine and Vermont
crying still for war."

The assemblage was estimated to be 100,000 persons and there
were representatives from all 36 states. Thousands not able to secure
positions in the square or the adjacent streets, stood on building tops,
windows, and balconies.

I and some other event speakers had been waiting in the Maison Doree Restaurant on East 14th Street and after the crowd had gathered, we were escorted to our positions. There were speaker stands from Fourth Avenue to University Place. The stand from which I spoke was East of Fourth Avenue. The *Herald* reporter listed those who spoke from that stand, some of whom were: Magnus Gross, Esq., Hon. John J. Freedman, Dr. Philip Merkle, Hon. Max Herman Schroeder Esq., and Hon. Max Goepp. " Some of the officers assigned to organize our grandstand area were also listed: "Charles E. Loew and Oswald Ottendorfer. There were mottos adorning all grandstands with such maxims as "With Malice to None, with Charity to All" and "Civil and Religious Liberty, the Rights of Man."

My oration, as usual, emphasized that the goal should always be equality for all and I referenced the United States Declaration of Independence which includes the phrase "All men are created equal." I further mentioned that the realization of that powerful concept cannot take place until differences among us are eradicated. (It is difficult to accept that it is now 1899 and bias is still evident.)

The event closed with an exceptional pyrotechnic show. Of the many incredible displays, I believe the most outstanding was of a figure representing President Andrew Johnson. He was surmounted by a rainbow with two figures on either side, one representing the South with extended hand, and the other representing the North, tending an olive branch. Underneath were the words "Peace and Reunion." The entire exhibit was surrounded by thirty-six stars representing the thirty-six states. It was a wonderful occasion in celebration of unity and peace. I hope the maxims presented will be realized.

Other happy occasions were christenings, weddings, and anniversaries at which I officiated. Most were simple occasions but a few I recall were quite elaborate. In 1895 I performed a christening for the prominent Schoneberger family. Frederick Schoneberger's five-month old daughter was to be christened.

I remember arriving at their enormous home, ringing the doorbell and as the door was opened, smelling the fragrant aroma of roses. I was escorted through the hallway to the huge parlor. Both areas were decorated with white ribbon streamers and pink roses. About 100 chairs were assembled in the room and people were seated, speaking quietly, while they awaited the family.

The Shoneberger family was well-known to me. I had officiated at the christenings, weddings, and anniversaries of every member of the family. Mr. Shoneberger reminded me that I had christened him, officiated at his wedding, at his other children's christenings, and now would be doing the same for his most recent child. She was a handsome baby and didn't cry once during the ceremony.

After the event, the child was taken by her nanny to the nursery. The guests were invited to the dining room for a buffet provided by a Delmonico chef. The table was immense and covered with a white crocheted tablecloth like Anna used to make. Here and there on the table were enormous arrangements of roses. The company and food were wonderful. A journalist friend of the Shoneberger's was in attendance and the details of the occasion were reported in *The Brooklyn Eagle*.

Another wonderful happening was the 50th Anniversary celebration of my longtime friends Mr. and Mrs. William Pfeifer. I had performed the marriage of the Pfeifer's 50 years ago in 1849. One of their grown children greeted me at the door and escorted me to a chair by a lectern in the immense parlor.

The approximately 40 guests were seated facing me and several, with whom I was acquainted, gave a slight wave which I acknowledged with a nod. The parlor was decorated with bouquets of sunflowers and a wreath of those flowers adorned the lectern. I learned later that Mrs. Pfeifer's favorite flower was the sunflower and coincidentally gold is the traditional color of a 50th jubilee.

The ceremony was arranged by the family to resemble a wedding procession. A string quartet performed Mendelssohn's wedding march to accompany the procession. The great-grandchildren entered first, then the grandchildren, children, and finally the honorees. It had been well-rehearsed and when they reached the lectern, I spoke some kind and humorous words, and then led the couple in renewing their wedding vows. It was a touching and joyful occasion. After the ceremony, we had delicious refreshments and I was able to informally speak at length to the family and guests. The event was also reported in *The Brooklyn Eagle.*

On another occasion I was asked to perform the marriage ceremony for a young couple. Details of the event were reported in the *New York Tribune* and the following is an excerpt:

> At 5 o'clock last evening Miss Ida C. Kramer
> was married to Louis Eltlinger, of this city, at
> the home of her father William Kramer.
> The Marriage ceremony was performed by
> the Rev. Philip Merkle who also married
> the grandparents of the bride.

These did remind me of how quickly time passes.

Another reminiscence was my campaigning for Grover Cleveland. I had the occasion to spend time in Buffalo, New York and become acquainted with many people there. Probably for that reason, the *Buffalo Daily Courier* wrote an article about me in 1883. The following are some excerpts:

> The Rev. Philip Merkle, M.D., one of the

New York Coroners, celebrated Friday the
fiftieth anniversary of his arrival in this
country. He has welcomed, christened, married and buried more human beings it is said,
than any other living German-American.
He converses fluently in Latin,
to say nothing of Greek, German, French,
and English. He has
inspected drugs in the custom house
and once was an excise commissioner.

The same year, an article appeared in the New York City newspaper *Whole Truth and Nothing But the Truth*, which reminded me once
again of my advanced age. The following is an excerpt:

THE OLDEST CITY OFFICIAL.

Coroner Philip Merkle celebrated his 73d birthday the other day and became the recipient of a
number of presents from a large circle of personal and political friends. The Coroner is the
oldest man holding office in New York City at
present, but his age does not prevent him from
being one of the most active.

Another exciting event was my being honored in a ceremony
commemorating the 25th Anniversary of Fessler Masonic Lodge which
I had founded. During the ceremony, I was presented with a silver
vessel on which was the inscription, "Dedicated to Brother Philip
Merkle, in appreciation of his unending dedication to the improvement
of mankind." This was a greatly appreciated gesture. Reports appeared
in *The New York Times*, March 7, 1890. The following is an excerpt:

> At the celebration of the 25th anniversary of Fessler Ledge,
> Dr. Merkle made an address to the 130 members
> in attendance in which
> he outlined the history of the lodge and elo-
> quently told the brethren that they must con-
> tinue to work in the cause of humanity with
> unabated vigor.

A few years later, I was surprised with a week of celebration honoring my humanitarian work during my tenure in many lodges of the Freemasons. In attendance were my family and many friends who welcomed me to the festivities they had painstakingly prepared.

Several newspapers as far away as Baltimore, Maryland reported the celebrations. On March 26, 1894, the *Baltimore Sun* printed the following article:

> Rev. Dr. Philip Merkle, now in his 83rd year
> has just passed through one of the most exciting
> weeks of his long life. With numerous Masonic
> Lodges of which he is a member, he has been
> celebrating the 50th Anniversary of his introduction
> into the fraternity. Dr. Merkle officiated at services
> frequently and his voice is as truly strong as ever
> it was and he can preach a very good sermon his
> friends say.

1895 marked another momentous occasion when The Sons of Hermann celebrated its 55th Anniversary. During the celebration I was presented with a beautiful mechanical pencil in remembrance of my founding of the order. I have made much use of the gift.

Below are excerpts from an article printed in the *New York Times* May 19, 1895 regarding the organization and referencing me and my constant emphasis on performing kind gestures and charitable work.

An Order with an Honorable Record
for Benevolence.
WORKS OF CHARITY QUIETLY DONE
The Sons of Hermann has won an honorable place in the
list of benevolent orders by strict adherence to its fundamental
principles. Its long roll of good deeds quietly done bears
evidence of its allegiance to the humane plans outlined by its founders.
The order was founded in New-York City July 20, 1840
by Dr. Philip Merkle and a few friends.

In 1896, Frederick, Marie, and I attended the annual singing festival of the Harugari Society in New Haven, Connecticut. At that time, the estimated Harugari membership was 50,000 and of them 20,000 were also members of the singing society.

I am pleased that the Order of Harugari, which I was instrumental in establishing in 1847 has continued to flourish. By 1896, there were 300 lodges and a membership of 30,000 nationwide. In addition, during the 1890s, women's lodges, estimated to have about 7,000 members, were established and became affiliates of the Order. I am proud that the motto of the Order of Harugari, "Friendship, Love, and Humanity continues to be met.

1897 marked the 50th anniversary of the founding of the Order of Harugari. During those 50 years, I am proud to report that $5,000,000 was donated to the needy. There were many celebrations and the following excerpts in *The New York Sun*, July 26, 1897 will give an idea of the elaborate celebratory events in New York City.

A LODGE CELEBRATION.

Members of lodges from
all over the United States will be here to
attend the festival, which will last four days.
A reception will follow in honor of the three
living founders of the society, Dr. Phillip

Merkle, Friedrich Germann, and Peter
Schnatz.
Since the foundation of the society more than
$5,000,000 has been paid out by the lodge and
large sums of money were collected to assist the victims
of the Chicago fire, and those who
suffered from yellow fever in New Orleans.

There were many other articles about celebrations, including the
following excerpts which appeared in the *New York Times,* July 26, 1897.

ORDER OF THE HARUGARI.

Jubilee Celebration in Honor of Its
Fiftieth Anniversary
Three of its founders are still alive,
Dr. Philip Merkle,
who was born in 1811, and looks well
enough to pass the century mark,
Frederich Germann, and Peter Schnatz.
The large hall was crowded with
representatives and guests.

A special award was presented in New York City to the three living
founders of the organization. It was a beautiful coin cast with engravings of our images and names.

Harugari Founders Coin Front View.

Harugari Founders Coin Back View.

For me, more gratifying than receiving honors and awards is recalling the charitable projects I initiated which resulted in alleviating

suffering, and fostering kindness, and benevolence. These projects were accomplished both monetarily and in volunteering to help those in need.

Through fraternal organizations, governmental positions, businesses, political organizations, dialogue with journalists, religious organizations, and orations, my goals and messages have been to foster charity and strive for equality. I am pleased that I was always voted into leadership roles to ensure that those objectives are addressed.

CHAPTER 36

Musings of An Old Man

AS ACCURATELY AS POSSIBLE, I HAVE CONVEYED MY EXPERI-
ences and observations during my life in Germany and the United
States (with help from the contents of my diary and journals). Without
them, I would not have recalled all that I have communicated in this
book. As I reflect about my life, the following are some final thoughts
and predictions from the musings of this old man.

The populous of the United States should understand and be
aware of how fragile a democratic government is to maintain. Look to
the countries that have histories much longer than the United States
and you will comprehend the concept. Without an understanding of
this, the wonderful free and democratic country which I adopted can
one day become a tyrannical one.

As long ago as the 12th Century A.D., a warning was predicted
through an artistic message regarding those in power. The Sienese
artist Ambrogio Lorenzetti painted the series of frescos *The Allegory
of Good and Bad Government*: good government depicted as content-
ment in a safe environment with happy citizens busily performing
productive tasks, while bad government is depicted as crime-ridden
with decaying towns and rampant disease. Lorenzetti was insightful
regarding government and offered a message through his frescos
which conveyed a warning to beware that a government of honest leaders can quickly change to a government of tyrannical ones. Therefore
we must not be complacent, but always vigilant and active in making
sure that moralistic and honest leaders prevail.

I also remember the wise words of philosopher Thomas Hobbs who
wrote in essence that a society in which men live, without other security beyond what their own strength and invention offers, is a society
that is solitary, poor, nasty, brutish, and short-lived.

As a result of a lifetime of observing countries that are or were ruled by dictatorial governments, including Germany at the time that I left, I must warn that if oppressors are strong, they often make the majority of the oppressed fearful to take action. Fear and indifference result in human suffering and the continued rise of demagogues and despotic leaders.

During my tenure in the United States, I have read as much as possible about its history. There were so many laws and acts passed for the betterment of society, but there were also those that, if they prevailed, could have led to the destruction of our democratic government. An example of laws passed as early as 1798, were the Alien and Sedition Acts. They gave government too much power and basically attempted to prevent freedom of speech. If one opposed those laws, fines and imprisonment could be imposed. While they were in existence, over 20 newspaper owners or editors were arrested. The content of some of the acts impacted immigrants by imposing stricter rules for deportation and raising the immigrant residency requirement from five to 14 years for eligibility to vote. All were repealed by 1802, the last, the naturalization ones. These types of acts must always be disputed and prevented.

The Federalist Party, who were responsible for passing the acts, were not the only anti-immigrant organization. There have been others during my lifetime, such as The Native American Party, the American Party, the Know Nothing movement and in this last decade of the century The Immigration Restriction League, all of which represented anti-immigration sentiments. I say to them, "Look at me, look at my circles of family and friends and you will realize the wonderful contributions which many immigrants have made to America that have improved your lives."

Although Abraham Lincoln won the United States presidency in 1860 (with no southern electoral votes), his eventual decision for a civil war might have been premature or unnecessary, and his course of action was unsettling for me. I believe Lincoln was a well-meaning leader and I spoke for his election. However, I also believe that the impending issues between the north and south were beyond manumission, such as the ramifications of southern farm crops versus the increasing economic industrial growth of the north, the issue of slavery in the territories becoming states, and the matter of states' rights. In short many of the issues were politically and financially motivated.

Admittedly, some of the matters had manumission overtones but none of them could be easily solved by simply pitting the north against the south. When I spoke with my journalism friends covering battle sites, the horrors observed and the hatred described made me even more convinced that more negotiations and other solutions might have been a deterrent.

It is estimated that over 600,000 died during the war. Such wastes of lives! After reading Walt Whitman's book of prose recollections, *Memoranda During the War* in which he graphically describes his observations of the carnage and the infinite numbers of suffering and dead young men, I was overwhelmed. Throughout the work, which he dedicated to the memory of the fallen United States Civil War soldiers, he does not only make reference to the dead, but also the living who must internalize the mass deaths and atrocities that occurred on this country's soil. He remarks that as our nation reconstructs, what remains is not only the named dead, but the tens of thousands of tombstones with the word "Unknown." "Northern dead leaven Southern soil and Southern dead, Northern soil." In short, Whitman aptly proclaimed, "The dead, the dead, the dead—our dead—or South or North, ours all."

Since the aftermath of the Civil War, as I expected, the goals of freedom and equality for colored people and the issues of governmental power have not been accomplished. There was no planning for those freed to take their rightful place in society. Instead, resentment, hatred, and inhumane treatment of colored people continued.

I had embraced the writings of John Locke and Jean-Jacques Rousseau regarding education as the key to equality, but now believe that their words are too simplistic. It is important for the colored race to gain empowerment through education, but due to social ignorance, it will need time and effort beyond formal education to attain equality.

Incidents which point out the power of human kindness as a strong motivation to erase difference occurred during the draft riots of 1863. It was learned after the riots that in the Five Points area there were colored merchants who had shown kindness to their Irish neighbors and the Irish rioters did not attack those merchants or their homes and shops during the riots. This emphasized for me that once positive interaction has taken place with another human being, the barriers of difference disappear.

Tolerance of religion and ethnicity was exhibited in the Magnus Gross Association. George William Curtis embraced transcendentalism, Joseph Pulitzer and Adolf Ochs embrace Judaism, Henry Villard had been a Catholic, but chose to follow the Reformed Church of Calvin, Henry Alloway embraces Quaker beliefs, and I free thought. Joseph Pulitzer, originated from Hungary, William Curtis and Frank Leslie from England, Oswald Ottendorfer from Moravia and Henry Villard, Magnus Gross and I from Germany. This certainly points to the fact that once you view a person without prejudice, you dispel bias.

People must view others as part of humanity and not see differences other than qualities that each possesses, and consider what each could contribute to humanity. This can occur through education only if the concept of acceptance of difference is a goal. Our Magnus group and other groups with which I was affiliated attempted to accomplish this through charitable acts and advocacy.

There are many good and well-intentioned people including those in leadership positions, not only in my native land and my adopted country, but in all countries of the world. We must remain vigilant so that democratic and compassionate leaders will prevail.

In further reminiscing, I recall when I was a young man, noting the ills of the Lower East Side, and expecting to cause change quickly. Age taught me that reform comes slowly and, at times, there are steps forward and sometimes steps back.

Whenever I was frustrated, I would recollect my father's words that in life there are givers and takers. As we pass through this world, always be a giver and leave with your head high having positively contributed even if only in a small way. Those words often helped me to persevere.

Along those lines, I also learned that the tolerance and ultimate meshing of differing races, ethnicities, religions, classes, and identities cannot occur, or at times even be addressed when people need food, clothing, and shelter, and are living in areas that are disease ridden. Survival then becomes the priority. One of my tasks therefore (which became an ongoing one) was to first attempt to ameliorate the suffering that was being witnessed, and then attempt to combat other injustices.

A favorite quotation that reminds me of the often slow progress and need for patience is by The German poet Friedrich von Logan who authored a second line to the Greek proverb and whose English translation was by the American author Henry Wadsworth Longfellow in his work, *Retribution.*

> *Though the mills of the gods grind slowly; Yet they grind exceeding small;*
> *Though with patience He stands waiting; With exactness grinds He all.*

There have been variations of the phrase such as:

> *The wheels of justice turn slowly, but grind exceedingly fine.*

I have analyzed and evaluated the results of my successes in causing positive change during my lifetime and offer some advice to those who follow. In my many orations to both large and small audiences, formal and informal groups, I was always sure to emphasize that actions and suggested legislation must be for the good of all, always striving for tolerance and equality. I also learned (in addition to promoting large audience awareness) that those in positions to cause change should be petitioned individually or in small groups. Finally, belonging to organizations is important so that through interaction with others, when the need arises for advocacy and philanthropy, there is the probability for positive results.

The diligent and tireless efforts that I and those around me have undertaken to dispel bias I now realize will need acceptance beyond what we have done. We laid the groundwork through our dialogue, advocacy, and actions so that the momentum for these causes might continue during the 20th century. Hopefully, bias and intolerance for difference will disappear and all will be seen simply as members of the human race.

By introducing my accomplishments for this developing city, I trust that in reading this autobiography, especially future generations, will understand that much of what is offered in New York City (hospitals, libraries, museums, concert halls, educational facilities, and entertainment venues) had their beginnings with many hard working, innovative, creative individuals (many of whom were immigrants) during the 19th century.

I commenced this autobiographical project in 1895 and have now completed it in 1899 marking almost four years since its undertaking and now completion. My purpose in writing my recollections is to offer an historical view of the time in which I lived and the contributions that I and many immigrants made. As a result, the reader should gain an appreciation of the hard work, ingenuity, and beneficence of many, and hopefully will be influenced and inspired.

EPILOGUE

Philip Merkle died May 3, 1899. Many attended his funeral service including Aunt Anna's relatives who had remained in communication with him even after he separated from her. Despite their separation, her family had respect and admiration for him, and could always seek his help and advice.

I am Philip Merkle's nephew, Frederick Bechtel. When I last visited Uncle Philip, three days before his death, he asked that I oversee the publication of his autobiographical manuscript and that I determine a title after reading it. I decided that MATTERS OF LIFE AND DEATH: The remarkable journey of Dr. Philip Merkle would best describe the content of the book. His life was interrupted so often by deaths and yet he always forged forward to continue contributing to mankind.

I asked permission of Uncle Philip to write this epilogue and he agreed.

He requested that when he died, I contact his family in Missouri. This I did and later helped facilitate the sale of Uncle Philip's home and property in the Bronx which he bequeathed to his nephew J.F. Conrad and his wife Sarah.

During my last visit with Uncle Philip, I thanked him again for his gift to me of a Steinway grand piano. Besides his constant support, it is the greatest gift he could have given me and again I assured him that I would bequeath it to a future talent. Uncle Philip also offered me a box of his papers and awards which I gladly accepted.

As the content of his book indicates, he always supported and advocated egalitarian principles never hesitating to address an injustice. He never cared about popularity only dispelling bias. In spite of that, he was admired by so many and influenced their thinking regarding the necessity of correcting wrongs being perpetrated against humanity. In every oration I attended, he spoke of the four "A"s that were needed to improve society: AWARENESS regarding injustice, ACKNOWLEDGEMENT of the problem, ANALYSIS of the situation, and ACTION to correct the discrimination.

Whenever I heard him speak, he was so enthusiastic, and his words so prudent, and convincing that people in attendance departed commenting about his wisdom (and his sense of humor). He never failed to indicate in his address summations (no matter what cause he was presenting) that we are all part of mankind and must respect each other's beliefs.

When Uncle Philip and I met after some of his orations, (as we often did) I always complimented his wisdom and commented that his speeches were concise and to the point. On one of those occasions he quoted Marcus Tullius Cicero who stated, "Brevity is the best recommendation of speech whether in a senator or an orator." Cicero was one of his favorite authors and Uncle Philip often quoted him. One other quotation I particularly recall is "The higher we are placed the more humble we should walk."

I attended his last oration and as I left, a group of people conversing outside the hall were speaking of his inspiring words and one commented (to the agreement of all) that Uncle Philip had the stamina and energy of five young men combined with the sagacity of his age. Without a doubt, he had a notion of charisma which made him even more effective in his constant quest to dispel discrimination and oppression.

He was also a visionary always suggesting future actions that would improve the plight of humanity. For example his summoning juries of individuals not only to return verdicts, but to recognize and influence the need for change in policy and law.

I believe the content of his book underestimates his contributions, but certainly introduces anyone who reads it to a better understanding of the conditions in Germany during the 19th century, (causing the huge exodus of so many who settled in America) the growth of New York City and St. Louis, Missouri, and the many 19th century individuals with whom he interacted.

The tireless work of Uncle Philip and his circles of family and friends concerning educational and cultural development, and their work in improving the health, employment, and living conditions were outstanding. They indeed should be praised for contributing a great deal to many aspects of our growing metropolis. His description of some influential and contributory individuals of St. Louis and surrounding areas along with the sites of that city gleaned from his visits and correspondences with his family are enlightening. His lifetime of encouraging the acceptance by all human beings of differences in ethnicity, race, religion, and non-traditional relationships was relentless.

After services, his remains were placed in a niche at the Fresh Pond Crematory, Middle Village, Queens, New York next to the niche where his "wife" Marie's remains had been placed. I will miss him greatly, but I am pleased that Aunt Anna is still on this earth and as alert, caring, and humorous as always.

Business card giving the address and agent of the NYC Conrad wholesale business.

Uncle Philip's nephew JF corresponded with me after Uncle Philip's death, not only because of my facilitating the sale of Uncle's Philip's house and property, but also regarding other cordial items. He wrote that he wished Uncle Philip could have lived longer to see his business expand to include a wholesale operation with an extended base in New York City (as he and Uncle Philip had discussed during JF's 1897 visit). He sent me a card regarding his wholesale location and agent in New York City and penned that the location on Worth Street was the area Uncle Philip had shown him and suggested he rent.

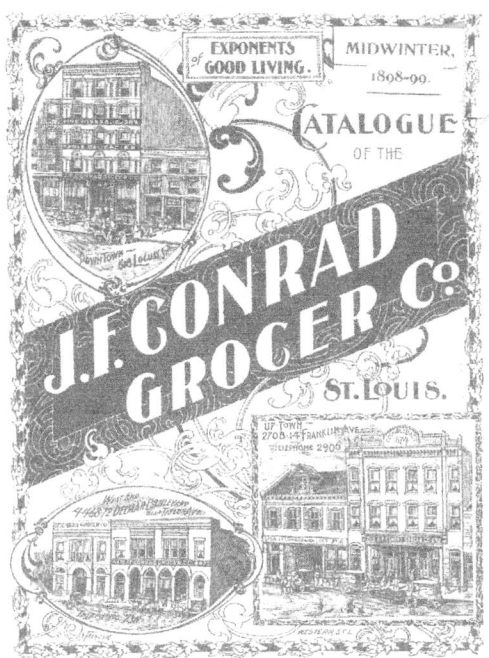

Cover of the 25th Anniversary Catalogue of J.F. Conrad Grocer Co.

In one of his missives he also enclosed a 24 page catalogue celebrating the 25th anniversary of his grocery business. It was amazing to see the quality products, inexpensive prices, and diverse and extensive offerings numbering over 500. That, too, he wished Uncle Philip could have seen.

After Uncle Philip separated from Aunt Anna, she kindly invited me to continue living with her in her home in Brooklyn. She set aside one part of her home for my use as a music studio in which I taught and presented recitals. What a wonderful hostess she was for my recitals even offering the attendees delicious homemade baked goods and beverages after the performances. I must add that even when Uncle Philip parted from Aunt Anna, both remained kind and caring to me. Uncle Philip made sure I had employment while I was pursuing my musical career and both encouraged me to follow my talent for music.

Aunt Anna was caring in a different way from Uncle Philip. She was always aware of people in need (both family and friends) and quietly brought food and other means of support to them. Being a tutor to any children who were having difficulty with school work or who were anxious to expand their educational horizons brought her joy. She too, had a wonderful sense of humor which the children enjoyed.

His companion Marie was kind, compassionate, and musically talented. I delighted in her company and very much miss her. Marie donated time to charitable endeavors and musical events. I do believe both ladies were disappointed with the lack of time Uncle Philip spent with them. In Uncle Philip's last two decades of life, he did spend more time with Marie and she indicated to me the enjoyment she derived during those occasions.

I was rather surprised when I witnessed at one point Aunt Anna reading an article about Uncle Philip's accomplishments. Perhaps it wasn't so strange in that they lived together as a married couple for about two decades most of which were seemingly happy ones. As time passed, she spoke to me about his work and even kept newspaper articles about him. When he became ill in the last few weeks of his life, she was upset which made me aware that she never stopped loving him. She even asked if she might see the contents of the box of memorabilia he had given me, and we perused it together.

After we finished, I told Aunt Anna that I was going to give the box to her niece who always kept in contact with Uncle Philip. She agreed that it would be a nice gesture and a means of passing information about his work to future generations. I also told her that I was leaving my Steinway piano to the daughter of the same niece because she (who was one of my students) was an excellent pianist and overall talented musician who intended to pursue a career in music. Aunt Anna was pleased.

I will close by sharing the last photograph I have of Uncle Philip which was taken two years ago in 1897.

Photograph of Philip Merkle (1897)

I hope his autobiography is appreciated and enjoyed by all who read it.

Frederick Bechtel

ABOUT THE AUTHOR

Mr. Seger possesses degrees in Economics, Instructional Technology, Library Science, and Jurisprudence. He holds advanced leadership certification, archival certification, and is a New York State licensed attorney.

His professional accomplishments include the practice of law for over 25 years, a professorship in Instructional Technology and Cyber Ethics in the graduate program at the University of Bridgeport and currently a professorship in library science and paralegal studies at the State University of New York Suffolk County Community College. Awards include the Hugh Behymer Award of Academic Achievement from Long Island University Palmer School and the Idahlynn Karre Exemplary Leadership Award from the International Chair Academy.

He is a published author whose topics include the history of citizenship for women and an analysis of Lincoln's decisions. For the past six years his timely and instructional proposals which have highlighted new technologies and their cyber ethical implications have been chosen by the International Chair Leadership Academy for presentation at their annual international conference. Mr. Seger has also had the honor of serving as president of the Division of Academic and Special Libraries (DASL) for 7 years.

Recently he was selected to be part of the team of DEG Productions to produce instructional paralegal videos. For his part, he created scripts and selected both experienced and recently graduated paralegals to present segments of the content. Throughout the video, Mr. Seger presents interesting cases and experiences from his personal legal practice to highlight the topics in his scripts. The videos are sponsored by Alexander Street Educational Video Series, a division of Pro Quest.

In addition to staying current with legal research and other current topics of importance, he also enjoys genealogical inquiry, historical exploration, and travel in order to experience diverse cultures.